Martin King has b[een a televi]sion journalist for tw[enty years. He] reports for *A Curre[nt Affair*, the] Nine Network Australia. In January 1992 King became the first journalist to interview Vernon Wayne Howell, by then David Koresh, on his Branch Davidian compound near Waco in Texas. The story that followed triggered media and government investigations that in turn led to the 28th February, 1993, shoot-out.

Marc Breault trained as a Seventh-Day Adventist minister in California and left that church to join Vernon Howell's Branch Davidian movement in Palestine, Texas, in 1986. He became the cult leader's right-hand man, but was later to flee the movement and initiate investigations that were to bring about the demise of the man who claimed to be the Son of God. Marc Breault married Elizabeth Baranyai, also a former cult member, in 1989. He currently lives in Australia and devotes his spare time to deprogramming former Branch Davidian members.

Preacher of Death

The shocking inside story of
David Koresh and the Waco siege

Martin King
and Marc Breault

A SIGNET BOOK

This book is dedicated to the memory of all
those who died or were injured at
Mount Carmel – especially the little children,
who had no choice, and the twenty ATF agents,
four of whom gave their lives in an attempt
to stop the insanity of David Koresh

SIGNET

Published by the Penguin Group
Penguin Books Ltd, 27 Wrights Lane, London W8 5TZ, England
Penguin Books USA Inc., 375 Hudson Street, New York, New York 10014, USA
Penguin Books Australia Ltd, Ringwood, Victoria, Australia
Penguin Books Canada Ltd, 10 Alcorn Avenue, Toronto, Ontario,
Canada M4V 3B2
Penguin Books (NZ) Ltd, 182–190 Wairau Road, Auckland 10, New Zealand

Penguin Books Ltd, Registered Offices: Harmondsworth, Middlesex, England

First published 1993
1 3 5 7 9 10 8 6 4 2

Printed in England by Clays Ltd, St Ives plc

Contents

Acknowledgments

Martin King would like to thank the Nine Network Australia for their cooperation in the production of this book. In particular, he would like to thank the "A Current Affair" crew that went to Mount Carmel in 1992 – David Rose, Rob Beck and producer Craig Walsh – for their professionalism and courage. Craig Walsh also played an integral part in the writing of this book. Andrea Lee-Steere must be thanked for the long hours she spent in research, and special thanks go to researcher Neheda Barakat, who convinced Vernon Howell to allow "A Current Affair" to film inside the Mount Carmel compound.

Marc Breault would like to acknowledge all the people who tried to prevent the disaster at Waco: his wife, Elizabeth Baranyai; Bruce and Lisa Gent; Ian and Allison Manning; James and Michelle Tom; Jean Smith; David, Debbie, Robyn and Jeannine Bunds; Bob Garcia; Joel Jones; David and Heather Jewell; Lois Jewell-Swaine;

Sandi Hayden; Mike Shimechero; Mark England; Darlene McCormick; and Emil and Pat Schneider, along with their children Sue, Shelly, and Sidnee. Special thanks go to Erna Baranyai, for all the meals and support, and to Marc's parents, Leo and Sachiko, and his aunt Therese and uncle Bob. Marc Breault and Elizabeth Baranyai thank *all* their friends for caring, especially the Webbs, Tsimaras and Steinkamps.

Preacher of Death

I am the Son of God. You do not know Me nor My name. I have been raised up from the north, and My travels are from the rising of the sun.

On January 30, 1987 a man named Vernon Wayne Howell sent a wedding invitation to members of the Seventh-day Adventist Church in southern California. It seemed a neighborly enough action – until they read the invitation.

I have seven eyes and seven horns. My Name is the Word of God and I ride on a white horse. I Am here on earth to give you the Seventh Angel's Message.

I have ascended from the east with the seal of the living God. My Name is Cyrus, and I Am here to destroy Babylon. I have come in a way that is contrary to your preconceived ideas. I will reprove you for your world loving.

I will scold your daughters for their nakedness and

1

pride that they parade in My Father's house, and by My angels I will strip them naked before all eyes because of their foolish pride.

The young men will abuse My kindness. They will take My life, but I will arise and take theirs forever more.

Your ministers will lament your foolishness. Your lost flock will tear you to pieces.

PREPARE TO MEET THY GOD.

The good folk of the Seventh-day Adventist Church declined the invitation. The world had yet to hear of Vernon Wayne Howell, but all that was about to change.

Chapter One
Meeting the Messiah

Somehow it just didn't seem right.

Would Jesus return to Earth wearing sneakers? What about a silver bracelet, prescription spectacles and looking for all the world like a scruffy advocate for flower power?

But there we were, Vernon Howell and I, in the cocktail bar at the Hilton Hotel in downtown Waco, and he's telling me in a thick, slow Texas drawl that he's the Anointed One. He's also telling me not to call him Vernon. "My name's not Vernon. It's David Koresh. I changed it by deed poll. It's all legal, okay?"

Okay. David Koresh is dressed in black stovepipe jeans and a white muslin shirt. As he sips a Miller beer, straight from the bottle, he doesn't waste time launching into tonight's divine mission: convincing me and my three companions that he's the only person in the world who can truly interpret the Bible, and who can faithfully teach it. Back out at Mount Carmel, the headquarters of his Branch Davidian cult, there are

3

140 true believers, he says, who will vouch for that.

Four of them are with him now, and, yes sir, they tell us, as they too drink Miller beer, straight from the bottle, it's a fact. This man, with his dirty mane of brown hair that looks as though it hasn't seen a comb in weeks and his four-day stubble, sure as Hell is the Messiah. You'd better believe it!

Oh, we did, because we had a divine mission too: to get out to the compound the next day and secure a world exclusive – the inside story on this self-styled Prophet of Doom and his loyal disciples.

So there we were, David Koresh and I, in the bar of the Waco Hilton. And we're having Bible study with the beers.

"Do you know about the Seven Seals?" he asks leaning conspiratorially across the table. "Everybody says they know God don't they? But nobody teaches the truth. They don't know the Seven Seals. And if they don't know the Seven Seals, they're going to Hell, aren't they?!"

He's getting excited now. As he becomes more animated his voice gets louder, and people are looking at us. We're talking about the end of the world here, as we move into the main restaurant for dinner. And the maître d' looks surprised. Dinner is a stand-off, with Koresh and his four disciples, who we later discover are his bodyguards, sitting along one side of the table. Facing them are network producer Craig Walsh, cameraman David Rose, sound man Rob Beck, and me, Martin King, journalist. This self-professed Son of God harangues us

4

continuously with scripture. His companions nod their silent assent. Praise the Lord. Have another beer.

"You know how the Bible says, 'I have the keys of hell and death'? You know who that person is that it's talking about, don't you? You know that 'Koresh' means death. He's the rider on the pale horse."

It was 9 p.m. on January 4, 1992. Koresh was in full flight and, barely drawing breath, he ordered the waiter to bring another round of Millers. The astonished young man was quick to oblige.

Koresh was determined to call the shots. As we perused our menus, he was already instructing the waiter on what we were to eat. And no pork, please, for the Branch Davidians. He told the waiter: "I don't eat pig meat because I'm Jewish." As the waiter left, Koresh smirked across the table: "I always tell them that because it's easier for them to understand."

As the seafood, steaks and salads arrived, our garrulous host declared: "Hey boys, this one's on me."

Vernon Howell, aka David Koresh, was just another small-time, small-town fire-and-brimstone preacher. None of us could have guessed then, as we sat opposite him in that restaurant, of the extent of his bloody ambitions. What we did see that night was the frightening power of the Koresh persona. The raw, mesmeric pull of the Koresh charisma in full flight.

None of us paid much attention to the waiter during

the four-hour scriptural onslaught. Revelation with the rolls, Psalms with the soup, St Matthew with the main meal, and Proverbs with the port.

Koresh paused for breath and looked at me for a reaction. But it was the waiter who responded. He sprang forward and looked earnestly at the cult leader.

"Sir," he said, "I have seen the Light! Every morning I get up and I go outside and I look to the East and I pray for the Coming of the Lord." Koresh looked pleased and began reciting passages from the Bible to the excited young man, who burst into tears, saying, "Sir, I am so thankful. I have seen the Light." The entire restaurant was stunned. Near the kitchen, the other waiters huddled and snickered.

Just another convert for the man who called himself "the leader of God's marines." Later, I can't help but wonder if that good-looking young man was one of those killed or wounded or incinerated when the Mad Man from Mount Carmel took on the firepower of the United States Government.

And I can't help wondering, too, if he witnessed the terrible crimes committed by Koresh: the child sex, polygamy, beatings of children and adults, and the mind control. Did he see the frightening arsenal of weaponry, with a stash of cyanide always held in reserve? And was he there for the horrifying, fiery finish?

David Koresh didn't pay for dinner that night as he promised. One commandment broken, nine to go.

What he did give us, though, was his blessing to enter the strange and alien world of Mount Carmel the next day.

Chapter Two

Mount Carmel

Mount Carmel rises out of tinder-dry prairie, a twenty-minute drive from Waco in central Texas. Actually, it's nowhere near the size of a mountain, more a slight swelling of the earth on the horizon. Around here, though, it's so unforbiddingly flat, anything that's more than horizontal is a relief to the eye, and if the cult members wanted to call it a mountain, that was up to them.

The cult headquarters was a huge, wooden, barn-like fortress encircled by dozens of small shacks and sheds. It took pride of place at the top of the rise.

On January 5, 1992 the compound was a swarm of activity. Many of the cottages were being torn down. In time they were all to disappear. It had been raining here for three weeks, and many parts of Texas were under flood, but that day the sky was so blue, it was almost navy. It was a cold Texas mid-winter's morning. There was no wind, and so little in the way of sound it was quite eerie.

Occasionally the silence was shattered by the din of construction. As the ramshackle collection of cottages diminished, the huge fortress expanded. Two men labored on the second-story framework. Below them a group of men used paint rollers to whitewash the timber walls. The women and the teenage girls were gathering rubble from the demolished cottages and loading it onto battered pick-ups for disposal.

As I waited for David Koresh to emerge from his upstairs hide-out, I took a walk around his kingdom, closely followed by three henchmen. The atmosphere was tense. As we walked among his people, there was an overwhelming sense of resentment and hostility.

What I hadn't realized was the level of paranoia among the leadership of the cult. In readiness for our visit, we learnt later, Koresh had spirited away dozens of his followers who he feared might damage his credibility in the eyes of the world: pregnant teenagers, people who couldn't be trusted to keep their mouths shut, people who could crack under questioning, people who couldn't lie convincingly. These flawed followers were sent as far afield as California and Florida. But the largest number were concealed on another property, deep within a pine forest, in Palestine, Texas. With them were secreted most of the guns and ammunition normally kept at Mount Carmel. Enough guns and ammunition to equip a 100-man army. It was that same arsenal that was to inflict such a terrible toll on agents from the

Bureau of Alcohol, Tobacco and Firearms on February 28, 1993.

But Koresh kept his most intimidating weapons here at Mount Carmel to deal with us: these were his justly feared "Mighty Men." These men, hand-picked goons who enforced Koresh's discipline, were openly antagonistic.

"We don't want you here, you son of a bitch," a tall, blond man with piercing blue eyes warned us. "We know why you're here. You're gonna tell the world we're just a bunch of crazies."

His name was David Jones. He was the chief of the Mighty Men, ex-United States Air Force and a crack shot with a rifle.

Nearby, a pretty, dark-haired woman in her mid-thirties was busy raking up rubbish. She paused for a moment, glanced at the camera, and cautioned: "Point that at me and I'll break it."

This bitter animosity wasn't entirely unexpected. Earlier that morning we had met the director of news at Waco's local ABC television station, Don Marion, who expressed surprise and concern for our welfare.

"They're dangerous people and Koresh is unstable. Anything could happen to you and nobody would know." So he had made a deal with us. "If you don't call me by five this afternoon, I'll contact the authorities. Good luck. You might need it."

Finally, back at the isolated 77-acre cult compound,

Koresh emerged yawning, and blinking his large chocolate-brown eyes in the bright sunlight. And he didn't do a lot to allay our fears.

"You guys still with us, huh? Haven't been shot by one of my guards yet?" Vernon looks smug.

"Not yet," I reply. It's a tense beginning. Maybe those guys back in Waco know what they're talking about. I look around and take in the atmosphere. Nothing for miles. God. Suddenly I feel disconnected from the world. I think of my wife and two little girls half a world away in Australia.

You can tell it in their faces – the Vernonites hate us. I can't help thinking that I hate them too and, straight-away, I feel guilty for doing so. But when people treat you like they wish you were dead, it's difficult to be objective. It's not hard, though, to get the feeling that anything could happen in this alien world and nobody would ever know.

The other boys and I talk about it as we film, and we all feel a long way from home.

Earlier, over breakfast at the hotel, we talked about Jonestown and joked about the possibility of not leaving Mount Carmel alive. But standing there, in the dark shadow of the Mount Carmel fortress and surrounded by these hostile fanatics, I remember that at Jonestown the reporters were the first to die. Former cult members had already warned us that they were worried that's the

11

*way Mount Carmel was headed – another Jonestown,
they said.*

*I've been in some dangerous predicaments in my
twenty-five years as a journalist – shot at, bashed and
had my life threatened more times than I care to
remember. But here at the compound, I honestly wonder
if my luck has finally run out.*

"Are we safe here?" I ask the cult leader.

*"It's not me you should be worried about," he says. And
he points at the Mighty Men. "It's them. These guys would
die for me." Then, almost as an afterthought: "And kill
for me, if necessary."*

We all felt it on that cold Texas morning, out there in
the middle of nowhere. The fear, the alarm, and the panic
we tried desperately not to show. Our predicament was
this: Vernon believed we'd traveled half-way across the
world on a public relations exercise so he could strike
back at his disenchanted former followers. That was the
only reason he had allowed us the world-first behind-
the-scenes examination of the Branch Davidian cult. The
truth was that we had come to Mount Carmel to expose
him as a cruel, maniacal, child-molesting, pistol-packing
religious zealot who brainwashed his devotees into
believing he was the Messiah, the reincarnation of Jesus
Christ, and who would eventually lead them into an all-
out war with the United States Government and, finally,
to their deaths.

12

We had come to Waco, Texas because Vernon Howell's ex-followers had made shocking allegations and even more terrifying predictions about this would-be Jesus Christ. And we had come from Australia because the tentacles of his Branch Davidian cult had reached right across the Pacific and poisoned the lives of men, women and children as far afield as that. It wasn't just Texans whose lives had been shattered by the cult. The trail of victims included Americans from all over the States, Britains, Canadians, Australians and New Zealanders.

It was people like Marc Breault, a Californian who had escaped to Australia, who had turned to the Australian media for help after his pleas to the American authorities and media fell on deaf ears. But Breault possessed more than allegations. He had supplied us with damning evidence – hard facts, affidavits and secret audio tapes, which revealed the evil world of David Koresh.

At Mount Carmel, in front of those people who'd kill for him, I had made a decision. I would humor him for the majority of our stay, film everyday life inside his Branch Davidian cult, and allow Koresh to present his sanitized version of life at the compound, if that was how he wanted to play it.

It was a dangerous balancing act. I hoped this strategy would win his trust and lull him into a false sense of security. Then, at the last moment, I'd bite the bullet and confront him with the irrefutable evidence.

So there we were, David Koresh and I, walking across the straw-colored fields of Texas, the fortress looming in the background and the waist-high grass crackling underfoot in the bright sunlight.

I ask Koresh if we can dispense with the Mighty Men who continue to shadow us. His reply is an emphatic "NO!". Gesturing to the Mighty Men, I ask him, "What do they think of you?"

"Well, you know what they think of me. They think I'm the Son of God".

"Do they?"

"Yeah."

"Is that what you think you are?"

" . . . it's not what I think, it's what I am."

Koresh is inspired. "This is a sick world out here. You do what you've got to do to make it. If you're a Hindu or Muslim or whatever you are – a pygmy – if what you know is right, you do it. Your own conscience is with you. Christ is your judge.

"I'm on no head game, I'm not the Pope, I don't walk around with no robes. I am humanity."

Around us and above us, work continued on the fortress. Black men, white women, even children and quite elderly women toiled like Trojans. Vernon said the old cottages were being pulled down because they were damaged in a wild storm, but it was obvious that something sinister was happening. You could feel it. But what exactly was it? I shuddered and walked on. *Tick. Tick. Tick.*

The men and women in their ragged second-hand clothes wouldn't talk to us, wouldn't even look at us. As they tore down the houses they were forced to live in derelict buses with tattered sun-faded curtains stretched across the windows. Why were they doing it? There was a wickedness you could almost taste. *Tick. Tick. Tick.*

A sense of inevitability. Something bad would happen one day, and I could tell that these vacant-eyed worshippers knew it too.

In fifteen months' time the entire world would know. The time bomb was ticking steadily by now.

Chapter Three

The Seven Seals
of Slaughter

In the distance, the ominous sounds of thunder. Then, they come. Four spectral shapes rise out of the night. Four horseman glide across the earth. They have no substance. Nothing can stop them.

The first rides a white horse, wearing a crown and wielding a bow. Men, women and children fall before him as his arrows pierce through flesh and bone. He conquers and no one dares oppose him.

These words are not the product of a drug-induced nightmare, but the essence of the Seven Seals, the basis of Vernon Howell's teachings. His recruiting strike-force - principally Marc Breault and Steve Schneider - were ordered to instil this Message into the callow minds of potential converts. It was with this doctrine that the cult leader brainwashed his true believers. As the seals were opened, they lead to Vernon's pet topic: the end of the world.

On January 5, 1992 we filmed Vernon leading Bible study at Mount Carmel. The Seven Seals, as usual, were the topic.

The second is blood-red. A gleaming sword swings in deadly arcs. Where he passes, slaughter follows. Men slay one another, brother against brother in deadly combat. Peace is removed from the earth.

It was vintage Vernon, but it wasn't original. The Seven Seals are part of the Bible's book of Revelation. Everything Vernon did, everything he taught, everything he prophesied, revolved around the Seven Seals.

Third, over the mound of the dead and the dying, comes the rider. He is mounted on a black horse, and his weapon is famine, the merciless, biting spectre of hunger. That which the sword has spared, hunger takes.

"Look the government has a new tax, a new law, a new tax. People are starving and hungry. People are being oppressed. So is religion oppressing its people. That's all right! When he comes again he has a book. Let him be oppressed, let him judge. People are fixin' to get an ass-kickin' . . ."

In the fourth seal, the terrible one comes. Silence is his shroud. He is pale, and his followers are riders from Hell.

Where he passes, no hope remains. His name is Death, and he must claim his own. Plague goes before him, and a fourth of the earth's inhabitants fall.

"Death is terrible. Believe me. You'll go through it one day."

In the fifth, and headless bodies cry out for justice. "How long," they ask. "How long must this go on?"

"Let them go ahead and rage. Let them go ahead and talk nasty. Everything secret is going to be revealed. Sure Noah's ark's been uncovered – big deal. It doesn't stop the world from sin. How are you gonna judge man? We'll see."

Sixth: The earth trembles. The sun darkens, and the moon appears as blood. Those who are left from the bow, the sword, the famine, and the plague, cry out in despair.

   He comes from the east, shining like the sun. A sharp sword comes from his mouth. Humanity cries to the rocks and mountains to cover them. Islands disappear, mountains tumble like trees in the wind.

"Matthew 23. What does Christ feel about churches? You know? The beautiful synagogue, if there's no truth in the walls of that synagogue, why do you need a synagogue?

You see these stones – Christ says to the disciples, not one stone will be left upon another, and I haven't changed."

The seventh and last seal, and Vernon's favorite.

Then, an eerie silence covers the devastated landscape, with corpses for company. Even the wind is dead.

Chapter Four

Marc Breault: Right-hand Man

The most important person in the life of cult supremo Vernon Howell, aka David Koresh, wasn't his wife, Rachel, or his three legal children. It wasn't his mother, Bonnie, his step-father, Roy, or his brother, Roger, all of whom had joined him as cult members.

The most important person was a 6' 3", 200-lb southern Californian named Marc Breault (pronounced *bro*, as in blood brother).

Breault, now 29, was more than the cult leader's right-hand man. A great deal more. Breault was his back-stop, his confidant, his troubleshooter, and, when necessary (and that was a lot), his peacemaker. Vernon thought the world of his genial soul mate. One thing he particularly admired in Breault was his ability to keep a secret. And with a character like Vernon, there were plenty of those.

So who better to tell a story like this about David Koresh than Marc Breault.

It was a warm spring evening in a town called La Verne, in southern California. It was 1990. Koresh had begun a systematic pattern of leaving Mount Carmel and his flock for brief periods to live in California. The reason for this was simple. Apart from his religion, Koresh lived for two things, and two things only: sex and rock 'n' roll. He got both of those here in California.

I loved music too. I was the keyboard player in his band. I remember many times, after we'd finished jamming in the early hours of the morning, Koresh and I would grab a few beers and walk out into the night together.

"You know, Marc, with our music we'll be rock stars, man. I'll have women begging me to make love to 'em," he'd say, and you could tell from the look on his face that he was still on a high from the music. "Just imagine, virgins without number, man, this is how we're going to do it."

But on that warm night in southern California, in that expensive house, in that quiet upper-class neighborhood, sex was the furthest thing from his mind, even though he was lying on a double bed surrounded by at least twenty young women.

Koresh was always claiming he was sick because of the sins of his followers. He would say that God was punishing him instead of punishing us. The message was that when we were bad he suffered for us. At that stage the sins ranged from eating french fries, watching television or using the telephone without his express permission. But this time somebody had done something really serious, although none of us knew what it was. Vernon's condition today? A broken back!

Koresh's face was white with rage. "You've lied to the Lamb! How could you do this?" he screamed. The thirty men and women in the room turned to the object of his outrage – a terrified 18-year-old girl. She cowered in the doorway too frightened to speak and prepared to accept whatever punishment the Son of God deemed suitable.

David Koresh never missed an opportunity to bludgeon his loyal disciples with scripture, even if he had to do it from his sick bed. Today, said this self-appointed Messiah, this girl had committed the ultimate sin. She had lied to the Lord.

If he had said it once, he had said it a thousand times to the faithful: "God in the flesh! Do you know who I am? God in the flesh! The Word of God in the book has been shown to you. The most powerful of all prophets, the prophet that's found in the books. Lo, in the volume of the book it is written of me, Psalm 40, I come to do thy will, Oh God. Thy law, prophecy, is within my heart. Now what better sinner can know a sinner than a godly sinner? Huh?" The girl was sobbing uncontrollably. No one dared speak, let alone come to her defense.

Koresh was ranting now. He moved his Bible into his left hand, and slid his right hand down the side of the bed. Thirty pairs of eyes watched in horror as David

Koresh produced a black hand gun from its hiding place. The teenage girl stiffened with terror as he leveled the gun at her face.

"God would not condemn me if I killed you now!"

In that bedroom, in that luxury house in southern California, time stood still. It might have been just a minute, but, for that poor girl, it was an eternity.

The girl's terrible crime? She had covered for a friend who had left the house to visit her mother, against the express wishes of this would-be Christ.

Two days later, the teenage girl – penniless, was thrown out on to the street by the divine decree of Koresh.

Miraculously, the next morning, the man who drummed into us that he was God in the flesh, jumped on his motor bike to cruise Hollywood Boulevard.

Conquering Hollywood was one thing, but Vernon, according to Marc Breault, had loftier ambitions – he wanted to rule the world, and, in his own words, he wanted to rule it with "a rod of iron."

Even more frightening was Vernon's belief that he was anointed by God to sire a master race. This was no idle daydream. Again, it was only Marc Breault who was privy to the finer details of how Vernon would create his own Fourth Reich on a 77-acre compound in the heart of the United States of America.

I remember one night about 2 o'clock in the morning.

Everyone else was in bed. Koresh came and woke me up and said he wanted to talk. He looked frustrated and discouraged at the same time. We went into the kitchen. He made some popcorn and we sat down next to each other with our Bibles.

"You're the only one who really understands the Truth," he said. "Even my own wife Rachel doesn't really know these things."

I didn't know quite what to say. I was still trying to wake up. "I guess you've just got to be patient with everybody," I said. "I mean, there's so much for people to learn that you can't expect them to grasp everything all at once."

"I guess you're right," he said. "I guess it's kind of like Hitler. Hitler said if you told the people the same thing enough times, they'd believe you. You know, we've got a lot of work to do. We've got our music, which will get the women in, and we've got our motor bikes and that'll get the men in."

We talked until dawn. He said the Bible told him he had to have sixty Mighty Men. These Mighty Men were specifically ordained to guard the secrets of his bedroom.

"No one can find out what I'm doing in my bedroom," he said. "The Mighty Men have to know how to use swords – weapons that is – and keep their mouths shut."

We talked about the sort of people we wanted to recruit, and where we would find them. Koresh wanted to ride bikes all over the country and talk to bikies. He also wanted to set up shop in California near Hollywood.

"Californian women are liberal," he said. "They're used to anything. If we try to get women in the Bible Belt, or some place like that, we won't get many. We're bizarre. California girls like bizarre things."

But in the grey light of dawn, nothing was more bizarre than what Koresh said next. He outlined his plan to create a super race, a pure race.

"Look at the way children of the world are today. Their parents are raising them up for Hell. They're into TV and candy bars and drugs. God's got a plan. I'm going to raise up righteous seed that'll rule the world. My children won't be like the world's children out there. They'll be righteous judges and rulers in the world, and they'll destroy all the Babylonian children."

Koresh's master race would come from his loins. He quoted the Bible: "Righteousness shall be the girdle of his loins." His seed would not only rule the world, but would eventually rule the universe. His holy seed would be as the stars of Heaven in number.

By now the sun was shining. We could hear people stirring. We would soon have company. Koresh gestured toward the sleeping quarters. He patted me on the shoulder. "I can tell you things direct like this," he said. "With the others I have to speak in parables. They're not ready for the meat; they're still babies, still on the milk. I have to show 'em from the Word. I can't just tell 'em these things or they'd freak out."

But what Vernon didn't know at the time was that his faithful friend, Marc Breault, had difficulty coming to terms with the enormity of this audacious plan. What he also didn't know was that Breault, who had trained to be a minister in the conservative Seventh-day Adventist Church, and who had joined the cult to get closer to God, was more than a little freaked out himself.

After discussions like this Breault was skeptical and not a little cynical. But what really frightened him was that the depraved dream of this guitar-strumming Holy Hitler was fast becoming a reality.

It was then that Marc Breault first glimpsed the Doomsday Clock, ticking inexorably toward Koresh's own Armageddon.

Chapter Five

Childhood of a Prophet

Born Vernon Wayne Howell on August 17, 1959 in a Houston hospital, David Koresh didn't know who his real mother was until he was 5 years old. Bonnie Clark was just 14 years old when she became pregnant to her 20-year-old boyfriend, Bobby Howell. Vernon, just like Jesus Christ before him, was the son of a carpenter.

"I was only born because my daddy felt something in his loins and lusted after my momma," said Vernon of his father. "There was never any love there. They had a feeling between each other and I was the result."

His parents were unmarried when he was born, and stayed that way. Two years later his father fell in love with another woman, and left home. Vernon rarely saw his father from then on and, in later life, never told any stories about him or indicated any desire to contact him.

In 1961 being a single mother in the South was not only unusual, but it held a terrible stigma. In Houston, Texas Bonnie Clark was an outcast, subjected to stares and whispers from people she passed in the street. This was, after all, right in the middle of America's Bible Belt. In those days having a child out of wedlock made her a fallen woman in the eyes of the generally conservative Southerners.

Bonnie just couldn't cope. Her main concern was for little Vernon's welfare, and she did what she thought was best for him – she gave him up. She placed Vernon in the care of her mother and an older sister. And so began a masquerade that was to last for the next three years. Bonnie visited her son from time to time, posing as his aunt, leaving Vernon to believe that his real aunt was, in fact, his mother.

In 1964 Bonnie married Roy Haldeman, a former merchant marine. Finally, she had the means to support her son. One day she visited Vernon as "Aunt Bonnie" and revealed to the child that she was his real mother, and that he was to live with her. "I was shocked! I was confused!" Vernon told his followers years later. "Here I was just 5 years old and my whole world was turning upside-down."

The family moved to the Dallas Fort-Worth area where Roy had a farm. But Vernon never got along with his stepfather. To make matters worse, Bonnie and Roy soon had a son of their own, Roger.

"Roger was always the favorite," said Vernon. "I was always getting whooped by Roy for everything while Roger got away with murder. When I saw my daddy take his belt off, I knew I was in trouble. My daddy whooped me hard, let me tell you."

Life wasn't any easier for Vernon at school. He had a learning disability, which he later claimed was dyslexia. He was always behind the rest of the kids in his class, and was finally put into a special class reserved for slower students. The other children teased him and his new friends, calling them unflattering names and saying they were mentally retarded.

"We got teased every recess period," said Vernon. "They was always saying 'retard, retard' to me every time I'd try to play ball with them, or do anything else. And if they wasn't calling me 'retard' they was calling me 'four eyes' on account of I had glasses."

"I could never learn the alphabet," he said. "The only thing I could remember was L, M, N, O, P on account of that I used to think of the word 'minnow.' I loved fishin' and I used to say 'LM*minnow*P'." That's how little Vernon with his Texas twang tried to master the alphabet. "I don't know how many times my daddy tried to teach me the alphabet but I was too stupid to learn it, I guess."

If being called a retard was hard on him, the way the neighborhood kids treated him was far worse. "One day after school some of the older boys came and grabbed my buddy and me as we was playing. They dragged us on our butts through the fields until they got where no one could see 'em. They held us down and did things to us that hurt. We was kickin' and screamin' and yellin', but we couldn't do nothin' on account of them being stronger than we was."

Vernon rarely spoke of this incident. However, one night in 1986 he was driving around Los Angeles with Marc Breault's girlfriend, Elizabeth Baranyai, a cult member who would later become Breault's wife. The two of them were talking about their childhoods. Then Vernon dropped a bombshell: "I was raped when I was a kid." Elizabeth, too shocked to reply, could not believe that God would allow such a terrible thing to happen to her illustrious leader. They drove home in silence.

But as Vernon later confided to Marc and Elizabeth, school life wasn't all bad. By the time he reached the sixth grade Vernon's status among his peers took a dramatic turn for the better. It happened entirely by accident at a school sports day.

Vernon was 12 years old at the time. He was slotted into a running race by one of his teachers, just so that he could participate in the competition. No one expected the school misfit to do well. To everyone's surprise Vernon blitzed the field. "I didn't know I could run fast," said Vernon. "Me and Roger used to run all the time on our daddy's farm with our two dogs. We didn't have any bikes or expensive toys to play with. We were used to running on rough ground. You know how farms are uneven. We built up a lot of leg strength. So when I ran against them city boys I ran 'em ragged."

After years of disappointment in the classroom, Vernon had finally found his forte. He became a sports fanatic, taking up body building, track and football. It wasn't long before Vernon became vain – and obsessive – about his strength, something that was to stay with him forever. Years later he entered an arm-wrestling tournament. He was so anxious to win that he wrestled his opponent fourteen times until he finally beat him.

With this new-found athletic prowess the teenager became popular. For the first time in his life he was asked to join teams, and the more successful he was on the sports field, the more popular he became. But Vernon Howell grew to be arrogant and patronizing.

His skills as an athlete brought a pleasing side-effect: his new-found muscles began attracting girls. Before, Vernon had gone to church to find peace and sanctuary from the bullies. Now, he found that church was a good place to meet the opposite sex.

School began to bore him, and, anyway, what was the point of attending classrooms when you knew more than the teacher? After struggling to finish the ninth grade, Vernon dropped out and joined the workforce.

———

Twenty years on, Vernon Howell had become David Koresh, religious cult leader, and we were filming in the middle of his Texas compound for our documentary. Koresh talked about the old days.

"I grew up. I failed school. I quit in ninth grade because I had other things I had to do."

"Like what?"

"I had to learn some things, I'm a student."

"What did you learn?"

"About people," and he gestured to his followers. *"That's what I do, I learn about people, about myself. These people, the majority of them were college students, they were raised by mom and daddy, they learned what mom and dad had to show them, they rebelled because they had their own minds as children. Some went into drugs and some went into partying and some into athletics – and finally they came to religion and they went to this religion, and that religion, and they heard, they got an ear load, and they gave those institutions time to show them this great God and this great salvation in Christ."*

But Vernon said they failed.

"I've equal opportunity also to show something."

I asked him what that something was.

"Well, let me tell you this. I have more knowledge in my little toe than all the great men, all the great scholars could learn in a lifetime."

But back in his teenage days, when he was still Vernon Howell and a mere mortal, life was a struggle.

He tried all manner of odd jobs in Dallas, such as roofing and tiling. He also trained as a mechanic, but it always ended the same way. Vernon got his bosses' hackles up with his arrogance and his holier-than-thou attitude. More often than not, it was Vernon who walked out, rather than take orders from those he saw as his inferiors.

Up until the age of 19 Vernon had a succession of girlfriends, but it wasn't until he met a 16-year-old named Laura (not her real name) that he first fell in love. That short-lived union produced a daughter whom Vernon has never met. Laura didn't consider Vernon to be a fit person to raise a child, so she moved away and refused to see him.

Vernon was devastated. It was that bitter experience that brought him back into the arms of religion where he had found peace and solace earlier. He became a fundamentalist born-again Christian. Later he joined the Southern Baptist Church where his Pastor was Billy Harris, an old and experienced minister of the gospel.

At this stage Vernon suffered from massive mood swings. One minute he believed he enjoyed a special and unique relationship with God. The next minute, in Marc Breault's words, "he considered himself to be a worthless son of a bitch, scum who was so evil that he was amazed God didn't strike him dead on the spot." In fact, Vernon once told Breault:

"Sometimes I was so scared I couldn't eat, and my bowels became so bound up that I used to have to reach in there with my hand and remove my waste that way."

In Vernon's first flush with his new-found faith he was overwhelmed by a sense of inadequacy. He went to Pastor Harris for guidance for a personal problem he found distressing: he was a compulsive masturbator. He felt this was a grievous sin against God and he wanted to stop. Pastor Harris advised him to pray and trust in Jesus, who would give him victory over his vice.

So Vernon put his trust in Jesus, but the problem remained. He deduced from that that the Southern Baptist Church lacked a true link with God, so he turned to the Seventh-day Adventist Church. In 1979, in Tyler, Texas he was baptised.

But Vernon's sexual problems persisted – he desperately wanted a wife, a spiritual, God-fearing wife. And in Tyler he believed he had found her.

She was Sally (not her real name), the teenage daughter of the Pastor of the local Seventh-day Adventist Church. While praying, he had a vision in which he drifted in the clouds. Soon, he saw Sally in the middle of those clouds. Then God's voice said: "I will give thee Sally." When Vernon came out of that vision he turned around and saw that his Bible lay open to Isaiah 34, and that this passage literally glowed.

> There shall the great owl make her nest,
> and lay, and hatch, and gather under her
> shadow: there shall the vultures also be
> gathered, every one with her mate. Seek ye
> out of the book of the LORD, and read:
> no one of these shall fail, none shall want
> her mate: for my mouth it hath commanded,
> and his spirit it hath gathered them.
>
> – Isaiah 34: 15–16

From them on Vernon used Isaiah 34 to prove that everyone in God's kingdom should have a spouse. And Sally was God's choice for him. Vernon claimed that she had become pregnant to him twice, but that she had miscarried "because of them tight jeans of hers. I was always trying to get her to stop wearing them tight jeans but she never listened."

The pastor forbade Vernon from seeing his daughter. Vernon defied his wishes, and kept insisting that God had given him his daughter for a wife. He continued to relate the experience of his vision to his Bible class. Not only did Vernon fall out with the pastor, but he fell out with the rest of the congregation as well. They were sick of Vernon's constant references to sex, even in his theology. One member, in this conservative Bible Belt, accused him of never thinking above his buckle.

In 1981 Vernon was finally thrown out of the church. From then on he maintained a vendetta against the

Seventh-day Adventist Church, and took every opportunity to ridicule it.

Once again Vernon Howell was a lost sheep, wandering alone in a spiritual wilderness. Then one day he suddenly saw the Light. And – Hallelujah! – it was just what Vernon needed. A woman.

Chapter Six

Prophet vs. Prophet

This time her name was Lois Roden. She was intelligent, she was popular, she was pre-eminent in the Christian world, and Vernon Howell was madly in love with her.

It didn't bother him in the least that at nearly 70 years of age she was old enough to be his grandmother. They were an odd couple: Vernon, a scrawny, raw-boned 22-year-old with unkempt hair and thick spectacles, and Lois, a matronly, eloquent and tough grandmother.

Whereas Vernon had never traveled, Lois was a globe-trotting ambassador for the church who mixed freely with the rich and famous. She was on first-name terms with many famous American preachers and Christian entertainers, including Pat Robertson, Jim Bakker, Jimmy Swaggart, Jerry Falwell, Sandi Patti and Keith Green. It wasn't just the rich and famous either. There were the infamous, too, such as the then President of the Philippines, Ferdinand Marcos.

More importantly for Vernon, Lois Roden had become

the leader of the Branch Davidian cult after the death of her husband, Ben Roden, in 1978. As the editor and publisher of her own religious magazine, *Shekinah*, which had a huge international circulation, she was also incredibly powerful in the Christian movement.

The world knew her as Bishop Roden. But to the forty-odd Branch Davidians at Mount Carmel in Waco, Texas she was hailed as a prophetess. Like Vernon, she was controversial. Lois claimed she had had a vision in which she was shown that the Holy Spirit was, in fact, the Holy Mother. She even began her prayers with: "Our Mother, which art in heaven."

It was patently obvious that Vernon was besotted with Lois. He followed her around the property like a love-sick puppy. But, at this stage, the feeling wasn't mutual. Lois relegated the new arrival to kitchen duty.

"I washed enough dishes to last me a lifetime. Everybody looked down on me. I was just the camp bum, the loser that did all the dirty jobs, the things nobody else wanted to do. It was always Vernon do this, Vernon do that," Koresh later related to his confidant, Marc Breault.

Again, young Howell found himself a misfit, and the object of derision by other Branch Davidians. It was his opinionated attitude and arrogance that made him an outcast. So Lois tried to bring him down to earth. She forced him to live in a tiny room with no furniture and just one naked light bulb.

"I used to go to my room at night and pray for hours," Vernon told Marc Breault later. "I used to cry out to God and I shed many bitter tears. I could hear the others laughing and making fun of me as they went past where I was staying." But no matter how hard Vernon prayed, he couldn't convince the good Lord to prevent his masturbatory instincts.

If nothing else, Vernon was an incredible survivor. He managed to turn his negative energies into positive action. The young man soon made himself indispensable to Lois and to the cult. He won people over by fixing their cars and trucks, without charging them a cent. He did odd jobs repairing the houses. He could be relied upon to fix anything, and he did it ever so willingly, you could almost say meekly.

What followed next, in just two years, was nothing short of miraculous. Vernon was living proof, in his eyes at least, of those words of Jesus Christ: "the meek shall inherit the earth."

But not, however, if George Buchanan Roden had anything to do with it. George was Lois Roden's eldest son. He was a huge, brawling bear of a man with a thick, black beard and a hide to match. George liked to wear two things: a 10-gallon black Stetson hat jammed on his head and a .38 revolver in a holster on his hip.

George and Vernon hated each other from the start. George referred to Vernon as a mosquito. Vernon sneeringly dismissed George as a tub of lard. But there was one thing Vernon couldn't deny: big, bad George would one day rule Mount Carmel when his mother abdicated or died, whichever came first. George, then in his mid-forties, was eager to take over the Branch Davidian cult, an ambition that caused furious arguments with his mother. One day Vernon heard them fighting about the leadership. Later, Lois told him that George would never lead the cult until he learnt to take orders from his mother.

Vernon had also harbored thoughts of taking on the top job – and now let this be known. Both men realized that what they were fighting for was absolute control of the hearts and minds of hundreds of people. Not only that, but they were also vying for control over millions of dollars in cash, property and other assets held by the Branch Davidians throughout the world. As leader, they would not only have direct control of the assets all around them, but they would also have the power to demand contributions from loyal followers, wherever they might live.

Branch Davidians were very organized. They had a constitution that included a series of by-laws that were along the lines of the Ten Commandments. Lois Roden's late husband, Ben, listed his powers in the organization's constitution so there was no room for doubt as to the absolute power of the prophet.

> Therefore as members of the Branch Davidian
> Seventh-day Adventist association, the mem-
> bership appoints (Hosea 1:11) the president
> Ben L. Roden, as holding in his sole possession
> all legal, moral, and scriptural ownership and
> rights of the association, all its assets and hold-
> ings, and to operate the same for the further-
> ance of the association's work at home and
> abroad: to execute and administrate the entire
> balances of the association, to judge and make
> final judgment in all matters concerning the
> association's works, assets, and holdings, and
> to be its chief and sole administrator.

When Ben Roden died, Lois assumed the presidency and wielded all the power. Now, both George and Vernon wanted to be president, so they too could reap the fruits, forbidden or otherwise, of that exalted office.

Later, Vernon Howell put his own interpretation on that holy decree: "It means that the prophet owns everything, your house, your money, even your under-wear. That means that when the prophet comes to your house at night and asks you to strip naked, you are obligated of God to hand over your underpants."

Vernon claimed his first pair of underpants from the grandmotherly Lois Roden. Literally, they were his ticket to the top. In 1983 Vernon began having sex with her. It happened like this: Vernon approached Lois as she

41

ate her lunch in the kitchen. He told her he'd had a vision from God, and quoted Isaiah 8:3, "And I went unto the prophetess; and she conceived, and bear a son. Then said the Lord to me, call his name Maher-shal-al-hash-baz." He told the 68-year-old woman that this was a clear message that they should get together and make love. He said God told him they would have a son and that he wanted to name him as directed in his vision. So for the next six months Vernon had a secret, sexual relationship with a woman more than forty years his senior.

Eventually the truth got out, George heard about it, and the Branch Davidians were plunged into civil war. Lois claimed she was pregnant to her young lover, Vernon. She declared that a pregnancy test put the matter beyond dispute. This was the last straw for George.

Vernon said that the pregnancy was a sign from God that he and Lois were the true prophets. Their joint rule, though, didn't last long. Lois and Vernon fought bitterly over control of the funds. The baby, if it ever existed, was never born. The reason for that, said Vernon, was because Lois was disobedient to God's wishes and so God had punished her.

Then, amazingly, Vernon said God had ordered him to marry a girl named Rachel. The marriage went ahead with the consent of her parents: cult members Perry and Mary Bell Jones. Rachel was just 14 years old.

Vernon and George were now sworn enemies.

George started patrolling Mount Carmel with a gun, and even tried to force cult members, at gunpoint, to sign a document declaring him to be president. Even so, George didn't see Vernon as a serious threat. To him, the ninth-grade dropout was little more than a hippie punk, who would be easily intimidated.

For his part, Vernon declared George the antichrist. Surprisingly, twenty-five of the forty members sided with Vernon. George ran them off the property at gunpoint. Deciding that the pen was just as mighty as the sword, George began printing his own propaganda newsletter appropriately titled "Rough Wind." On February 17, 1984 the second edition of "Rough Wind" included the following.

> The seed of the adulterer and the sorceress and the whore, maybe this is Vernon because we know he is an illegitimate son, and you know what the world calls him. The seed of the adulterer is a bastard and prohibited from the congregation unto the tenth generation. He may be the seed of the sorceress because we know he is a rock 'n' roller musician and a satan worshipper who use their tongues for sex. If you have ever seen the rock stars called KISS, you will see them jut out their tongues which is their symbol of oral sex.
>
> He says. . .that the people at Mount Carmel

> keep their hand over their mouth NOW, lest
> they GET A ROD ACROSS IT. He says that the
> rod he is using to rule the nations is his genitals,
> the rod below his belt. He is not adverse [sic]
> to doing any kind of sex, because all kinds of
> sex is legitimate now since he is ruling the
> nations with it. This way you don't have to be
> righteous in his kingdom, anything goes.

George was no saint himself. He bought an Uzi sub-machine-gun and he wasn't afraid to use it, even against children. When Vernon left the property to look for somewhere for him and *his* followers to live in Waco, George lost control. One day, a bus loaded with Branch Davidian school children drove up the long winding driveway leading to the main building. When George realized that some of the little ones were the children of Vernon's followers, he opened fire with his Uzi. Luckily, nobody was killed.

With George on the warpath, Vernon and his followers decided that discretion was the better part of valor. They packed their meagre belongings into a caravan of run-down buses and roamed central Texas like a band of gypsies. The group supported itself with social security benefits, which were given to Vernon. Some of the young men worked as they moved from town to town. Eventually, this sorry rag-tag band of believers managed to scrape enough money together in 1985 to send their revered leader to Israel. His child-bride, Rachel, was already pregnant as they left for the Holy Land.

In Israel Vernon tried to recruit members to bolster his following back in Texas. While there, he had a vision that was to change the course of Branch Davidian history. God revealed to Vernon that he was the modern-day Cyrus. Two-and-a-half thousand years ago, Cyrus the Great took the lowly Persian tribes from barbarism to world dominance, conquering the empire of Babylon. Vernon saw himself doing exactly the same in the 1990s. On their return to Texas in April 1985 Rachel gave birth to a boy, Cyrus ben-Joseph Howell.

Vernon and his followers purchased a 40-acre property deeply secluded in a pine forest at Palestine, a safe 90 miles from George Roden at Waco. After all the hard times this was paradise, even though there was no running water, no electricity, no toilet facilities and no accommodation as yet.

It was then that Vernon vowed that one day he would return to Mount Carmel and reign as king. All he needed now was an army.

Chapter Seven

The Recruitment of Marc Breault

Perry Dale Jones was the highest-ranking soldier among Vernon's growing legion of believers, as well as his father-in-law. His mission was to recruit new blood from behind enemy lines – in this case, the Seventh-day Adventist Church that had given Vernon a dishonorable discharge four years earlier.

Perry was an unlikely mercenary for the Messiah. Aged in his mid-fifties, he was frail and effeminate but, at the same time, incredibly fervent about the cause. Perry Jones, with his wispy gray hair and spectacles, looked every inch the polished academic that in reality he was. He was a college-educated writer who had been the chief journalist for Lois Roden's religious magazine, **Shekinah**, but quickly transferred his loyalties to Vernon when he saw what was happening.

On a chilly January 1986 morning in Loma Linda, California Perry spied a new target. And he wasn't hard to miss, as he paused to select a can of beans from a supermarket shelf. For Marc Breault , it was the classic case of being in the wrong place, at the wrong time, in the wrong frame of mind. His downfall was his conspicuous black tee-shirt sporting the unmistakable logo of the Dallas Cowboys. Breault recalls what happened in that supermarket.

"I noticed your shirt and I was wondering if you were from Texas," Perry said to me.

"No, I'm just going to school here at Loma Linda. I'm going for my graduate degree to be a Seventh-day Adventist minister."

Perry suddenly brightened. He became animated and it was obvious that he saw me as a prize catch.

"Oh well, that's interesting. We have a few things in common then. I'm a religious journalist who reports a lot on church and state and the government's involvement with religion."

"That's great," I said, and I was genuinely interested. "That's an area I think is important because of people like the Moral Majority who are trying to take control of the government."

"So what do you think of the Moral Majority?"

"I think they're wrong."

"I've talked to Jerry Fallwell, you know. He's really quite an interesting man."

It was 1986 and fundamentalist Christianity was really on the march. Under the conservative Reagan administration it appeared that the Moral Majority, with leaders like Pat Robertson, Jerry Fallwell and Jim Bakker, could easily hijack the political agenda of the United States.

And I said to Perry, right there in the middle of the supermarket, in the canned beans department: "I don't trust these guys. You've met them. What are they like?"

"Well, as an Adventist you know what the book of Revelation says about churches trying to control the state, don't you? I believe that too. I believe the book of Revelation warns us not to let these men do what they say they want to do." Perry was getting intense now and he leaned close to me. As far as he was concerned, we were the only two people in that supermarket.

We talked about the book of Revelation then. We talked about the beast with seven heads and ten horns. We talked about the people who would be alive when Christ returned to earth. They're known as the 144,000 – 144,000 because that's how many there'll be – and we discussed how the Seventh-day Adventist Church didn't care about what the Moral Majority was trying to do right under their noses.

"I want to talk to you some more," he said to me. "You're a really unusual young man. I've got to go to a religious conference in Washington, D.C. this week but I'd like to get in touch with you when I get back."

"That's great," I said. I gave him my phone number and address. I really wanted to talk to this friendly

journalist who seemed to know all the right people, and have all the right words.

The next time we met, a few days later, Perry was full of stories. I was fascinated. We talked about the same things we spoke of in the supermarket, only in greater detail. As he was leaving he turned to me and said, with an apprehensive look on his face: "I'd like to introduce you to a young man only a couple of years older than you. I think he has inspiration from God."

I was startled that a journalist would believe someone had special revelations from God. That is what I understood him to mean. "By 'inspiration' do you mean you believe this guy has special communications from God, like the old prophets of the Bible?"

For the first time, I saw Perry nervous. "Well, yes, I do," he said, and waited for my reaction.

"Who is he?" I asked. I was very curious by now.

"He's my son-in-law," said Perry quietly. I think he expected me to tell him to go away. My first thought was, "Oh yeah, all in the family." But I wasn't about to miss this chance at meeting a real live prophet.

"Well, the Seventh-day Adventist Church was founded by a prophet," I said smiling. "Who says God can't raise up another one. Sure, I'll talk to him."

Vernon didn't waste any time in getting to know me. The very next day I met him outside my apartment. And my first reaction was one of shock. I expected to meet a long-haired, rough-looking, sandal-wearing berobed

John the Baptist type, with a tongue of fire.

Instead, this man, who would later render impotent the military might of the most powerful nation on earth, drove up in a small, battered green and white van. John the Baptist was a loner, but this puny prophet was accompanied by a pretty blonde girl, who I later learnt was his 16-year-old wife, Rachel, and their baby son, Cyrus.

Vernon climbed down from the driver's seat, smiled and shook my hand. He was dressed in a pair of faded, worn-out brown pants and a blue short-sleeved shirt. With his short hair and spectacles, he reminded me of someone who'd just got out of the army.

He couldn't have been more friendly. Immediately I liked him. One thing that impressed me was that Vernon knew where he was going and what he wanted to say, and, by God, did he say it!

"I will show you more in three hours than you've learnt all your life," said the man who was about to change my life – forever.

We all went inside to my apartment and Vernon conducted his promised three-hour Bible study. He hammered me over and over with the same message, that God always worked through prophets, and he quoted me this passage: "Surely the lord God will do nothing, but he revealeth his secret unto his servants the prophets." The secret that Vernon claimed God had revealed to him exclusively was the total understanding of the book of

Revelation, the book that talks about the end of the world.

He impressed me with his command of the Bible, and after a few Bible studies I decided to follow him. It was the biggest mistake of my life.

Chapter Eight

Australia and the New Recruits

Marc Breault, however, was just one of hundreds of people who would follow Vernon over time. In January, 1986 it all seemed like the start of a wonderful adventure.

It was not much of an adventure for George Roden, though. He was still engaged in a vicious guerilla war with his nemesis, Vernon W. Howell. With Vernon on the run, George was keen to stamp his own imprimatur on Mount Carmel. With typical modesty, he renamed it Rodenville.

The battle for the hearts and minds of the Branch Davidians moved from the prairies of Texas into the international arena. As George mailed his poisonous anti-Vernon literature to Canada, Great Britain, Israel, New Zealand, Germany, Africa and Australia, his enemy took the personal approach.

In February 1986 Vernon Howell stepped off a Continental jumbo jet at Tullamarine Airport in Melbourne, Australia. His great recruitment drive had begun in earnest. Close behind, carrying his bags, was Clive Doyle, a former Australian who had become an American citizen through marriage. Clive was valuable to Vernon for two reasons. First, he was in charge of printing all Lois Roden's literature, and, second, he was responsible for receiving and sending mail, which meant that he had access to a long list of names and addresses of people all over the world who were sympathetic to the Branch Davidians. Later, there was something else that pleased Vernon very much about Clive, and his family. It was Clive's pretty 14-year-old daughter, Karen.

But his quest on this mild Melbourne summer's day was to win over the Australian contingent of Branch Davidians. Dressed in a cheap, light-brown suit, with an expensive Ovation acoustic guitar in one hand and a black leather-bound Nelson King James study Bible in the other, Vernon was greeted, not by a bevy of followers, but by a congregation of irritating flies.

Elizabeth Baranyai was Vernon's first Australian convert. She met him at the airport. "Even then," she recalls, "he was a know-all. He kept insisting there must have been a farm next door to the airport because of all the flies, but I kept telling him there wasn't. He wouldn't take no for an answer."

The next day Vernon met a group of Australians, some of whom would join him in America. But for a prophet, Vernon's message wasn't all that clear. The Australians couldn't understand what he was talking about. Everyone was confused. In frustration, Vernon, mid-sentence, tossed his Bible on the floor and picked up his guitar. He pulled his chair up close to Elizabeth and tried to woo her with his version of romance – a song he'd written called "By the Rivers of Babylon."

"It was the most embarrassing thing I had ever experienced," Elizabeth recalls. "Everyone in the room was laughing at me and making jokes about what a lovely couple we made. I just wanted him to stop singling me out for attention." But the serenade was merely a prelude in Vernon's ambitious pitch for power over his followers. Vernon said he wanted to start a band to spread his Message all over the world. He said it was part of God's plan, and it helped that Elizabeth played the piano.

Another musician present that day was Lisa Gent, step-mother of 18-year-old twins, Peter and Nicole. She also had two other children from a previous marriage: Ian and Michelle Manning. Like her best friend Elizabeth, Lisa Gent was a longtime member of the Branch Davidians. Of particular interest to Vernon was Lisa's husband, Bruce, who was a builder. Bruce fitted in perfectly with Vernon's plans to build an alternative cult headquarters at his new property in Palestine, Texas. The only trouble was that Bruce was totally unimpressed with every aspect of Vernon, and wanted nothing to do with him.

"My first impression was that I didn't like him," recalls Bruce. His wife, Lisa, felt the same way. "We got exhausted just listening to him. I remember we were running shifts. Some of us were listening, some of us were walking out the door. Others were walking outside having a smoke, coming back in. It was like turning on a radio that you couldn't turn off. He just kept on and on and on."

"We said we'd give him a hearing, so we did," said Bruce. "It was funny, you know. He didn't look anything special. In fact, he looked like a hippie. He was dressed like he'd just come off a park bench." In particular, Bruce and Lisa noticed his scruffy, unwashed hair and dirty fingernails. "He was a guy you'd just walk past in the street," Bruce said. "He wanted to impress us that he had something important to say, but he had a funny way of showing it." Lisa adds that Vernon came on so strong, he was his own worst enemy. "To wrap the whole thing up," she said, "We couldn't understand his point. We couldn't *find* his point even after all those hours of listening to him."

But one thing was clear: "He was saying he was there right through the whole history of the Bible. He was basically there at Noah's time. He was trying to prove that he was the Holy Spirit." Lisa sums up her feelings towards him in three words: "He was weird."

When Lisa and Bruce didn't immediately agree with his Message, Vernon became aggressive and insulting. "At one stage he called us all dirt piles. He said all people are dirt piles. And he pointed at the pictures of our children on the wall and said, 'They are dirt piles too'."

Then Vernon had a dire warning for the Gents. He told them that if they weren't in Palestine for Passover in 1986 they would be lost eternally.

"Why didn't you simply wipe him off as a maniac?" I asked.

"I don't know," Lisa replied, shaking her head.

But, ever so gradually, Vernon wore the Gents down and won them over to his cause. "It was through the studies," Bruce said. "It was rather incredible. He made it obvious that the materialistic aspect of our society, that money ruling society, was bad. I mean, there were a lot of points that made a lot of sense. I didn't want to go to America. I didn't want to sell up my house. But as we progressed along he gradually pressed the right buttons in each and every one of us. Each person has got their own buttons, their own Achilles heel. He was able to turn a light on for us."

Vernon made the Gents feel guilty about owning a nice home and a swimming pool. Lisa was beset by doubts. "Well, I thought, 'what have we done for God? Nothing'."

"Once the wedge has been started, blow by blow by blow, the wedge goes in," Bruce said.

You could call Vernon's visit to Australia moderately successful. He'd signed up Lisa Gent, Elizabeth Baranyai, and a woman called Jean Smith, and they all travelled to America to be with him.

Elizabeth Baranyai, who worked at Melbourne University and who now makes a living as a hospital scientist, gives her insights into how this rude and arrogant man managed to win her over.

"What people don't realize is that Jesus also divided families," she says. "The very fact that he preached something that not everyone agreed with caused that division. The Bible is full of stories of people who suffered terrible punishments from God when they disobeyed the prophets. Vernon used his Bible knowledge to convince us he was a prophet. Once he managed that, we did what we did out of fear, even though we didn't like him or his attitude. None of us wanted to go to Hell."

One person he couldn't convince, though, was Lisa Gent's attractive daughter, Nicole. Lisa says Nicole was repulsed by the man whom George Roden described as the "masturbating Messiah."

And little wonder Nicole was repelled. On February 28, 1986 while in Australia Vernon had a vision and wrote it down for world-wide distribution. The following is an extract.

GET READY! GET READY! GET READY!

Yes, this morning my faith was severely tried. I was dreaming, and in my dream I saw a young man who was very unruly. He had in his hand a razor, but to me it appeared he was too young

---

to shave. I attempted to take the razor from him, and so he began to cut my arms with it. I then had to overpower him and discipline him. The young man was about 17 or 18, but when I punished him all of a sudden he became as a little child. He cried out and told me that he was going to tell on me. I knew that his worldly father was coming to check on his cry, so I feared on what I would answer him. I knew that worldly people did not raise their children properly, so I feared that the father would be more apt to listen to the child that now appeared to be as a baby, than to listen to me. The father came into the room, and looked at me very angrily . . . I awakened from my sleep; it was pitch black. I was fully awake, but I knew something was wrong. I could hardly breathe . . . As if I had a sword in my hand, I swung into the darkness before me with the words, The Lord rebuke thee, Satan; I have acknowledged that I am lost already, but I know that God has promised to save me, and to heal me from all sin: Get thee hence. As I spoke these words, a surge of strength entered into me; it seemed for a second as if all heaven were watching.

But for many Australian Branch Davidians, this was the Word of God. They had belonged to this movement that was led by prophets for years. Thus, their minds had been filled with promises of glory and eternal life. To them, the Branch Davidian church was the only true church in a world of sin and darkness.

And now, with George and Vernon wrestling for control, they feared for the survival of the organization. Vernon's audience believed that their eternal destiny hung on which prophet they chose to lead them. While George was far away in Waco, Vernon had come to Australia to personally argue his case. For all his arrogance, at least Vernon cared for them.

Vernon told the Australians that his Message was one of life or death. The Passover was coming quickly. Something big was about to happen. They must go to America, or die.

Chapter Nine

Prophet of Polygamy

It was an ultimatum they couldn't refuse. Branch Davidians from all over the world assembled among the pine trees in Vernon's new kingdom. There were now fifty followers and their children, and the converts had come from throughout Canada, America and far-away Australia (including Elizabeth Baranyai, Lisa Gent and Jean Smith). Together they celebrated Passover, the holy festival that commemorates the night the angel of death slaughtered all the first-born children of Egypt before Moses led his people from slavery to freedom.

By now Vernon and his converts had been living at Palestine for a year. It was a spartan existence. Elizabeth Baranyai says she'll never forget it.

We had no electricity, no heating, and no running water. We all lived in tents and broken-down school buses. Some of those buses didn't even have wheels. The only real building in Palestine was a large log cabin that served as kitchen, church, and meeting area.

We didn't have any toilets either. I was freaked out at first because I had never been camping. All we had was a shovel and a roll of toilet paper. We had to go out into the woods and find a secluded place and dig a hole. And you had to be quick about it with all the ticks that were around. When you were finished you had to go back to where you were staying and check that you hadn't picked up any of the ticks while you had been squatting over the hole.

Things improved somewhat a year later [1987] when plywood shacks were built. Then we could use a bucket in the privacy of one of the shacks, although you often had to share a bucket with someone. I shared mine with a girl from Hawaii.

We had a designated spot for burying our waste. We used to dig a hole and pour it in. Then, we would put the shovel in the next spot in line for the next person. Sometimes you'd be walking in that area and you'd feel your foot begin to sink into the ground. You knew that underneath you was excrement, so you'd try to get out of there as quickly as possible.

At night we used kerosine lamps and Coleman stoves. We had no refrigeration. The only way we could bathe was with a sponge, although some of the more creative of us eventually constructed portable showers.

Lois Roden had defied her son, George, who remained at Waco with his handful of adherents, and made the two-hour trip to Palestine from Mount Carmel. Now it was Lois who was acting like a love-struck teenager. About to turn 70 years old, Lois was still romantically inclined towards the guitar strumming guru. But Vernon only had eyes for his newest lover, the slightly built virgin daughter of Clive Doyle, Karen, who was just 14 years old. Karen became Vernon's second wife.

Marc Breault recollects.

We now had the unbelievable situation in which Vernon had taken two 14-year-old wives. I should explain that once Vernon had sex with a female, under his law, she automatically became his wife.

In Rachel's case, she was legally married to Vernon. This allowed him to portray himself as devoted family man. But in Karen's case, and it was to be the same in all future conquests, there was no formal wedding ceremony. And this suited Vernon just fine, because then he could dump his women, or girls, as it pleased him, with no legal repercussions.

If you're wondering where the parents of these two child-brides were, they were right there in Palestine, members of the cult. I remember that Vernon had claimed that Clive Doyle had given him permission to have sex with 14-year-old Karen. But that was a lie. Vernon, in fact, had committed statutory rape, and he did it while Clive was in Australia. When

Clive found out he went through the roof.

Vernon explained it away like this: he had a vision. God had told him: "You must give seed to Karen." Vernon claimed he was shocked and alarmed at this revelation. He told Clive that he loved his wife, Rachel, and his son, Cyrus. He knew that if he made love to Karen it would jeopardize his relationship with Rachel.

"I begged God not to make me do this," he told Clive, "but the truth was just too overpowering. I studied all night to see if this was really God's will, and it was." When it came to acting, Vernon was without peer. Clive was convinced and gave his blessing for the union to continue. But did anyone ask this innocent child what she thought?

The first Karen knew about her marriage to the Messiah was a tap on the shoulder in the early hours of the morning as she slept in a large bus that was home to four people. Vernon whispered to Karen: "The Lord has something for you to do. It's very important that you be faithful. God told me that I am to give seed to you."

Karen replied: "I will do whatever the Lord wants."

From childhood this quiet, shy girl had been brought up to worship the man who was now stealing her childhood in the back of a bus. She had been taught that whatever this man said was Gospel and must be obeyed.

But what of Vernon's legal wife, Rachel? Vernon had banished her to California on the pretense that God wanted her to go there to experience life in the big cities. In a bizarre twist of fate, the same night that her husband was seducing young Karen, in California Rachel had a dream. She heard God telling Vernon to do something terrible. If he disobeyed the command of God, he would die. Vernon was one lucky son of a gun! He could even blame God for making him commit sins of the flesh, it seemed.

The next morning Rachel telephoned the wily Vernon and told him she was worried about him. Vernon said he was fine and thanked her for being so considerate.

Rachel's dream reinforced Vernon's belief that he was the Chosen One. He believed that God was giving him the green light to practice polygamy. It was the beginning of Howell's infamous harem of women that he called the House of David. They'd later be known as the Brides of Christ.

Chapter Ten

The Hawaii Connection

Vernon was now recruiting on two fronts: first, to build up an army so he could retake Mount Carmel, and, second, to form an elite guard to protect the secrets of his bedroom. And again it was Marc Breault to whom Vernon turned. Breault, as a Seventh-day Adventist, had the qualifications to be a minister, and Vernon wanted to use him as a crack recruiting officer.

All Vernon's followers, except for Breault, were long-time members of the Branch Davidians won over from George Roden. His past attempts to recruit Seventh-day Adventists had met with confrontation and violence. His recruiting methods were two-fold: passing out literature, and approaching people cold in the street.

Literature evangelism consisted of sneaking in and out of church parking lots, displaying signs and offering pamphlets while trying to avoid the police when they were called, which they often were. Breault found there was a real art to disseminating Vernon's propaganda outside a church. The enemy here were pastors and ministers who did their level best to repel the interlopers. Often they would engage Vernon's ambassadors in conversation. They weren't really being polite. It was their way of saving the passing souls from contamination.

But Vernon was always a step ahead. He sent his followers out in teams of two. While one passed out Vernon's divine Message, the other was free to deal with the church elders. For their trouble, these Messianic martyrs were often beaten, ridiculed or thrown bodily off church premises.

But this was kid's stuff compared with what happened when the self-styled Messiah appeared in person. On a recruiting drive in January 1986 Vernon had gone to San Diego. Listening to a sermon in a Seventh-day Adventist Church, he heard the voice of God telling him to go outside to his van and eat a banana. Naturally, Vernon obeyed. Minutes later he returned to his pew, but God was not finished with him. Vernon was told to stand up and present his "seventh Angel's Message."

And Vernon being Vernon relished the opportunity.

"Excuse me, sir," he called out as he jumped to his feet.

The church went dead quiet as Vernon delivered The Word. He told the shocked congregation that he was the Messiah, that they didn't know their Bibles, and that they didn't know God. His unwilling audience was so stunned that he was able to bombard them for five solid minutes. Only then did the church elders take action.

Two angry men strode down the aisle and grabbed Vernon by both arms. He was dragged unceremoniously to the door and hurled into the street, closely followed by threats of jail. Through all this, Vernon continued his dissertation.

Next, it was Breault's turn. Vernon's right-hand man flew to Hawaii to spread the Good Word and gather some disciples.

It was June 1986 when I arrived in my home town of Honolulu, Hawaii. Except for a few summer vacations, I had been away for nearly six years.

My plan was simple: contact my best friend, Steve Schneider, and convert him first. Steve would do the rest. He was a born evangelist, the best I had ever seen. Steve could not keep his mouth shut. Once he got enthusiastic about something, there was no stopping him.

Steve, who was 36 years old then, taught a comparative religion class at the University of Hawaii. He was a respected teacher at the Diamond Head Seventh-day Adventist Church, about fifteen minutes from Waikiki beach. He was also the resident expert in the book of Revelation, so I told him about this weird new religion, and asked him for his opinion. I told him Vernon had said some amazing things during Passover. Although I believed Vernon was the anointed of God, I wanted Steve to affirm my new-found beliefs.

I must admit that Vernon's Message took a lot of

explaining, and Steve wasn't very receptive at first. He had been raised a Seventh-day Adventist, and I was telling him things that went against everything he believed in. But, in the end, Steve, to use one of Vernon's cliches, "caught the vision."

Vernon taught that God would shortly return to earth with fire and lightning and establish a kingdom in the Holy Land of Israel, along with a king, who naturally would be Vernon. His subjects would be a mighty army of immortals who would slaughter all the wicked of the earth, starting with the Christian church.

Steve became convinced that this was the truth, and he had a good reason to feel sympathetic to another faith. He'd given up years of his life to train for the ministry only to be beaten to the pulpit by an inferior candidate. The selector just happened to be the other candidate's uncle.

Schneider was to become second only to Marc Breault in Vernon's cult. And it was the same Steve Schneider who negotiated with the FBI on Vernon's behalf during those long harrowing weeks after the February 1993 bloodbath at Mount Carmel.

From the outset, Schneider was an invaluable asset to Vernon. He was Vernon's passport to at least thirty converts in Great Britain alone. In his early twenties Schneider had studied theology in Nottingham, where he was still well connected.

Enter Judy Schneider, Steve's loving wife. She was so smitten with the polished young man that she pursued him for ten years before they were married. Judy trusted her husband implicitly and followed him blindly into the cult.

Another convert was Paul Fatta, a wealthy Honolulu businessman, who not only gave his mind to the cult, but he gave his money, too. Fatta was only too willing to bankroll Vernon's every whim from a $25,000 Corvette Classic sports car to tens of thousands of dollars of musical equipment and, the most sinister series of gifts, an ever-growing arsenal of sophisticated weaponry.

And there were other wealthy benefactors as well. One elderly Chinese couple sold their expensive Hawaiian home and gave the entire proceeds – almost a million dollars – to the self-professed Son of God.

Marc Breault's home town of Honolulu was a gold mine for Vernon Howell. Tourists flocked there and they were easy prey for the smooth-talking Marc Breault and Steve Schneider. After they left Hawaii the Message spread like a virus, infecting the minds of hundreds of people who were searching for spiritual enlightenment. Like a mini plague it swept through Australia, Canada, England, New Zealand, continental Europe, Hong Kong, the West Indies and Africa. The United States, though, was still the biggest hunting ground. The myopic Messiah, Marc Breault and Steve Schneider criss-crossed America selling the word and establishing bases in San

Bernardino, California and Miami, Florida. Breault estimates they converted people from twenty states.

This trio of fast-talking evangelists perfected a strategy that was nigh-on invincible. Their skeptics, usually conventional ministers and pastors, were left shell-shocked. Now Vernon had amassed an army of recruits. He'd achieved half his equation. He'd taken their minds. In the case of the women, it was time to go after their bodies.

Chapter Eleven

Howell's Harem

There's only one Hard-On in this whole universe that really loves you, and wants to say good things about you. Remember Mary and God? Yeah. God couldn't make any advances because the world would misjudge.
– Vernon Howell, Mount Carmel, October 1989

Vernon Howell was deeply in love with himself. And when it came to the opposite sex, this God of Lust was in Heaven. Vernon's sexual tastes knew no bounds, and his appetite was unquenchable. Thirteen-year-olds, 68-year-olds, and anything in between, were fair game. If you were female, and you had a pulse, Vernon was interested.

Even if he had to travel half-way across the world to Australia to add another notch to his belt, Vernon would do it. But it was a lot more convenient if it happened in his own backyard.

Take Michele Jones. In September 1986 Vernon was so captivated by this blue-eyed blonde, he drove 1700 miles from the San Bernardino base in California to Texas to seduce her. Vernon loved to tell this story, so here it is, in his own words.

God told me to drive to Palestine to bring Michele back to California with me. She was supposed to sing in the band. While we was driving back I had this overpowering temptation to take her clothes off and make love to her right there in the van.

I pulled over to the side of the road and told her to wait for me. I went a short distance off and I says to God, "God, what's happening to me?" I mean I wanted to fuck her. That's all I could think about.

Anyway, God helped me overcome my fleshly lust and I drove with her to California.

Then I'm studying the Song of Solomon. I read about this girl with no breasts. She has a sister. God showed me that this was my wife, Rachel, and I was to have her sister with no breasts.

So I go to Michele, right, and I climb into bed with her. She thinks I'm trying to get warm. I reached for her underwear to take 'em off. She didn't know what I was doing so she struggled. She didn't know what I was trying to do with her. But I was too strong and I was doing this for God. I told her about the prophecies. That's how she became my wife.

Michele Jones was wife number three for this sexual

tyrant. Michele Jones was his sister-in-law. She was just 12 years old.

Perry Jones had already lost his older daughter as a teenager to Vernon. Ironically Perry had always believed that his younger daughter would be safe from Vernon because it was against biblical law for a man to have sex with his wife's sister.

Thou shalt not commit adultery – unless your name was Vernon Wayne Howell, and then that gave you the right to break any biblical principle when it suited you. That was Vernon all over. If he committed a sin, he was quick to find a passage in the Bible, and deliberately misinterpret it to get him off the hook, as he did at Palestine at Passover in 1987.

The people of the world, Christianity, worship the Bible. They idolize these men who lived 2000, 3000 years ago. Yet look at the Bible. Look at what it's saying. Abraham had more than one wife. David had more than one wife. Solomon had a thousand. Can you imagine a thousand wives?

Just imagine Solomon taking his wives down to McDonalds. How much would that have cost him?

Yet these stupid Christians, with their stupid scholars, will condemn me one day for having more than one wife. They don't even know the damn book they say they believe.

Vernon believed that he was the modern-day King Solomon. And he was doing his best to get the same batting average. Vernon turned to the Song of Solomon for his biblical inspiration.

> There are threescore queens, and fourscore concubines, and virgins without number.
>
> – Song of Solomon 6:8

In Bible study Vernon taught that one of these threescore queens and fourscore concubines, or in other words, sixty wives and eighty sex slaves, would be chosen to marry Jesus Christ himself. (Vernon, in those early days, taught that God had two Sons – Jesus was one and he was the other. In fact, he claimed he was the younger brother, Cyrus. Later, Vernon promoted himself to the one and only Jesus Christ.)

Vernon's need to acquire so many wives defies description. He believed that in 1995, or thereabouts, he would go to Israel and be killed by the American troops that had invaded the country. His glorious death would widow his 140 wives, allowing them to remarry Jesus Christ.

This was how 17-year-old American Robyn Bunds became the fourth member of Howell's Harem. She was attracted by the notion of marrying Jesus Christ.

Robyn was a striking, dark-haired teenager with a winning smile and sparkling personality. She was born and bred a Branch Davidian. Her parents, Don and Jeannine Bunds, had both been cult members since the 1960s. Her older brother, David, was a member, and one of Vernon's original converts. From birth, Robyn had been trained to obey the Branch prophets. She fell for Vernon's threescore queens and fourscore concubines line in a big way. Her attitude was that you had to be in it to win it, and she wasn't going to let anyone get between her and the divine jackpot.

Robyn, though, had one big problem. Vernon said she was overweight, and he liked his women thin. The thinner the better. At the time, Robyn weighed around 140 pounds. Vernon set her a target of 120 pounds before he would allow her to enter the House of David.

Robyn practically starved herself in order to make the weight. When she wasn't exercising, she was studying her Bible. She studied it more than any of Vernon's wives. She genuinely wanted to marry Jesus. She tried everything she could to learn about the Lord because Vernon had told her if she married him, she could then marry Jesus after his death. She wanted a perfect husband. She wanted him so badly she was even willing to put up with Vernon, a man who was definitely not her type. Robyn Bunds lost the 20 pounds and gained admittance to Vernon's exclusive harem. Eighteen months later, she gave him a son, whom Vernon named Wisdom.

It was 1986 and Vernon was alternating between the

main camp at Palestine, Texas and the run-down rented house he used as a base in San Bernardino, California. Where Vernon went, the House of David went too. It moved whenever Vernon got the urge to travel.

To keep control of his followers Vernon searched for their Achilles heel. He worked it so that everyone was forced to rely on him, and him alone. All previous bonds and attachments, family or otherwise, meant nothing. His rationale was that if they had no one to depend on, they had to depend on him, and that made them vulnerable.

> If any [man] come to me, and hate not his father, and mother, and wife, and children, and brethren, and sisters, yea, and his own life also, he cannot be my disciple.
>
> – Luke 14:26

Howell used scripture like this in his Bible studies to divide and conquer families. And it worked: the Australian contingent left Palestine in 1986 and returned to Melbourne to recruit their families and friends.

Vernon didn't confine himself to single people either. In fact, his speciality was splitting up married couples. That there were children to consider was no consequence to him. During my stay with the cult leader at Mount Carmel in January 1992 Vernon was totally unrepentant about this cruel practice. By then he was demanding to be called David Koresh. Here is part of my television interview with him.

KING Have you separated couples?

KORESH *I have separated couples.*

KING You have?

KORESH *You better believe I have.*

KING Why?

KORESH *For the same reason . . . any time you present a truth and the truth comes to a family, the family has to decide if they're are interested in it or not, whether it's a perception, true or false. There are those who say "yes, this is the truth," and go with it. And there are those who say "no, this is not the truth." There's not a religion on earth today that doesn't cause that. To say I don't separate families would be a lie.*

KING Why do you separate them though?

KORESH *Why does what I teach from the Bible separate them?*

KING But what right do you have to separate families?

KORESH *I work in regards to trying to take the person who doesn't want to hear and I say, now, look, let's take a look at these things. And if they don't want to look at the Bible, that's their right, but if their spouse wants to look*

	at the Bible, it causes trouble in their home.

KING You split them up!

KORESH *Then what happens is, I'm one of the agents that has given a truth, like Luther, split up a lot of families didn't he! Luther split up lots of them.*

KING How long ago was that?

KORESH *That was in the 15th century.*

KING Yeah. This is 1992.

KORESH *Yeah, this is 1992 where drugs, music . . .*

KING And what gives you the right?

KORESH *Uh, uh, uh! . . . drugs, music, AIDS, disease, TV, hey what the kids are learning today splits up families!*

But what did the children learn under the tutelage of this know-it-all prophet? Among other things, they learnt that separation of parents was normal. They learnt that Vernon was their great and only provider. And, for the little girls, they learnt that the ultimate honor in life for them was to become his wife.

Vernon was not sensitive with his young lovers. One girl, for example, was too small when Vernon tried to penetrate her. So he advised her to use large tampons so she could stretch a little to accommodate him.

Another of Vernon's young conquests was 13-year-old Aisha Gyarfas. Vernon also had sex with her on one of his visits to Australia a year later. It happened in the home of Bruce and Lisa Gent, with the consent of Aisha's parents.

During my interview, I tested him on that too.

KING Do you know Bruce Gent?

KORESH *Yes, I know Bruce Gent.*

KING And his wife?

KORESH *I know his wife.*

KING They told me that you slept with a 13-year-old girl in their house.

KORESH *OK, why didn't they put me in jail?*

KING Because they believed in you.

KORESH *They believed in me? That's what they told you? They believed in me.*

KING Did you do that?

KORESH *No, I did not!*

KING Were you there with the 13-year-old girl?

KORESH *I was there with a lot of people – thirteen, ah, what's he talking about – Aisha? Was it, ah Nicki, let's see . . .*

KING I think the girl's name was Aisha.

KORESH *Was the parents there? Her parents were there.*

KING Did you do it?

KORESH *No, I didn't do it!*

On March 9, 1993 the FBI reported that Aisha, now 17, had told them she was not only one of the cult leader's wives, she had also borne him two children.

The indoctrination of these innocents began when they were as young as ten years of age, when they were told to sleep in the same bedroom as Howell, while he slept with their mothers. Vernon often said that if he didn't take these little girls to bed, someone else in the world would, and that wouldn't be right. Better to have sex with Jesus, than just anyone.

Women were always scrambling over one another to get Vernon's attention and approval. Once, Rachel, his legal wife, even wrote a short document describing how women should prepare themselves for love making with Vernon. The document described how they should bathe and perfume themselves. Vernon was pleased with that effort.

Although Rachel's primary reason was to impress Vernon, a secondary one was to prevent the spread of disease. Because hygiene was a problem at both Palestine and Mount Carmel, infections developed easily and, with Vernon sharing himself around, spread rapidly. In one instance at Palestine thrush or monilia (*Candida albicans*) spread from one woman to several others in Vernon's harem. Vernon himself fell victim to this condition and it caused him considerable discomfort – an almost intolerable itch in his genitals – that persisted for weeks. Naturally, sex was off the agenda once Vernon's symptoms became apparent. Many of the men thought it was a great joke at Vernon's expense. The general feeling was that if you lie down with dogs, you get up with fleas.

This condition presented Vernon with a real problem. Showing up at a clinic with several women, all with the same complaint, wasn't conducive to the isolation Vernon sought. He had, therefore, to find some natural remedy. He chose garlic. Vernon made every woman in the camp consume an entire corm of raw garlic each day until the malady cleared up. We're not just talking about a clove, but an *entire* bulb.

Vernon was also afraid that one of his new wives would have a more serious sexually transmitted disease of one form or another. "You think it's easy having all these women? I have a lot of worries. What if one of my wives has AIDS? What if she has VD? I have to trust in God's strength to keep me free of such things."

Apart from his paranoia about AIDS, Vernon had many other sexual rules. Although Vernon's method of choosing a partner for the night seemed solely based on whim, he stipulated that he would never bed a woman who was in the middle of her period.

Vernon also tended to dump women after they gave birth to his children. On one occasion Vernon told the then 14-year-old Aisha Gyarfas not to get pregnant because he liked her the way she was.

In keeping with the Hitler image, Vernon was an ardent racist, especially when it came to women, and he wasn't ashamed to admit it. He had strange ideas about racial differences between women. It was known that he did not like black women, and only tolerated them because they were human beings in God's eyes. He related his views in Bible studies in England, Australia, and the United States. He preached his racial theories incessantly.

God has made the four races of women different. Red, yellow, black and white. They're all different. I know. I have the experience.

Black women are ugly. They were designed by God for life in the jungle. But God is merciful. He made up for their ugliness by making 'em well endowed where it counts. They're good lays in bed and they make their men happy. That's all men want. Make 'em happy in bed, and they'll put up with a multitude of sins.

Oriental women, you know, like your Japs and Chinks, they're real ugly in the face most of the time. They all look the same anyway. But God made 'em small and compact to make up for their ugliness. Have you ever noticed oriental women often have real tight breasts? Real nice. Real firm. And they're good in bed too.

White women, on the other hand, were prettier than Asian women, but were not as good as Asians in bed, he claimed. According to Vernon, white women had small clitorises because the Roman Catholic Church had so devalued and discouraged sex during the Dark Ages that they had actually managed to genetically alter that aspect of female anatomy.

Vernon believed that, in general, a woman's ability to please a man in bed is inversely proportional to her beauty. Vernon would go on in this vein for hours. He started this kind of teaching in England during his first recruitment drive there in the summer of 1988. This may have been because many of the English prospects were black.

This man, who said he was sexually abused as a child, also had very firm opinions about the sexuality of men.

You know, though, God wanted to show the children of men that this world is vanity. God made the oriental women to please their men, but he made their men with small dicks. You know what I mean, small horns. When the Bible says horns, it means dick doesn't it? The scholars know this.

So these poor oriental women had to put up with men who had small dicks that couldn't satisfy 'em.

And God is fair, you know. He's a just God. The black race was downtrodden through the centuries. You know, they was slaves and everything like that. So God gave them something to be happy about. God's merciful. God made the negroes so they could enjoy each other in bed. Their women are good, and the men have big peters to make 'em happy.

This sexual Samson was a mere mortal, nothing special according to his women. In fact, when it came to displaying his body, Vernon was very private and shy. He was very unhappy with the body God had given him. In particular, he was obsessed with the spindliness of his legs. He was once caught in the kitchen with his pants down, literally. It was just before dawn and the woman was reporting for kitchen duty. Vernon darted back to his bedroom and later denied the incident. To any of us this would seem a petty occurrence, but to Vernon it was a huge embarrassment, and later he castigated the poor woman publicly for spreading the story among the rest of the group. What's amazing is that this man, who was so prepared to engage himself sexually with so many women and girls, would make such a big deal out of nothing.

But that was just one of his many idiosyncrasies.

> In my body has been desire, but it deceived me. I looked upon the desire and said, this is love, but once that love came through my testicles and left out of the head of my mind and went into their body, my body turned into hatred, my body found no more desire and my body ached, my stomach grabbed a hold of me and says, you don't love these girls. I said, God, what is love! God said "no man knoweth love, nor hate, by all the things that he sees under the sun." And I persevered. I continued my work, feeling dead, feeling lonely, feeling like a dirty

dog, cause God said that they that bear the
vessels of the Lord shall triumph.

– Vernon Howell, Mount Carmel,

October 1989

Vernon was walking a tightrope. Because he was
having sex with so many women, he was worried that
the camp minders, the Mighty Men, would become
jealous and turn on him. In public, he would often say
things like: "It ain't easy having all these wives. I know
what all of you men are like. Everyone of you sits back
and wishes you was the Prophet so you could have all
these women. But none of you men knows the pain that
I endure to do God's work. These women are always
jealous and they always complain about how they don't
get enough. They're always wanting to be the one to
come to my bedroom for the night. They don't understand. I get tired. I suffer. Sometimes I don't want them.
And then they cry and say I don't love 'em. They just
don't understand my work. They haven't caught the
vision. They're not in the spirit."

But in private, it was an entirely different matter.
Vernon said having so many women was like being a
little boy in a candy store. Sometimes, though, little boys
in candy stores eat too much and get a belly ache. And
Vernon knew that feeling all too well, as Marc Breault
explains.

One night after we had finished a gig, and everyone else had gone to bed, Vernon came up to me and said he needed to talk.

"I've got a real problem," he said. "I don't know what to do because I've tried everything I could think of." He looked real worried, about as worried as I had ever seen him.

Now I was worried too. Vernon told me that he was impotent.

"I just can't get it up sometimes," he said. "You know what it's like? These women have expectations and all, and then I just can't give 'em what they want."

I couldn't help being a little curious, even though I was quite shocked. Vernon was always talking about sex and this admission must have really been hard for him to make, even to me.

I said: "How are the women reacting?"

"They say they understand. They're real polite and they ask if there's anything they can do to help. But I know different. I know they're disappointed."

Vernon then told me all the things he tried to do to cure this problem. He used everything from herbs to combinations of food. That explained a lot to me. Vernon was a walking pharmacist. He took so many vitamins and herbal capsules. Now I finally knew what they were for.

I didn't know what to say. I'm no expert. I told him

that maybe he needed a rest. "Maybe you're just worn out," I said.

"I can't rest," he said emphatically. "I've got to do my work. I've got to triumph in the work of God's hands. I've got to anoint these women with oil."

Sometimes the problem became so serious that a public explanation was required. Once Vernon said that God had told him to kill one of his wives. No one in the cult knew why. Vernon said he disobeyed God because he loved his wife too much to hurt her. God, Vernon said, was extremely displeased and punished him by making him impotent and said he would die of cancer.

Only Vernon could explain how he managed at other times to be what he called "the ultimate sex machine." When describing his sexual activities with women his favorite words were "take" and "submit." He liked to be in total control of his relationships with women.

Because he had so many, women either did as he commanded or were relegated to the scrap heap. It was important to Vernon that his women said that he was the best lover they'd ever had. He made them feel guilty for previous relationships and emphasised that they were with him only because of the goodness and kindness of his heart.

For a man who was so private about his own body, Vernon was fond of detailing the sexual habits and inclinations of his paramours. He did it in public, and in the presence of children. He publicly berated one woman, charging that she did not know how to do anything right. This God of Love told the dumbfounded gathering that she was "awkward and even repulsive." That is, he explained, until he, with patient endurance, taught her the right way to make love.

But Vernon wasn't always heartless and derogatory to his women. He could be charming, captivating and romantic. He sang to them, he praised them in public, he bought them little gifts, which, even though they were cheap trinkets, were treasured by the Brides of Christ.

When Vernon was feeling particularly romantic, he'd take his lover of the moment out to dinner. Nothing too fancy, mind you. Usually she'd find herself gazing into his eyes under the harsh glare of the fluorescent lighting at Burger King. If Vernon really wanted to take her to Heaven, the starry-eyed lovers would romance each other over the salad bar at Sizzlers.

It was his charisma, coupled with his power as cult leader, that caused Vernon's women to compete for his affections. Life among Vernon's women was often vicious, with intense rivalries. Some of his lovers even formed cliques.

The growing harem became composed of groups of women, teenagers and girls who would do almost anything to please him. When Vernon targeted a woman for his harem, he put her on a pedestal, saying she was special. The other women became insanely jealous. The lucky woman would enjoy that status and flaunt her position as head of the harem until Vernon's mood changed, and he chose a new queen.

But Vernon was capable of jealous rages, too. He flew into an uncontrollable fury on one occasion in March 1988, claiming that 13-year-old Michele Jones (his third wife and the sister of Rachel, his legal wife) and another girl, Shari Doyle, had been flirting with two men, one of them the millionaire Paul Fatta, the other Peter Hipsman, a convert from New York. The flirting was, in fact, an act of innocence and kindness: the girls had massaged the feet of the two men after they came in from a hard day's manual labour. Vernon threatened to expel both Michele and Shari from the House of David. He publicly castigated the two men, accusing them of committing adultery.

> Thou shalt not covet thy neighbour's house, thou shalt not covet thy neighbour's wife, nor his manservant, nor his maidservant, nor his ox, nor his ass, nor any thing that [is] thy neighbour's.
>
> – Exodus 20:17

Marc Breault says that at no time during his four-year reign as second-in-line in the cult did he see anything more pathetic and degrading than Vernon's treatment of the little Australian girl Aisha Gyarfas. It's worth remembering she was only 13 years old when she joined the ranks of Vernon's lovers.

Aisha was completely captivated by Vernon. She was like his little puppy dog tied to his leash. Aisha would do anything for Vernon. She even slept in front of his door when he was sleeping with someone else. Aisha pandered to Vernon's every whim and followed him around everywhere. Vernon really enjoyed that.

But what he really enjoyed was having sex with her. Once Vernon said to me privately:

"You think 13 and 14 year olds aren't good for sex? People think that. But let me tell you, boy I'll tell you. They're ready at that age. They're ready and willing. They're so eager. They get all hot and they pant and their little hearts beat so fast you can hear 'em."

Whenever Aisha did something Vernon didn't like, which could be something as simple as wearing the wrong colored pants, he spanked her and sent her away from him crying.

I witnessed one beating. Vernon had an upstairs bedroom at Mount Carmel. It also doubled as the music studio because it was so big. I was the keyboard player so I had free access to his bedroom when he wasn't sleeping there.

Vernon was out one morning so I went up to practice. He came back later and was really upset when he saw that Aisha had forgotten to take some of her clothes with her. He yelled out the window for someone to get her. When she came he started yelling at her. He told her never to forget her clothes again. It was important when she left his room that she should take her clothes with her. He told her to bend over and he started to spank her. She sobbed uncontrollably and you could tell she wanted him to stop but she was too afraid to ask him to. Vernon sent her away, and she didn't come into his presence for two days. The poor girl was devastated.

There was a strict set of rules for Vernon's girl lovers. Vernon didn't want anyone to talk about his wives. He even forbade his wives to talk to each other about him. But the most serious offence was talking about what he did with little girls. Vernon could not tolerate that.

When he took a little girl to bed, he made sure the girl would leave his bedroom very early in the morning, before anyone in the camp got up. He didn't want us knowing about the children.

"I'll be put in jail for this one day," he confided in me when he knew I was aware of his activities.

On another occasion when someone had talked about him behind his back about child sex, he threatened that if there was any such talk in future the offenders would have their tongues personally torn out of their heads by him.

But even though Vernon was paranoid about his child-brides, their existence was common knowledge. I wasn't the only one who was worried for the mental and physical welfare of these little kids.

Many of us noticed that, after joining Vernon's harem, the children's behavior changed dramatically. Before, they were happy, bouncy and full of life. One thing about kids is that they're so adaptable. They can cope with bad situations better than adults. But, afterwards, they became sullen and withdrawn. Once you belonged to the harem it became a sort of secret society. They tended to stop associating with the other children and didn't join in their games. It was as though something had been taken from them – and, tragically, it had.

Something else that bothered people like Marc Breault was that in Vernon's sealed world there were few of the trappings of childhood. The only toys allowed were those they possessed when their parents joined the cult. For most children, a Barbie doll, Lego or the latest Nintendo game is an exciting gift, but, in the isolation of Texas, Vernon's version of a great prize for these young girls was a cheap gold-colored pendant – the Star of David.

The girls were taught from an early age that this pendant was the ultimate gift from their leader, and they lived for the day when this honor would be bestowed upon them. Their own mothers, some of whom belonged to the harem, impressed on them that their sole aim in life was to receive the cherished Star of David and have babies for the Lord. That cheap piece of jewelry signified that a female belonged to the exalted House of David and was destined to become a handmaiden to the Lord.

The exclusivity of this symbol suddenly became meaningless to the cult when Vernon feared the authorities would use it to determine who belonged to his harem. From then on everyone wore one, even the men.

With total control now over all his subjects, it was time to move from the bedroom to the battlefield. It was time for war.

Chapter Twelve

War

In October 1987 Vernon decided it was time to challenge the enemy, George Roden. The object? To invade and conquer Mount Carmel. Like Moses leading his Israelites to the Promised Land, Vernon prepared to lead his disciples the 90 miles from Palestine to Mount Carmel.

When it came to abnormal behavior, George was right up there with his nemesis Vernon Howell. Among other things, George, also a polygamist, claimed that he was the modern-day reincarnation of King Solomon and always finished prayers "in the name of George B. Roden, Amen." George also thought he was the Son of God – and he knew Mount Carmel wasn't big enough for two Sons of God. One of them had to go, and it sure as Hell wasn't going to be George, if he was to have anything to do with it. George was still seething over Vernon's dalliance with his late mother, Lois. She had died of cancer in hospital in 1986, leaving the Branch Davidians divided and in danger of self-destructing in civil war.

In the three years since he had run Vernon off Mount Carmel at gunpoint, George had been busy. After renaming the property Rodenville he erected a series of makeshift barricades. George claimed these were designed to stop car bombs sent by the hated Vernon. "This is what they should have had to protect our boys in Lebanon," George was often heard to say, referring to the 1982 car-bombing of the US Marine headquarters in Beirut. The Middle East theme seemed pertinent to George. "It's basically a holy jihad, Khomeini versus Israel, that's what Vernon Howell has with me."

Roden wasn't content, though, to be the President of the Branch Davidians. He had already run for the highest office in the land – the Presidency of the United States – in 1976 and was to do so again in 1988. Both times he couldn't get enough people to sign his petition to get his name on the ballot. Perhaps voters were put off by some of George's policies; they included the legalization of bigamy and a nuclear first-strike against the then Soviet Union.

George now also turned to the American National Football League. He approached the Dallas Cowboys and told them he had a message from God that would ensure they would win the Superbowl. Like voters across the nation, the Dallas Cowboys sent him packing.

By 1987 George was keen to show the world that he was the true leader of the Branch Davidians, the king of Mount Carmel. He issued Vernon with a challenge that would settle the leadership issue once and for all. Whichever of them could first raise the corpse of Anna Hughes, dead for twenty years, said George, would prove that he was indeed the Son of God.

Anna Hughes died at 85 years of age. She was buried in a huge steel casket in a marshy corner of the Mount Carmel property. This desolate piece of land, bordered by broken-down barbed-wire fences and thick with waist-high prairie grass, was the final resting place for a dozen or more Branch Davidians. There were no crosses or headstones to indicate this was a cemetery.

When I interviewed Vernon in 1992, he was only too keen to recount the events that led to all-out war with George. Walking through the graveyard with the man who by then was calling himself David Koresh, we stopped at a depression in the ground, and I noticed a huge hole half-filled with black, fetid water. The hole was Anna Hughes's grave. As we stood on the edge of the plot, the cult commander recounted the grisly details of the challenge.

KORESH   *Well this here is where George had dug up an 85-year-old woman from this plot of ground . . . he called me up and challenged me to see who could resurrect her.*

KING   What did you say?

KORESH   *I didn't know where he was coming from. So I said to him: "Well, no George, not*

today," not realizing at the time that he had
actually dug up a lady and was going to
resurrect her. He put the casket in the church
and prayed several times . . . Three times
he tried to resurrect her . . . but of course
she didn't resurrect.

KING Could you have done better?

KORESH *I don't think so, could you? Could anybody?*
Twenty years ago [she died] – there was
nothing really left to resurrect. She was just
like bones. But anyway, just one of the
many things that religion gets involved
in . . . you know who's got the biggest magic
wand, and it shouldn't be that way. But
some people make it that way.

Vernon told his lawyer, Wayne Martin, what had happened. Martin, a loyal Vernonite, was incredulous. He told his friend that George could be charged with corpse abuse. Vernon couldn't have prayed for a better opportunity to get back at George. So he went to the McLennan County Sheriff and made a formal complaint.

But officials said they needed proof of the crime, at the very least a photograph of the old lady's body. Vernon later claimed the authorities gave him tacit approval to go onto the property, with a warning to be careful of George and his followers.

"They're a bad bunch of boys. You'd better make sure

you can protect yourself," Vernon said the Sheriff told him.

Over the next few weeks Vernon went on a big shopping spree. So as not to attract curiosity from the police, Vernon and his followers traveled all around central Texas to buy their arsenal. He purchased dozens of guns, mainly .22s, shotguns and Ruger .223 rifles, not to mention an assortment of hand guns and hundreds of rounds of ammunition. Along the way they dropped into discount department stores and outfitted themselves with camouflage clothing and flashlights.

Vernon hand-picked his team of commandos. The eight Mighty Men included ex-US Air Forceman David Jones, the millionaire Paul Fatta, Jimmy Riddle, Greg Summers, Stan Sylvia, Floyd Houtman, Mark Wendel and Peter Hipsman. To prepare for battle, Vernon ordered his Mighty Men to start eating massive amounts of garlic, to put them in peak physical condition for the coming conflict. He believed garlic was a super amphetamine, which would make his soldiers tense and alert. In fact, its nett result was that when the Mighty Men entered stores for their military supplies all they did was attract attention to themselves. (Later, witnesses would say all they could remember of the cult members was the overpowering odor of garlic.)

With the day of battle nigh, Vernon established a command centre just 2 miles to the south of Mount Carmel. For two nights running, armed to the teeth and reeking of garlic, the Vernonites conducted reconnaissance missions of the property.

On the afternoon of November 3, 1987 Vernon led his eight commandos into the Mount Carmel complex. The first objective was to take photographs of the old woman's remains, which were in a dilapidated church. But no one in the raiding party had taken into consideration George's dog, which got a good whiff of them as they wriggled on their bellies through the long grass. The dog raised a huge racket. George, startled in mid-prayer, ran out of the church with his Uzi and, recognizing the enemy, opened fire.

The Holy War of Waco was on in earnest. George and the Vernonites exchanged fire for fifteen minutes. Outnumbered nine-to-one, George and his trusted Uzi sought refuge behind a large tree. Later, the Sheriff would find sixteen slugs embedded in the bark.

The sound of gun-fire carried for miles, and it wasn't long before the Sheriff and his men joined the fray. Vernon and seven of his Mighty Men were arrested and charged with attempted murder. But Mark Wendel managed to escape, eluding a police chopper. The attackers were dubbed the "Rodenville Eight."

George, who'd been shot in the hand, ended up in jail. He declared that Vernon was getting far too much sympathetic publicity, and feared his rival would be let off. George had good grounds for believing this.

While the other six raiders languished in McLennan

County Jail, unable to raise bail, Vernon and Paul Fatta raised almost $100,000 bail the day after their capture.

On his release Vernon employed the acting skills he used so successfully to manipulate his adherents in the cult and, with the help of the television, radio and the print media, became a folk hero. He turned the situation around so that he, and not George, appeared the victim.

As Vernon and Paul Fatta became free men, poor old George was doing the opposite. He was sentenced to six months' jail for contempt of court. His crime? He'd sent letters to Texas Supreme Court judges, threatening to inflict them with AIDS and herpes should they show leniency toward the man he hated.

Facing attempted murder and conspiracy to commit murder charges Vernon strangely decided to pursue a career as a rock star. With his right-hand man and confidant Marc Breault, he went to a music studio in downtown Waco called "The Big Planet." For the first time in his life, he recorded a song he'd written himself. It is all about George, and it would have enraged his now-jailed rival. It is called "Mad Man in Waco."

Please please please won't you listen,
It's not what it appears to be.
We didn't want to hurt anybody,
Just let our old people free.

In the light of the darkness,
Risking our lives for the Lord.
Helping the women and children,
To their houses restore.

There's a mad man living in Waco,
Bowing his knee to Baal.
Won't you help Mr Sheriff,
So we won't fail.
We won't fail.

This is for the little children.
God knows how it should be.
Stars and stripes are flying,
Give us justice and liberty.

There's a mad man living in Waco,
Praying to the Prince of Hell.
Won't you help us Lord now,
To pay our bail.
Pay our bail.

Breault and Howell spent all night in The Big Planet, with Breault playing the keyboard, bass and drums, while Vernon put down the guitar tracks. Flushed with his success in the recording studio, Vernon commissioned Steve Schneider to book a concert hall in Waco so he could perform live and, at the same time, pick up some new converts. Steve managed to book a 5000 seat hall but Vernon's bid for stardom failed when he couldn't put together a complete band in time.

But Vernon treated this setback as a learning experience. He put his superstar ambitions on hold, and focused his energies on beating the two serious charges levelled against him.

The trial of the Rodenville Eight began on April 12, 1988. Although Vernon Howell and Paul Fatta had been free on bail since November 4, 1987, the day after their arrest, their six cohorts were not so lucky. For the six months between the shoot-out and the trial, they had remained confined in prison.

It looked like an open and shut case: nine heavily armed men dressed in battle fatigues trespassed on another person's property and engaged the owner in a gun-fight. But, in court, the Branch Davidians looked more like Quakers than criminals. Most of the women wore dresses flowing to their ankles and blouses buttoned to their necks. The men wore ill-fitting, second-hand suits. The Branch Davidian children clung to their mothers during the long days of evidence and legal argument. Before the trial began, Judge Norman Fitts inquired if there were any witnesses in his court who should be sworn in. He was greeted with silence. Vernon's attorney, Gary Coker, tried to help. He looked pleadingly at the Branch Davidians in the gallery, and urged potential witnesses to make themselves known.

The Branch Davidians stayed put. Cult leader Howell rose to his feet.

"It's all right," he said, and he raised a hand. "You've done nothing wrong. Stand." The cult members stood as one, everyone wanting to be a character witness for Vernon.

On the other side the prosecutors had a real problem. Their chief witness was George Roden, who came to the courtroom straight from the county jail.

Roden told the jury he had tried to raise Anna Hughes from the dead. He did it, he said, with a prayer that ended: "in the name of George B. Roden. Amen." Roden didn't help the prosecution case by informing the open-mouthed members of the jury that he had the power to inflict AIDS and herpes at will, and to cure both diseases.

George was the loose cannon in this court battle. The defense could not have hoped for a better prosecution witness. Vernon's commandos were acquitted, but the jury could not reach a verdict on the leader himself. Later, charges against him were dropped. Of the twelve members of the jury, nine sided with Vernon and only three were against him.

Out at Mount Carmel in 1992 Vernon talked to me about the trial. Winners are grinners. He was still getting a kick out of George trying to raise the dead.

I'm a guy where if you dig up my grandmother out of the grave I'm going to punch you out. I'm going to find

*out what you're doing. I am an American citizen . . .
If that was your grandmother out there, somebody dug
her up, would you come and confront those individuals?
You'd better! Or you wouldn't be my friend. My friends
aren't sissies. If they had a gun and they stood over her
and said "you're not gonna to move her body," what
would you come with? Stop and think.*

*The individuals here, some have sat with me confront-
ing religious leaders. They all have a Bible these people,
the religious leaders have a Bible, I got a Bible. It's like
in a game of war. In the movie you got a gun. I've got
a gun. Everybody's got a gun. It's all equalized . . .*

*I don't look like the Lamb, do I? I don't look like Jesus,
do I? Don't act like Jesus. Would Jesus have a gun? No,
but he has a sword though.*

It was then that this Prophet of Doom issued me a
warning.

KORESH *Don't pass over lightly what I'm trying to tell
you for your sake.*

KING Everybody's got a bit of bullshit in them.

KORESH *I sometimes have to use those means but
that's also written in the book and I'd some
time like to show you.*

KING Like I said to you before, I'm not going to
ask you patsy questions. People have made
serious allegations about you.

KORESH *Definitely . . . I can show you my gun, or Steve's guns. I just think it's irrelevant . . .*

KING Where are the guns now?

KORESH *Some of the guns are sold.*

KING You have guns?

KORESH *Yeah, we have some.*

KING Can you show me?

KORESH *In some of the houses, you know.*

KING Can we see that – is that OK?

KORESH *I guess, if you want, you know.*

David Koresh shoots me a black look. He's thinking hard. Then, a long, long pause. He looks at me.

KORESH *No. This right here is what I told you in the beginning. You know what the public thinks about guns. In this country right now the legislation is to ban all guns, and it makes nobody's business if we have a gun or not at this place.*

Guns are the right of Americans to have. They came and took these weapons away from us because they said we were bad people. Two weeks after the trial they gave us the guns back . . . So you know I want you to understand that bringing up guns . . . y'all don't have guns in Australia – your government says your people are

KING   *not supposed to have them. Our government says we can.*

KING   So you keep your guns?

KORESH   *Yeah, we got a gun here and a gun there. Most of the guns were sold. A lot of people say: "He's got guns, that makes him bad, that makes him a cult." It's just a raw deal in this touchy subject we're dealing with.*

KING   Would you use a gun if somebody trespassed?

KORESH   *They come in here with a gun and they start shooting at us, what would you do? Tell me, be realistic. This is America. This is not Australia. This is not Europe, not where a country overthrows a bunch of people, takes away their weapons so the people cannot argue any issues. Our Constitution states every citizen in America has the right to rebuttal the government. Guns? Yes, we have guns. Yes, we have knives and forks, yes, we have a bus. Yes, we use toilet paper.*

George might have had his doubts, but he still couldn't believe the verdict would go against him. He stood devastated outside the courtroom in his black Stetson and matching black vest and announced to the world: "There's no justice in these courts."

Fifteen months after the trial, George split a man's

head open with an axe. The man died. Only two people know the true story leading up to the murder – Marc Breault and Vernon Howell. Marc remembers:

It was a hot Waco summer in 1988. Things were quiet and life was pretty much routine. A man named Dale Adair came to Mount Carmel out of the blue. Dale was an old-time Branch Davidian who had become an alcoholic. Now, he told us, he wanted to get back to God. He came to the only religion he had even know, ours.

We talked to him for a couple of days. He seemed interested in what we had to say. But Vernon wanted to make sure. On the afternoon of the third day, Vernon took Dale aside and started giving him a Bible study. I was the only other person there. Vernon tried to show Dale that he was the Messiah. Vernon said Dale had to listen to him in order to be saved.

Suddenly, while Vernon was speaking, Dale got a glazed look in his eye. He stared up toward Heaven and said: "My God, my God. After all these years I understand. I'm the Messiah, I'm the David. Now I know why I've suffered all these years." Dale lost his sanity right before our eyes. He walked out then and left Mount Carmel.

A short time later Dale confronted George to tell him he was the true Messiah. George became enraged. Two Sons of God were bad enough. He didn't need a third one. George killed him with an axe. Dale was a nice guy who had a screw loose.

George got life, and Vernon got Mount Carmel. But it wasn't quite as easy as you'd imagine. With almost $70,000 in back taxes that George had neglected to pay, the state of Texas was about to seize Vernon's dream and auction it to the highest bidder. But fate, in the form of the elderly Chinese couple Vernon had recruited in Hawaii, stepped in. They wrote a check, and finally Vernon could claim his Holy Grail. At last, he was king of Mount Carmel.

Chapter Thirteen

Vernon the Rock 'n' Roll Star

Vernon's new domain was dirty, run-down and weed-infested. In fact, in May 1988 Mount Carmel resembled a disaster area. But while his subjects cleaned up the camp Vernon headed to Hollywood. He was feeling pretty self-satisfied now that he'd beaten George Roden and the Sheriff had handed back his arsenal, and it was time for a change of scenery. He'd decided he wanted to be a rock star.

Vernon took Marc Breault, Steve Schneider and Paul Fatta along for spiritual support, and a couple of wives for physical gratification. He knew that if he was to make it big in Hollywood, he needed two things: a slick manager and a production company. Vernon had the former in the person of Steve Schneider. The latter he had to invent to impress the cynical music moguls of Tinsel Town.

Vernon had instructed Schneider to locate the top managers in Hollywood and convince them that his music was the best thing since The Rolling Stones. He suggested Steve contact Madonna's manager, or Joe Satriani's or Mick Jagger's. Steve was to pose as a big-time manager and he was to push Vernon as the best act – and he'd worked with them all – he'd ever managed. Schneider had gilded plenty of lilies in his time, but even he was daunted by this particular mission.

With the help of millionaire Paul Fatta, Vernon was able to purchase huge amounts of musical equipment. It wasn't unusual for Vernon to walk into Hollywood's Guitar Centre, one of the largest music chains in southern California, and buy more than $20,000 worth of equipment.

Marc Breault was Vernon's keyboard player. "Vernon wanted everyone to know he had a lot of money," Breault remembers.

He figured that he'd have a good chance of converting salesmen, and especially saleswomen, if they knew they might be writing up a receipt for $20,000. Vernon would spend anywhere from two to eight hours in music stores, talking to both customers and staff alike.

It was just the usual Vernon bulshit. He'd tell them that God was going to bring about the Apocalypse through rock music.

"Have you ever listened to a sermon? How many of them do you remember? You don't remember, huh? You

hear 'em but they don't sink in right?" he would ask his astonished quarry.

"But God's got a plan, right? I mean a real plan. He's gonna tell the world about the God nobody knows and he's gonna do it through music. That's what I'm here for. That's what Marc's here for."

By now the hapless shop assistants wondered what the Hell had hit them. You could tell that they were really fascinated.

"Marc was a minister but he found out the churches don't have nothin'. God has given us prophecies that are written in the book. Everybody says they know the Bible don't they? We're putting the prophecies to music, hard rock music."

After these harangues everybody felt uncomfortable and embarrassed. I remember one day in the Guitar Centre the young manager was just about to throw us out until Vernon produced a little bit of magic – he whipped a check for $50,000 out of his money belt and condescendingly slapped it on the counter. The manager saw the Light!

Vernon only bought the best. He had a collection of about fifteen guitars, both acoustic and electric, that he was proud of showing off. He had two favorites, both white Charvel Jacksons, which he nicknamed "Adam" and "Eve." Vernon's expensive musical taste was not confined to guitars for himself, though. With Paul Fatta's money he bought Breault thousands of dollars worth of superb keyboard equipment.

People came over to where the cult members were staying in Hollywood to audition, and it would take them a few minutes to recover from the sight of so much gear. Most would-be rock stars are lucky if they can manage a guitar, amp, and keyboard. Vernon had it all.

Vernon needed a singer, and wanted it to be a woman. He advertised in the classifieds of local Los Angeles newspapers and music magazines under the name of Cyrus Productions. More than a dozen hopefuls answered the advertisements, but none of them worked out, because the cult leader said they simply didn't reach his lofty standards.

When the musical Messiah set his sights on something, he set them high. One night he said he heard a voice from Heaven. It said simply: "I will give thee Madonna." Now Vernon had some real competition. He wanted to meet Madonna, convert her, and live with her at Mount Carmel, where she would take pride of place in the House of David. The irrepressible Steve Schneider actually managed to speak to someone high in the Madonna hierarchy. The reply from Madonna's management was negative, as you'd expect

It didn't deter Vernon, though. He was absolutely infatuated with the "material girl." He prophesied that one day Madonna would come into his arms. She was put on earth for him.

Until the end of 1987 Vernon had had to be content with his ever-growing coterie of wives (there were ten by then). He couldn't bear to be without them so he had bought an old airport shuttle bus. The bus transported his lovers and other cult members between Mount Carmel and his new love nest in Pomona, a downmarket town about an hour's drive east of Los Angeles.

The expansive house, owned by Robyn Bunds's parents, Don and Jeannine, had been purchased for Vernon to use as he liked. Don was a well-paid designer engineer with over twenty years' experience. Vernon liked him immediately. Jeannine was a nurse, and later she would fulfil a critical role for the cult back at Mount Carmel. When Vernon's wvies began having prodigious numbers of babies for the Lord, it was Jeannine who delivered them. For the moment, the Bunds were content for the cult leader to have sex with their daughter in their own home, which became Vernon's home away from home.

The house may have been large, but there were only two bedrooms; the garage served as a dormitory. While sometimes up to twenty-five people slept in the small attic on top of the garage, Vernon took over the main house. At any given time there were no fewer than five women sharing this modern Solomon's bed chamber. Marc Breault stayed at Pomona, too, and he tells this story with distaste.

Vernon was on the floor of his bedroom with two of his mistresses lying next to him. He told me he was trying to sleep. I shrugged my shoulders. He didn't have to explain anything to me.

On the double bed was another of his wives. She was a fairly recent addition and she slept there alone. I don't know why but she was really unhappy and depressed. I think that the sharing was starting to get to her.

The two women on the floor felt sorry for her and the small dark-haired one said: "Why don't you go and be a husband to her? She needs you."

This surprised Vernon. He was used to his women squabbling and fighting for his attention. To have two of his women urging him to give his seed to a third blew him away.

It's one of the few times I've ever heard of this man doing what he was told. Usually it was he who gave the orders. But, in this case, he was only too eager to obey.

When Howell wasn't making love or making music, he was writing it, with his co-composer Marc Breault.

Vernon was a talented musician. He was good at coming up with ideas for songs, but he could never really finish them. Just imagine trying to form a band with the Son of God. The Son of God is never wrong. He never makes any mistakes. When he misses a beat, or plays a wrong note, it's never his fault. Sometimes, he would even claim

114

that His Father said that's the way it should sound.

I used to get frustrated with Vernon's inability to finish any of his countless religious love songs. Some of them were real doozies and I guess it's just as well they never made it into the Top Ten. Jimmy Swaggart would have come to him for lessons!

Some of the more lurid lyrics he penned for one song about the joy of sex were:

> *Six Inches into Heaven,*
> *I'm going to be in Paradise tonight . . .*

Cyrus Productions officially never existed. But that didn't stop Vernon promoting it as one of the biggest new names in music. He used Cyrus Productions as a front to attract talented musicians, whom he then tried to convert to his apocalyptic vision. The closest Cyrus Productions ever got to being a real company was the printing of its business card. The name was later changed to Messiah Productions.

Vernon was now about to embark on a new phase of his Grand Plan: the second wave of recruits from America, Australia, Great Britain and Canada. Before leaving for Hollywood he had given specific instructions to his father-in-law, Perry Jones, that Mount Carmel was to be ready for their reception. Jones and fifty followers toiled from sunrise to sundown, clearing the property of rubbish, removing rusting car bodies and repairing the small houses that were scattered around the 77-acre compound.

Vernon returned from California and was well pleased. As he stood with Marc Breault beside one of the two lakes, he surveyed his domain and told his right-hand man how good it looked, and how good it felt, now that Mount Carmel was theirs. So good, he said, it was as if they ruled the world. But even in Vernon's moment of triumph, Breault noticed a trace of unease on his ruler's face. Vernon talked about having to build up numbers, to expand the sect in order to protect Mount Carmel – and the secrets of Solomon's bed. His greatest fear was being exposed as a paedophile, a polygamist and an adulterer. And to secure his secret from the unwelcome gaze of the authorities the new leader of Mount Carmel began to arm his mob of Mighty Men in earnest.

Using some of the weapons given back by the Sheriff and newly acquired shotguns, semi-automatics and hand guns, Vernon introduced 24-hours-a-day, seven-days-a-week guard duty. To start with, the Mighty Men, including David Jones and Jimmy Riddle, stood watch from an existing shack. But Vernon still wasn't satisfied. He needed more troops.

It was time for another invasion.

Chapter Fourteen

The Second Wave

Let them give glory unto the LORD, and declare his praise in the islands.

– Isaiah 42:12

Vernon began his campaign with two thrusts: in June 1988 he went to Australia and Steve Schneider set sail for Britain. Marc Breault held the fort.

In contrast to most evangelical campaigns, which rely on PR and pomp, Steve Schneider flew into London's Heathrow Airport armed with nothing more than a Bible, a duffel bag and a silver tongue.

Schneider targeted his former Seventh-day Adventist college, Newbold, in Berkshire. The students and their conservative teachers were no match for the sophisticated smooth-talking American. He came alone and left with more than twenty converts, most of them young students who were impressed with his biblical prowess and his promise of meeting a real-life prophet who could change their lives forever. His new disciples weren't confined to naive young students. Three senior theology students and a full-blown pastor signed up four weeks after Steve's arrival.

Schneider's method was simplicity itself. He arrived, unannounced, in the lounge of the men's dormitory. He had no money, and nowhere to stay. His hope was that the good folk at the college would take pity on him and invite him in, and they fell for it, hook, line and sinker. Schneider then worked on the family of one of the students. The tragic result is that there is one man in England now, Samuel Henry, who lost his wife and his five children to the cult.

Steve purposely began missionary work exclusively with the male students of the college. Although his real objective was new women for Howell, he was afraid to show his hand directly. Once he had converted the men, he told them to invite their girlfriends, sisters and wives to hear the new truth. Again, it was all part of the Grand Plan – Vernon's ambitious breeding program, with him the only sire.

Meanwhile, Vernon flew into Tullamarine Airport, Melbourne, Australia for the second time in two years. He'd had another vision. The same voice that had proclaimed "I will give thee Madonna" thundered down from Heaven: "I will give thee Nicole." Vernon headed for the home of Bruce and Lisa Gent, parents of 19-year-old Nicole.

Whereas on Vernon's first visit to Australia, when his

appearance had appalled the Gents and repulsed Nicole, this time he was a different man. Lisa Gent was most impressed. She recalls: "Vernon was dressed to kill. He went out of his way to impress. He was all muscley. He was really brown, his hair was done nicely, his glasses were gone and he was wearing contact lenses, and he was here to influence Nicole."

Nicole already had a boyfriend. She had come to Melbourne for a holiday and was staying with her parents. Bruce Gent now says it was a case of being in the wrong place at the wrong time. "Nicole didn't have any chance. She was captivated. He worked on her day and night for three days. Once you're in that environment with Vernon, with that manipulation, it's very hard to break that charisma."

After three days, Nicole approached her parents and asked them: "Vernon wants me to ask you if it's okay for me to be his teddy bear for the night." They said yes.

Nicole became wife number eleven.

By another quirk of fate, Nicole's twin brother, Peter, was also there with his parents. He'd been bashed by a gang of bikies and was recuperating. "Right at that time Vernon was there, he turned Peter's head around completely," Bruce says. "He pushed all the right buttons with Peter, and Peter said, 'Yeah man, I can see that.' And he was away. There was no stopping Peter. He would move mountains to find out more and more and more. Peter had no chance at all."

Even while Vernon was "honeymooning" with Nicole he kept his mind on the job – and recruited the Gyarfas family. But Vernon's real interest lay in the youngest member of the family – Aisha, who was 12 years old.

Meanwhile, Elizabeth Baranyai, who had been Vernon's first Australian convert in 1986, had left the cult when it moved to Mount Carmel after disagreements with him. Elizabeth had even dared to hang up the phone on this self-styled Son of God while he was in mid-sentence. Howell retaliated by forbidding all cult members from having anything to do with her. The others obeyed. Elizabeth was shocked that her longtime friends could treat her that way.

Now, in mid-1988, and only a couple of months after her departure, Elizabeth wanted to rejoin the cult, not because she adored this rude Messiah, but because her boyfriend, Marc Breault, was still a disciple. The only way she could get to him was through Vernon.

Elizabeth, one of the few single women (including Michelle Manning) who had resisted Vernon's carnal advances, decided to test the supposedly all-seeing and all-knowing cult leader. She wrote him a letter, appealing to his vanity. To ensure her letter was obsequious enough, Elizabeth drew on dialogue from a television soap opera she had videotaped earlier that day.

Dear Vernon

I hope you take the time to read this letter, but if you don't I wouldn't blame you. I realize that you are the chosen of God and that God directs everything you do. If I have wronged you, I'll completely understand if you won't take me back into your heart.

These past few weeks have only served to make me understand how much pain you've suffered because of me. All the defiance and rejection I made you endure must have been torture for you.

I beseech you now, from the bottom of my heart and the core of my soul, to forgive my selfishness and misplaced pride. I implore you, as the Chosen One, to intercede with God on my behalf. Perhaps he'll listen to his Son.

It's only now I've realized just how much you've meant to me and just how much I've hurt you.

Yours in hope and fervent prayer
Elizabeth Baranyai

For Elizabeth, her letter was a sardonic joke, but Vernon was exhilarated. So exhilarated, in fact, that he read the letter to the entire following in Australia, as proof that he was always right.

Elizabeth recounts: "I thought that if God was with him, He would tell his prophet what I was up to. I still

121

thought Vernon might be right, but I wasn't sure. I did know he was extremely vain, however, so I appealed to his narcissistic nature. It worked and I was allowed to rejoin the cult and, more importantly, be with Marc. One thing about Vernon, he was always willing to take an ego trip." While she had rejoined the Branch Davidians, Elizabeth decided to stay in Australia rather than return to Texas.

Before he returned to Mount Carmel Vernon also converted Graeme Craddock, a 26-year-old Melbourne science and mathematics teacher.

The first June Craddock knew of her son's involvement with Vernon was when she opened her front door to a taxi driver. Graeme left for the airport with barely a goodbye.

The second international recruiting drive had been a resounding triumph. Thirty-five Britons and Australians made their way to Mount Carmel with Howell and Schneider. They were promised a religious paradise, but what they got was a Hell on earth.

Chapter Fifteen
The Swearing In

You stupid idiots! Get it in your minds! He says His heart has declared a teacher! If you don't follow the truth you're going to Hell! Psalms 90! You'd better start fearing God, 'cause he's going to burn you in the lowest Hell! His love! He's trying to show you he's going to kill you! If you don't listen!

– Vernon Howell , taped Bible study, 1989

On arrival at Mount Carmel the new recruits were sworn in during Bible study, a procedure that was witnessed by Marc Breault. What the Britons, Australians, Canadians, New Zealanders and Americans who made up the majority of the cult were about to experience was one of the most awesome demonstrations of mind control since Jonestown.

Listen to the Lord! You don't know his fear now! You don't know his terror yet! You haven't seen His anger! But you go ahead and dare Him!

The new recruits were herded into the front of the chapel. They sat on rough-hewn, wooden tiered benches close to the floor that forced them to look up at their would-be savior. The old hands had heard it all before, but the new converts had never witnessed anything like it in their Seventh-day Adventist colleges back in England and Australia. It wasn't what they came to hear, but at Mount Carmel there was no such thing as a democracy.

Calling another fellow brother a fornicator, or a thief, or a liar, you stand in the judgment of God! What's God going to call you one day?! How much evidence does He have against you, poor weak dust!?

The dictator was really angry. Screaming. Out of control. And the inductees were rigid with fear.

Get wise! The man on the white horse comes first! That's Psalms 1, that's Psalms 2, that's Psalms 3, 4, 5, 6, 7, 8! Learn 'em! That's what God says is going to happen! Do you hear?! Do you understand! It's war! These governments of this world are coming to an end. The minds of men are going to be focused upon a fact! Go ahead and laugh! Go ahead and muse in your minds. And see what happens to you, fools!

Vernon Howell stood behind a wooden pulpit and surveyed his audience with scorn. He was dressed in dirty, black stovepipe jeans, a creased blue shirt unbuttoned to the waist and a pair of stained sneakers. Just when they thought they couldn't take any more, their ruler suddenly returned to serenity.

It was dead silent. Then Vernon started to speak. Softly. Ever so slowly.

Now go contrary to that revelation of truth, and I guarantee you I'll kill you one day.

He wasn't joking. After fire-and-brimstone sermons like that the Vernonites were conditioned for anything. And that's exactly what was needed to survive life on that desolate piece of ground, a twenty-minute drive from Waco, Texas.

How long could it take one person to have absolute and total control over the mind of another human being? In most cases it took Vernon Howell just four weeks. And who were these people who so readily allowed themselves to be brainwashed into believing that whatever Vernon said was Gospel? And what were they searching for in life? Perhaps the best man to answer both these questions is Marc Breault. He not only fell into the vortex of lies and deception himself, but he propagated them throughout the world on behalf of his leader.

In my case I wanted to know God. There was something

inside me that said there had to be a God. But I didn't know him. I was raised a Roman Catholic but then became a Seventh-day Adventist when I thought they possessed the truth.

But after a while my Christian experience went dead. I was badly mistreated by the Seventh-day Adventist Church. After four years of college, and having spent thousands of dollars in the process, I was told repeatedly that I was unfit for the ministry because of my poor eyesight. I was left stranded with no job prospects and a useless degree. I decided that I had had enough. But I still felt a longing to know and understand God.

I think all the people recruited into the cult were of a similar mind. They had usually had rough childhoods. Many were abused and used throughout their lives. They wanted something better for themselves and for their children.

One girl, who became one of Vernon's wives, had seen her sister murdered before her eyes when she was only 5 years old. One of Vernon's Mighty Men was beaten repeatedly as a child. We all saw so much hate and suffering in the world. We turned to religion for answers.

And when we turned to religion we often found that it didn't solve much. Sure, we felt the initial high of new conversions, what Christians call First Love. But after a while, we found out that we, along with all of our other church brethren, were just like everyone else.

Vernon used the Bible to accomplish one thing, and one thing only. He used it to convince us he was a prophet, someone chosen by God. Vernon used many different angles and tactics, but that was his sole aim. Once a person thought he was a prophet, he had them. Once a person thought he was God, there was no turning back. Most people knew just enough about the Bible to fall victim to its misuse. The Bible is full of stories about people leaving their homes and loved ones to follow God.

Once Vernon established himself to his recruits, he used fear.

"You'd better listen to the prophet," he would say. He would refer to stories like that of Korah, who disobeyed Moses, only to have the earth open underneath him and bury him alive. He referred to Elijah calling fire down from Heaven to burn up 100 men who mocked him.

These are stories actually in the Bible. Many people don't realize they're there. And those who do often sanitize them to such an extent that their impact is lost. But Vernon, Steve and I were very good at bringing the emotional feel back to the biblical stories.

"Look at Jesus," Vernon often said. "Think. Here's a man who says he's a carpenter's son. He's just another guy. He comes up to you and says, 'sell everything and follow me.' What are you going to do? What are you going to tell 'em? You're going to say 'Get lost!' aren't

you? You're gonna tell him 'Who do you think you are? God?'

"Yet that's what Jesus did. Read it in your Bible. That's what Jesus told people. And here are these Christians today that talk about loving Jesus. 'If I was there when he walked the earth 2000 years ago,' they say, 'I would have followed him.'

"Bullshit! Look how they treat me. They say I'm rude. They say I'm arrogant. Those same people who say they'll follow Christ are the kind of people that would have been saying 'Crucify him! Crucify him!' Come on, get real!"

So once these people believed he was a prophet, they did whatever he said out of fear. Once you believe someone has a direct phone line to God, you're in trouble.

And trouble was something there was plenty of at Mount Carmel. Vernon couldn't call fire down from Heaven, but he could certainly mete out retribution on the hard, unyielding soil of his kingdom.

Chapter Sixteen

Rules, Rules and More Rules

In 1989 "routine" at Mount Carmel for the one hundred or so adherents was synonymous with child sex, child beatings, polygamy, secret births, the hoarding of weapons, military-style training, food and water deprivation, violence, mind control, and a series of insane rules and regulations.

Life at Mount Carmel began at 6 a.m. with guard duty. Kevin Whitecliff, a former prison guard, was the custodian of the watch and was armed with a Ruger .223 rifle. His orders were to shoot first and ask questions later.

Kevin spent his four-hour shift in a small run-down guard shack, with only a torn, flea-infested couch for company. Beside the shack was a large swinging gate that was always locked. No one went in or out without clearance. Whitecliff's responsibility was not only to keep people out, but, more importantly, to keep people in.

Guard duty was inordinately popular, the reason being that it was the only excuse tolerated for missing Bible study. It was rostered 24 hours a day, seven days a week. Nobody was immune from guard duty, even women with babies (including those who were pregnant) had to undertake it.

This level of security was unnecessary, according to Marc Breault, who volunteered for the watch as much as possible so that he could read and listen to music in peace. The biggest threat at Mount Carmel was Vernon's paranoia.

The most important rule in the Branch Davidian cult was never to admit to anything when questioned by outsiders, particularly any figure of authority. They were told in Bible study to get on the offensive if anyone asked questions. Vernon told them to make the questions look ridiculous, to turn their questions back on the inquirers, to confuse them. If that didn't work, he said, they were to send them to him.

Instructions on how to counter questions about the leader's polygamy were given. These were necessary because cult members were constantly questioned by concerned relatives or curious workmates, if the cult member was one of those allowed to work in Waco. The more people knew about the activities inside the compound, the greater the risk that Vernon would be exposed. He had a few very close calls, the closest of which was an FBI investigation initiated by Paul Fatta's father, Gordon. (It was 1987 and the FBI didn't believe the allegations could be true as they seemed too far fetched.)

Another rule was that the majority of cult members were banned from working. Vernon didn't trust them once they left his sight. Some were privileged enough to work as they earned good salaries and Vernon needed the money for his ultimate goal of setting up his own totalitarian state within the borders of Texas. Douglas Wayne Martin was a lawyer in Waco. He followed his wife and children into the cult in 1984 and provided Vernon with free legal advice throughout his reign. Along with Steve Schneider, he was one of the main cult members to negotiate with the FBI during the fifty-one day standoff that began on February 28, 1993.

Jeff Little was a highly successful and highly paid computer programmer. His salary topped $50,000 dollars a year, and in December 1989 he purchased a house in La Verne, California that became known as the "White House." Apart from being huge and painted white, this mansion was specifically acquired as a love nest for the President of the Branch Davidians.

Then there was Sherri Jewell, a school teacher recruited from Anaheim, California. Her young daughter Kiri would later figure prominently in Howell's downfall. For her part, however, Sherri was the most loyal of wives.

Other professions represented in the cult included a landscape supervisor, nurses, builders and restaurant owners. At first these professionals gave the cult leader money whenever he required it. Later, Howell didn't bother asking – he simply took it.

For those not working, Mount Carmel was a prison. No one could go into town without first clearing it with the cult leader. This clearance was not easily won. Members had to specify their reasons for leaving, as well as the duration of their time away from the compound. Howell kept close watch to make certain that no one stayed in town any longer than was necessary.

When Vernon was absent from Mount Carmel, a strict chain of command was put in place to ensure that no one slipped away unseen. Marc Breault remembers what it was like.

When Vernon was present, no one could go to town on their own initiative. Some people did have set schedules, however, that they were allowed to follow unless Vernon stopped them for any reason.

Being so close to the man, I didn't need permission to do anything. If you like, I ran my own race. And if I did happen to tell Vernon where I was going it was only in case he needed me for something. I didn't see why people had to be so strictly controlled. So when I was put in charge of letting people in and out, I allowed anyone to go whenever they wanted. Asking my permission was more a formality than anything else.

Vernon got angry so he put three others in charge of camp administration: Perry Jones, Novelette Sinclair, and, the worst, his mother Bonnie, who had joined the cult in 1986 (her husband and their son Roger followed in 1988). She was really strict and stuck to the letter of her son's law.

Aside from accidental encounters with those asking questions, Vernon's greatest fear was that people would eat the wrong kinds of food. He was paranoid about people buying french fries at, say, McDonalds. You weren't even allowed to go to the supermarket to buy yourself juice.

"All of you are gluttons," he would say. "If I relax the rules even for a minute you'll all go out there and eat Babylonian food."

Vernon became obsessive about what his followers ate. There were so many inane rules that even Vernon couldn't remember them all. It made life at meal times a nightmare for the cooks. One day bananas were the most nutritious fruit God created. The next they were banned because he feared pesticide poisoning.

Oranges could be eaten with grapes at the same meal but not with raisins. Fruit could not be eaten with vegetables, unless the vegetable was freshly cooked corn or the fruits were lemons, pineapples or avocados. Apples could be eaten with vegetables provided they were stewed first, as Vernon believed the chemistry of the apple changed when cooked. White bread was banned at all times. Brown bread was allowed, as long as it wasn't combined with corn, avocados or potatoes.

While some foods were prohibited because of their

chemical additives, hot dogs were highly recommended. But sometimes hot dogs were given the thumbs down because Vernon decided they looked too much like penises to be allowed at the table.

Like everything else, meal times were highly regulated. Breakfast was gruel – sloppy oatmeal – and a piece of fruit. Everyone ate at the same time and in the same place, a huge kitchen filled with trestle tables. No one was permitted to take food to their own homes. There were special exceptions, such as when someone got off work at a time that didn't coincide with a meal time.

Vernon didn't join his flock for breakfast because he often stayed awake until 3 a.m. or later watching television or videos with his welter of women. Usually, he would emerge in the early afternoon, and one of his first tasks would be to conduct an hour-long Bible study.

Cult members were required to study twice a day. The first study at the third hour from sunrise, and the second at the ninth hour from sunrise. This was a rigid rule. If Vernon was asleep for the first study, which was often, Marc Breault led the troops through the scriptures.

Lunch was always exactly at 1 p.m. Again, everyone had to eat in the commons area. Lunch was the best meal of the day, usually salad consisting of lettuce, tomato and onions. There were beans and bread, too. If Vernon was feeling particularly magnanimous, chicken would occasionally grace the table.

Like guard duty, kitchen detail was rostered. It was strictly women's work. The food was set up on tables that were attended by the women on duty. The diners lined up, bowls in hand, and filed past.

Dinner, without exception, consisted of popcorn. On the odd occasion the Vernonites were permitted to put a combination of brewer's yeast and safflower oil on their popcorn. Butter was banned. Marc Breault to this day cannot explain why popcorn had been chosen, except, perhaps, that it was cheap.

Vanilla, strawberry and praline-flavoured ice cream was acceptable but chocolate ice cream was on the banned list. So were chocolates in general.

Drinking water or fruit juice was not allowed for one hour after meals, because Vernon said it would neutralize the digestive acid in the stomach. Sometimes, though, he relaxed this rule and allowed his followers to drink Coca-Cola, pineapple juice or lemonade with meals. Alcohol was banned at all times, unless he gave permission, which was rare. And even then men were forced to drink beer and the women, wine cooler.

Smoking, too, was banned, until Vernon decided to take up unfiltered Camel Kings. Even then, followers needed his permission.

If you were pregnant, which was a common condition at Mount Carmel, the rules and regulations were even more confusing. Pregnant women weren't allowed to eat onions and were only permitted a very little starch. Spaghetti was banned. The wretched women could only eat foods that were specially labelled by Howell. But he rarely remembered to label the foods. The women spent most of their nine months stressed because Vernon continuously upbraided them for feeding his future demigods garbage.

> Therefore thus saith the Lord GOD, Behold, my servants shall eat, but ye shall be hungry: behold, my servants shall drink, but ye shall be thirsty: behold, my servants shall rejoice, but ye shall be ashamed:
>
> – Isaiah 65:13

Vernon was now becoming erratic. By May 1989 his constant companion, apart from Marc Breault, was an AK-47 semi-automatic, which he slung arrogantly around his shoulder. But his AK-47 wasn't the only weapon at his disposal. Vernon used food and water deprivation with devastating effect. An early example of this form of punishment, and perhaps the worst, took place in February 1989 and concerned his own son. Three-year-old Cyrus had been a naughty boy. Marc Breault was there.

Vernon felt his young wife Rachel wasn't educating their son Cyrus properly. He thought the Australian Nicole Gent was more cultured. He took Cyrus away from Rachel and sent him out to California so Nicole could raise him. About a week later, Vernon and I arrived in Pomona and Vernon wanted to see how Nicole had fared with the little boy.

He was initially pleased. In fact, he was so pleased, he tried to get Cyrus to disown his own mother, and say that Nicole was in fact his mother.

Cyrus started to cry immediately. He kept saying "Nicole isn't my mommy. My mommy isn't here. She's at the other place." Vernon became enraged and tried to inflict his usual punishment on the child – violence. Vernon grabbed his son by the arm, and hauled him over his knee. He pulled the little boy's pants down and said: "Don't disobey me, son. Say that Nicole is your mommy."

"No daddy, no daddy, no daddy." Vernon began to spank the child hard – really hard – on his bare bottom with a large wooden paddle. I tried to stop him. I was getting angry because I liked Cyrus and I felt Vernon was being a real bastard. Vernon told me it was his son and that I should mind my own business.

For the next twenty minutes, this man I looked up to as a prophet beat the living daylights out of his own flesh and blood. Even Nicole, who was normally a fanatical follower, started to cringe. She didn't dare intercede.

Vernon and I were yelling loudly at each other by now and I was seriously contemplating physical violence. But our yells were drowned out by the loudest screams

I've ever heard come from a child's throat.

"I want my mommy!" he kept saying over and over again.

That poor little kid's bottom was so red and full of welts it made me feel sick. To the little boy's credit, he still refused to admit that Nicole was his mother.

Vernon finally stopped beating him and told the now sobbing Cyrus that he should think about what a bad boy he was being. But Vernon couldn't just leave it at that. He had to scare the poor child into hysterics. Just when little Cyrus was wiping the tears from his face, Vernon told him to sleep in the garage, alone in the dark. Cyrus looked stunned. Then Vernon told the boy that there were huge rats in the garage and that they would eat him if he continued to disobey. Cyrus wanted to know what rats were, so Vernon told him – huge animals, as big as Cyrus himself, with sharp claws and teeth. Then the child began a fresh round of screaming that lasted nearly as long as the first. He begged Vernon not to send him out into the garage. He was shaking with fear.

Vernon ordered another cult member to prepare a place for the child in the garage. The poor boy was beyond fear now. He just kept sobbing.

Eventually Cyrus had to be dragged screaming to the garage. I went outside with him and whispered in his ear not to worry about the rats. I told him I hadn't seen any in the garage and that if I did I'd make sure they didn't hurt him. He calmed down a little after that but he continued to whimper.

I was so upset I didn't want to be around Vernon for a while.

Marc Breault spent the next three days away from the cult. He had begun to have serious doubts about the man who said he was the Messiah. His doubts were confirmed two weeks later when a senior cult member took him aside and told him about the most appalling aspect of Vernon's punishment of his son.

Little Cyrus had decided to stay, as any child would, with his real mommy. But Vernon wouldn't be defied by a 3-year-old. He sentenced Cyrus to undergo food and water deprivation until he acknowledged that Nicole was his mother.

For the next two days Cyrus didn't eat a morsel of food or drink a drop of liquid. At midnight on the second day Vernon had a conversation with God, who told him that he should give Cyrus a glass of water. Vernon went to his sleeping son, woke him, and put the glass in his hand. The child was too weak to even raise his head so Vernon had to force the water down his throat.

Vernon believed that children should be "spanked" from 8 months of age on. This was a divine commandment, as far as this prophet was concerned. Poor Cyrus was Vernon's guinea pig. When Vernon once asked Cyrus if he loved his daddy, the child's honest "no" drove his father into an absolute frenzy, which led to a thirty-minute beating. Finally, the little boy whimpered that he did love his daddy.

Children were spanked for any reason: crying during a sixteen-hour Bible study, refusing to sit on Vernon's lap, or daring to defy the prophet's wishes. The spanking was always the first line of discipline. Each child had his own special paddle with his name written on it. Whenever it was time for a spanking, the child was required to fetch his own "helper," as they were called, and bring it to whichever adult was meting out the punishment.

Some women thought the best way to please their Son of God lover was to be especially severe when dealing out discipline. Some women developed an enhanced reputation in this area. But sometimes it wasn't easy for the adults to spank the children. They couldn't find a spot on the child's buttocks that wasn't black and blue or bleeding.

Until now food and water deprivation had been common among the adults, but Vernon's rule was entering a frightening new phase. Violence and cruelty to children was soon to become commonplace.

Vernon went further with his food and water punishments. If somebody broke one of the raft of petty rules in the compound and was too frightened to own up, he directed that his entire following fast until the offender confessed. Usually this ended with an admission from the guilty party. The rest of the group resumed eating and drinking, while the culprit continued his or her penance until God was satisfied.

At this stage nobody was courageous enough to stand up to Vernon. They were confused because there was only one rule they knew for sure: that the rules would change according to Vernon's whim.

> I will also save you from all your uncleannesses: and I will call for the corn, and will increase it, and lay no famine upon you. And I will multiply the fruit of the tree, and the increase of the field, that ye shall receive no more reproach of famine among the heathen. Then shall ye remember your own evil ways, and your doings that [were] not good, and shall lothe yourselves in your own sight for your iniquities and for your abominations.
>
> – Ezekiel 36: 29-31

Howell used passages like this from the Bible to punish the heathen among his flock. If somebody ate an item of food without permission, Vernon decreed that they should be force-fed with the same food until they were sick. He even included Marc Breault, the man he trusted and respected more than anyone, in this punishment.

Vernon gave orders that no one should eat hot dogs. Scott Sonobe, a longtime member from Hawaii, didn't know about that order. So he ate a hot dog. When someone told Vernon of this blasphemy, he got really savage. He ordered a "solemn assembly," as he liked to say, and told everyone that a grievous sin had been committed.

I wondered what it was that would make him so angry. When he told us I couldn't believe it. I told him that Scott didn't know about his orders and that he shouldn't be punished for something he didn't know about.

But Vernon would have none of it. He was determined to teach us all a lesson. He began frying hot dogs on the grill and ordered everyone to keep eating until he stopped. This applied to both men and women.

We sat there for about an hour eating hot dogs. After the first four, everyone started to go as slowly as possible. The women were really suffering when they hit their seventh.

Big Joel Jones didn't consider this a punishment at all and that really pissed Vernon off, because the more Vernon fried, the more Joel ate. Vernon finally ran out of hot dogs after both Joel and Scott put away twenty-six between them. Joel was still smiling, and even told Vernon he was still hungry.

But Vernon had the last laugh. For the next week, Joel was constipated.

If there was anything Vernon hated it was being directly defied. Joel Jones, however, continued to annoy his leader. The blond-haired, blue-eyed Joel Jones, brother of chief Mighty Man David Jones, stood 6' 3" tall and weighed 210 lb. It was all muscle. You didn't give lip to big Joel. Most people were frightened of him.

Joel was sick and tired of the endless stultifying rounds of Bible study. He decided Vernon could preach all he liked, and for as long as he liked, but he'd be doing it without one Joel Jones. One day, when all the converts of Mount Carmel were sitting expectantly in the chapel waiting for their daily dose of dogma, Vernon noticed Joel was missing. He flew into a rage, walked out of the chapel and strode across the compound to the small tin shed that the big blond man called home.

Vernon flung the door open, ready to have it out with Joel. When he saw the big man sleeping sound as a baby with his blanket tucked up to his chin, he lost total control. He set upon the sleeping giant and punched him mercilessly and repeatedly about the head. Joel woke in fright, and began cursing his leader. Vernon yelled at him that he had to hit him, that it was the only way he could save him. It was God's way, he said, of telling him he loved him. Joel had no choice but to take the blows, both verbal and physical. If he'd retaliated he would have been torn limb from limb by the thirty Mighty Men.

There are many other examples of Vernon's sadistic

behavior. Now, even the most faithful of his followers were beginning to doubt him. His performance during Passover, April, 1989 gave even more reason to be concerned. Howell completely sealed the compound, gathered his congregation in the chapel, and regaled them with a dream he had had about devil worship the night before. He even recorded it on cassette for sale.

> You know, we've got to, we've got to sacrifice to serve our Devil. We've got to have something, you know what I mean? And so I, I knew what he was really asking. He didn't. He wanted some, just some, human help for now. You see? He wanted just some comfort for the time then being. You know he has hunger, and desire and need. He has fantasy and wickedness. Everybody does and I knew there was only one way to help him. That was to help 'em all.

Vernon was really on the edge by now.

Chapter Seventeen
On the Edge

It's unique, it's bizarre and it's scary. Very scary. But I have had to exercise by many different ways by the Spirit of God to prepare for fear, anxiety, torment, torture. The scriptures to me have become not so much a thing of fantasy but a thing of reality. The lessons are very clear.

– Vernon Howell, Mount Carmel, April 1989

In April 1989 Vernon Wayne Howell had a dream. A bad dream. It was a nightmare that ushered in a treacherous new era at Mount Carmel. There was no turning back after this one.

We're going to the supermarket. And I am really frustrated. And this supermarket, I'd never been in it before. But it was, it was colossal, it was, it was unreal. An unreal, colossal supermarket.

Men, women, and little children sat in their Bible study

145

waiting for the next bulletin from God. They'd heard many things here in the chapel at Mount Carmel but this was a revelation. Not about the Bible, though. They were learning about their leader.

And I'm walking down the aisleway, you know, and I'm looking and I'm really, I'm hating life. You know. You know this big supermarket, yeah it's fine, but I'm not caring about eating, I'm not concerned about food. And I see this one long . . . it looked like a . . . like a skinny . . . like a . . . like a thing, like a, what do they call it? Well the impression was to me I just know that it was long and skinny, you know, wrapped up real tight. And, and I go over and I can't make it out because it's just a long thing wrapped up, you know, and I look over at the actual thing on it, you know, and it's been there for a while and it's kind of like, you know . . . the thing is a human cadaver. And I'm going to myself, "Aw, sick." I said, "Man, sick." I looked at it again, and I kind of looked at it and said "Oh, man, sick." And I got really teed off and I turned around and I walked down the hall and I saw this woman over there and she's, like, taking care of some juices or something . . . and I said "Ma'am, will you come over here and help me? What is this?" And she goes, "Why, that's, that's, that's human meat." I said, "What you saying?" "Well," she goes, "these people, they, they donate their bodies for this." You know. I says, "You mean

146

there's people who eat other people?" She goes, "Yeah. This store has everything."

Vernon's dreams were contributing more and more to his already perverse theology.

And I grab this girl and I pushed her around like that, in front of all those girls and even Judy [Schneider]. Judy was going . . . And I grab her and I'm pulling her clothes off and I wack it right to her. And I turned myself over and I watched the TV set. And I came out of my dream.

The subject was rape – violent rape – and the message was: those who laugh at Vernon now, suffer later. In Bible study, he commented on his dream.

Now that is a dream, isn't it? Huh? Now that is a dream. Well these baby girls they had a lesson to learn, didn't they? Right? I grabbed her little hanky and tied it through some knots she never dreamed possible, turned it into a star.

She thinks that's interesting. They're amazed at that . . . And all of a sudden their smiles all left 'em. And, uh, I grabbed her little butt, and I threw her clothes off and the other girls was looking there and I just wack it to her, boy! There ain't one person in that room doing anything to me.

I have a look over and I start watching TV like I'm

not even concerned about what I'm doing. Know what I mean?

By now, this Holy Hitler was teaching that his Mighty Men would not only guard the door of his bedroom but that they would embark on a rampage to rape the women and murder the men who mocked him. The children were not to be spared either.

KORESH   *"Everyone that is found shall be thrust through." With what? Our sword right? "And everyone that is joined unto them shall fall by the sword" . . . That's the Babylonian children . . . "And their wives ravished." Babylonian girls, what happens to these Babylonian girls with this mighty army?*

CLASS   *They get ravished.*

KORESH   *What does that mean in English terminology?*

CLASS   *Raped.*

KORESH   *Is that what your Bible says? These girls must be worth nothing in that time, huh?*

Couldn't the lawyers, school teachers, nurses, engineers and accountants among the followers see that the new kingdom Vernon had promised them had turned into a Temple of Doom? Incredibly, no. And that is why, in

October 1989, after two months' intensive teaching, Vernon Wayne Howell was able to turn his attentions from the young girls and strip the men of their last remaining dignity. He took their wives. He did it with his own special brand of mind control.

In January 1992, when we were filming at Mount Carmel, I asked Vernon whether he taught his followers – or brainwashed them.

I show them. I sometimes tell people this. People come here skeptical. And they say, hmmm, we're going to figure this guy out. And I say, point blank, "When you come here, you have your mind filled with all kinds of thoughts and opinions . . . You're going to learn the Revelation of Jesus Christ. You're going to learn words. And if those words cleanse your mind, those opinions, and puts in your mind the truth, then the opinions are going to be washed away." If that's brainwashing, yes . . . Doesn't Christ brainwash you? Gets rid of the filth and puts in the good.

That afternoon Vernon allowed us to film his mind-control classes. The followers of this man with the fatal charm appeared zombie-like in the large wooden chapel. They sat there, soaking up the Word. Vernon played them like a fiddle. They chanted their responses in unison. He reminded me of a school teacher that lectures by rote. The response of his adherents came as one voice, in a low monotone. The responses lacked energy, and everybody looked very tired.

KORESH *When a man comes again, what's he gonna bring?*

CLASS *The book.*

KORESH *Those who want to learn – are they gonna live?*

CLASS *Yes.*

KORESH *Looks like someone's gonna get a butt-whipping in the near future, aren't they?!*

It was high-powered stuff, delivered at machine-gun pace, but the only things blown away were their minds. The message was simple: Vernon would eventually die in glorious battle against unbelievers. The world would end and all those who died for him would join him in Heaven and help him rule the world. The rest of us would perish. Vernon taught his followers that he was the only person in the world who could reveal the exclusive secret of the Seven Seals, which the book of Revelation (according to him) says will lead to the end of mankind.

Vernon liked to refer to himself in the third person.

"The guy's tough, he's got more than guns, he's got God." He strides from one side of the chapel to the other, posturing and posing. The people are transfixed. "How come religion's not weeping? Here's a revelation of Christ

150

nobody knows. For 2000 years men have suffered and died, taught theories, spoken their own inventions, and people have risen up empires, spent billions. Yes, Luther had an ideal, too, and when Luther began to spread his message to the Catholic Church, which was the political power of his day, BLOODSHED! INQUISITION! DEATH! MURDER! KILLING! That's religion, that's the church for you."

Marc Breault offers insight into that religion. The story begins in August 1989.

We had just arrived in California after a long three-day drive from Texas. Vernon's car was experiencing mechanical difficulties. Whenever we traveled between Texas and California we took the southern route, sticking to Interstate 10 the whole time. During the summer the weather could get extremely hot, especially through the deserts of Arizona and California. That was the case this time. Only this time the heat wave seemed to be all through the South West. We drove non-stop through the first night. The weather was so hot during the day that Vernon's red Chevy Camaro kept overheating and we had to stop at the side of the road to let it cool.

By the time morning of the second day had dawned, we were nearing exhaustion. We kept going, however, until early afternoon. Then it became evident that neither the Camaro nor our bodies could take much more of the 100+ heat. So we decided to stop at a hotel in New Mexico until nightfall. This would allow us to travel during the cooler night.

But we were so tired we simply lay down and went to sleep. Vernon and 13-year-old Aisha Gyarfas went into the only bedroom, while Ian Manning and I slept on the living room floor. It galled me that a girl so young was the sexual plaything of a man who was then 30 years of age. The poor kid believed she was destined to be queen of God's new universe.

I could tell that Ian Manning, Lisa Gent's oldest son, wasn't thrilled either. He was going to California to rejoin his wife before coming back to Australia. I remember Ian telling me that he couldn't wait to get out of there. I remember, too, thinking how strange it was to want to leave the Messiah's presence, when we were supposed to love God as well as the Word of God. Still, I envied Ian his permission to fly to Australia, as far away from Vernon as possible.

I was trying to get to Australia as well. My wife, Elizabeth, to whom I had only been married for four months, was there waiting for me. (We had married in April, when Elizabeth had come to the States on a holiday visa.) But my visa had not been processed yet and I wasn't certain whether I would be able to go even if I got permission to migrate to Australia.

The next morning Vernon came out of the room where he and Aisha had slept. He told us in a serious, *calm voice that he had just had a vision from God. According to Vernon, God had told him to masturbate. When Vernon had asked why, God had told him that it was to show that he must give his seed to the world.*

That was strange! What was stranger still was the way Vernon told us about the vision. He said that it was to be a secret. No one else was to know about it. To Vernon, this was some sort of major revelation. When Vernon went to take a shower, Ian and I both looked at one another trying to figure out what was going on. Something was cooking, there was no doubt. Vernon had been acting more abnormal than usual over the past month or so. He seemed preoccupied with something and he wasn't as talkative as he usually was.

After we eventually made it to the Bunds house in Pomona, California Vernon spent all his time emphasizing his mission to fill the world with righteous children. On the day that Ian and Allison Manning were scheduled to leave for Australia, Vernon made the comment that all the women in the world should want his seed. Allison asked Vernon (in somewhat of an alarmed voice) whether he meant that spiritually or literally. Vernon became enraged and castigated Allison for asking such a question. Vernon said that the question was ridiculous, since she was a married woman. But the fact that Allison had expressed such shock and alarm at the possibility that the remark had been meant literally had bruised Vernon's ego.

Vernon did not like the fact that some women preferred other men. He was very conscious of his appearance and his shortcomings. Allison obviously did not want to belong to Vernon in any way other than a spiritual one and Vernon obviously did not like that.

Ian and Allison Manning flew to Australia that same night. Once again they confided in me that they could not wait to be on that plane. "This is nothing personal against you, Marc," Ian said, "but I can't wait to get out of here."

When I woke up the next morning I had serious doubts. On the one hand Vernon could be the Messiah. On the other, he could be a man with a psychological disorder who believed that God told him to masturbate as a symbol that he must give his seed to the world. Or, worst of all, he could simply be a paedophile who hid behind a Bible. Which one was it? To a normal person the choice would be obvious. But I was not a normal person on that morning. I was a man fighting against the intense conditioning and brainwashing I had experienced for over three-and-a-half years. It had taken time for my good sense to break through, but, once it had, the struggle was on. I was making a decision that would affect my eternal life. One wrong move, and I would be lost forever, consigned to the flames of Hell without even the slightest hope of liberation.

As the others began to stir in the dormitory in the garage, I put aside my doubts and fears, as I had so many times before. The day was warm and sunny and it lulled me into a false sense of security. I went outside and was soon joined by Steve Schneider, my best friend and the best man at my wedding.

Steve and I engaged in small talk until the others got up. Today was Saturday, our Sabbath, so no one had to get ready for work. The atmosphere was pretty relaxed and friendly. Suddenly Steve decided to call some old friends of his in South Carolina. Dale and Carol Krohn had listened to Vernon's Message in 1987 and had invited Vernon over to their home in 1988. They eventually rejected his teachings as heresy. Steve wanted to try one last time to bring them back into the fold.

He got through to Dale on the first try and started telling him how awesome the message was and how it was going places. I knew that Steve was just giving a sales pitch. But he was so good at doing this, I almost believed him myself. Steve tried to get Dale to come down for one more try but he couldn't manage to get any kind of commitment out of him.

Steve was really worried about his friend. What is difficult for the reader to understand is that Steve believed Dale and his family were on their way to Hell. Dale and his wife had rejected the Truth. They had gone against the Light. To Steve's way of thinking, people could be friendly, helpful and considerate of others but still burn in Hell simply because they rejected a set of doctrines. Steve had tried his very best to sell the Message to them, but he had failed to impress them.

Worrying about the eternal salvation of someone can be a terrible burden and Steve did what he always did when this happened. He started questioning the Wisdom of God. "Of all the people in the world," he said, "why did God have to choose a bum from Texas who can hardly speak English and who is always so rude to people?" That was Steve for you. Steve and Vernon had a sort of love–hate relationship. On the one hand, Steve believed Vernon was the Messiah, the Son of God. On the other, he disliked Vernon as a person and totally disapproved of his methods and character. When Steve recruited people, he painted Vernon and the group as the best thing since satellite television. When he talked candidly, however, a whole different perspective emerged.

I spent most of that morning talking to Steve, wondering where we were going and what we were doing here. Vernon had been promising, for example, that our music would "take off" soon, but nothing had happened. Every time we started to get somewhere in that area, Vernon would do something to stop our progress. We seemed to be caught in an endless cycle of taking one step forward, and two steps back.

Of course, Steve and I couldn't talk like this all the time. Others were around and one wrong word could land a person under the stick, literally. Vernon had been beating people since early 1989. It was then that Vernon *had actually had people beaten for disobedience. Some cult members had been traveling from Texas to California in two vehicles. Vernon had ordered them to stay together. During the course of the trip they had become separated, and arrived in California hours apart. As punishment, Vernon ordered one of his strong men, Floyd Houtman, to beat the disobedient ones with a large stick. From then on Vernon meted out this punishment to everyone who disobeyed. So when Steve and I talked negatively about Vernon and the Message, the way we were doing now, we had to make sure that no one else was around.*

I was not in the mood for a long Bible study that day so I hoped Vernon would sleep late into the afternoon. But, as luck would have it, he got up at around 1 p.m. Aisha had been his woman. I could tell because she came out with him looking the way people do who get up in the afternoon after a late night. Vernon went and ate his lunch. On this occasion, he was eating spinach straight out of the can. During this period Vernon had a thing for canned spinach. He seemed to think that spinach would increase the iron content in his bloodstream and thus boost his sexual potency, something he was having trouble with then. At least, that is what he used to say.

As usual, people hung around him, trying to get his attention. I had grown out of that phase by then. I was hoping that he wouldn't give a study today but I reasoned that would be unlikely. It was Sabbath and we almost always had a study on Sabbath. During the week Vernon didn't really care about people having to go to work, but on Sabbath that barrier was removed. At around 3 p.m. Vernon called everyone for a study.

Vernon started by reading large portions of scripture. He tried to scare us. He said: "Do you think that just because you are in this Message you will be saved? Many are called but few are chosen. God will shake out most of you." I noted, with apprehension, that Vernon was getting revved up. Oh no, I thought, this is going to be a really long one.

After telling us how difficult it was to be saved, Vernon went on to teach that, in fact, no one was saved at all except for himself. He did this by showing us that no human being was living up to the Christian standard. He used scriptures like, "Be ye therefore perfect, even as your Father which is in heaven is perfect" (Matthew 5:48). "If God were to judge you according to that scripture," he said, "you wouldn't stand a chance. You'd go to Hell." When I say, "Vernon said", I mean he really got into it. The guy was charismatic. He went into detail concerning why we were not living up to the Christian standard. He'd yell out: "How dare you claim the blood of Christ can save you, when you don't do what Christ said for you to do."

Vernon was good at making people feel guilty. He would ask: "Are you really a Christian? Do you have the *fruits of the Spirit? The apostles of old used to heal the sick and raise the dead. They were Spirit-filled men. What about you? Do you do those things today? How can these stupid churches talk about the gifts of the Spirit when they don't even do what the apostles did 2000 years ago? How dare you, or anyone, claim to be led of the Spirit?*

"*Everybody claims God talks to them. 'Oh the Spirit leads me,' they say. But nobody knows what the Spirit really teaches. Nobody knows the prophecies. Nobody is perfect like Christ said to be perfect. So they sin against the Holy Ghost. They commit the unpardonable sin because they claim to be led by the Spirit, when they are actually led by the Devil.*" *(In Matthew 12:30–32, Jesus Christ defines the dreaded unpardonable sin as blasphemy against the Holy Spirit. Here, Jesus teaches that God can forgive any sin except for this one. Hence, it is called the unpardonable sin.)*

Because Vernon was the "Messiah" by everyone's standards, people would confide intimate things to him. Being the Judas that he was, Vernon would then go to Bible study and blab these secrets to the whole group. Those with the secrets would sit there ashen-faced, squirming on their seats. Vernon would have made a lousy priest.

Today's targets were the married couples. He was saying stuff like: "Why did you marry your wife? You had a feeling between your legs and you wanted to satisfy it. You had lust in your heart and you fulfilled it by fucking your wife. You didn't really love your wife did you, did you?!"

Vernon often talked like that for hours. Why didn't the guys tell Vernon to jump in the lake? Because Vernon was the Messiah and everything he said was direct from God himself. So when you said "No Vernon, that's not true" you were telling God that He was a liar. And, really, what person who believes in God wants to say "Hey God, you're full of it!"? That's not generally considered a good idea.

So Scott Sonobe and Mark Wendel, who were copping the brunt of this, were thinking that since God said they only married to satisfy their lust, then it must be so, even though their own minds told them that wasn't true. Of course, Vernon also said things like, "You loved your wives according to how the world feels love. Now it's time to love them the way God wants you to." So at least it was a form of love instead of pure love.

What surprised everyone was Vernon's definition of loving one's wife God's way. After Vernon was finished drumming into everyone that they were lost, he stressed that he, the Lamb, owned everything. He kept calling himself "the heir of all things." The only way we could be saved was through him. Only he, the Lamb, was worthy. And why was Vernon worthy? Simply because God said so. And because he was worthy, and the Lamb, God had given him everything and everyone. That meant that everyone who had married had married one of his wives. And since they had married before they met Vernon, according to his twisted logic, that meant they'd been running around marrying Vernon's women without his permission.

"All you men are just fuckers, that's all you are. You married without getting God's permission. Even worse, you married my wives. God gave them to me first. So now I'm taking them back. I'm the only one that can produce righteous children. The rest of you are just shit."

People looked at each other, stunned. They were in total shock. But Vernon wasn't finished. He went on to say that when he made love to our wives, we could experience it through him.

It took Vernon sixteen hours to finish this Bible study. He kept saying things like: "So Scott, how does it feel to know you're not married any more?" I couldn't believe that he was teaching this to people. He was losing me fast. The funny thing was that all of Vernon's "wives," the single girls, thought this new tack was great entertainment. They'd sacrificed and suffered all these years, so why shouldn't someone else? But Judy Schneider, Steve's wife – boy, was she upset.

If anyone ever loved her husband, it was Judy. She knew exactly what Vernon meant, but her husband, Steve, refused to believe it. He kept saying that we must have misunderstood Vernon. He was in total denial.

But there was no denying it. Vernon was emphatic.

As he talked, he would suddenly stop and stare off into space as if in direct communication with God. During these periods he would stay things like: "Oh my God, this is beautiful!", "It all makes sense!", "I understand now!" and "What a truth!". When Vernon did this it was positively scary. It was almost as if God himself were in the room. I could see the looks of fear on everyone's faces.

At one point, Vernon laughed at us. He said (after coming out of one of his "visions"), "All these years my wives have sacrificed to be with me. They have shared me around among themselves and you said it was okay because you didn't have to suffer. You didn't have to sacrifice. Well, now you have to sacrifice. How does it feel?"

I must confess that my first reaction upon hearing this teaching was to feel sorry for the others. Maybe something in my mind clicked and I said to myself: "I'm never going to do this so why should I worry about it." You would think that I would have felt outrage and indignation that someone could be teaching what he was. But I was really in shock and I knew that my life would never be the same again after that day. I think everyone was in shock too, especially the married ones.

After the study he asked for questions. But after sixteen hours everyone was too shocked and exhausted to even think straight, let alone challenge him. One married woman simply said, "I'm with you Vernon, I just want you to know I'm with you."

I know I belonged to this organization and went along with many things. But this theology was too crazy – even for my then twisted and warped mind. It was garbage.

I confronted Vernon and accused him of teaching adultery. He became enraged and yelled at me. "How dare you accuse the Son of God," he ranted. I responded by saying, "But you used to teach . . ." Vernon interrupted me and shrieked: "That's what the Lamb taught yesterday but today he teaches something else."

I knew that this rift between Vernon and me would never be healed. I saw myself standing on a small patch of ground. All around me were the fires of Hell. Soon my patch of ground would be consumed as well but I had nowhere else to go. Wherever I walked, I would be engulfed in the flames. I somehow knew that everyone would eventually accept Vernon's new teaching and that I might do so as well. I cried out in despair.

The whole room was silent. Everyone, including Vernon and Steve, was staring at me. It was around 6.30 in the morning and I must have dozed and dreamed all that bit about the flames and the shrinking patch of ground. In a cult with a history full of prophets and visions, everyone wanted to know what had happened to me. For the first time, Vernon actually looked a little worried. His bold and intimidating demeanor left him and he ended the study then and there. He went to the kitchen to get breakfast. I just sat there dumbfounded. What a time to have a dream like that!

I would like to say that I stood as a tower against evil and heresy. I would like to say that I defied Vernon and everyone else boldly and without fear. A few months later, I would start to exhibit those characteristics. But on that morning I was timid and tired. Instead of a warrior shining in the battle armor of faith, so to speak, I was a weak-kneed man who might run away at any moment.

The first thing I did, in fact, when Vernon finally went to bed, was call Elizabeth in Australia. I did not use the phone in the house for fear of discovery. Vernon had commanded us not to tell anyone of the night's proceedings. I was, by this time, bordering on hysterics. I told Elizabeth that Vernon had flipped out and gone crazy. I told her what Vernon had been teaching. I told her everything.

I was all for leaving the group then and there. I didn't even want to pack. I just wanted to get out of there as fast as possible. Elizabeth, who must have felt like a ton of bricks had landed on her, told me to stay for a while just to learn Vernon's "new light" better. Elizabeth, who had been following Vernon for years too, wasn't sure that Vernon was wrong. After all, she hadn't heard his study. I might be jeopardizing my eternal salvation for all she knew. So we decided that I would stay for a while longer and report back to her.

The next day, Steve, Judy and I went to the park. As soon as we settled down in the grass Judy burst into tears.

She sobbed uncontrollably for several minutes and nothing Steve and I did could make her stop. It was terrible to watch. Steve and Judy weren't just husband and wife, they were the best of friends. They were, in my book, the perfect couple. I remember praying to God that, when I got married, I would have a relationship like theirs.

Steve and Judy had no children, even though they had been trying for years. "If Steve and I had a baby," Judy sobbed, "maybe I could handle this better. But all I have is Steve. How can God be saying all this?"

"Maybe God isn't saying this," I said. "Maybe Vernon is teaching error." I wasn't sure, of course. For all I knew Vernon could be the Messiah. But that study was like a splash of cold water. I had been asleep for years, but now my eyes were beginning to open.

Chapter Eighteen
Marc and Elizabeth

Marc Breault met Elizabeth Baranyai in April, 1986 when she arrived in America to investigate Vernon's message. It was love at first sight. But the cult leader would have none of it. He did everything he could to separate the two.

Vernon wanted Elizabeth for himself. His tactic: tell her that God had ordained her to be the keyboard player in his band. So he ordered her to go back to Australia, sell all, and return to the cult.

When Elizabeth returned to America, Vernon began applying the pressure. He told her that the success of his entire mission on earth depended on her joining the House of David. Elizabeth recalls: "He used to single me out in Bible studies. He used to accuse me of not wanting to make babies for God. He did everything he could to separate me from Marc. We weren't allowed to sit next to each other. We weren't even allowed to talk to each other. Even his other women tried to get me to join the harem. A lot of them looked down on me and ridiculed me for wanting a mere mortal instead of the Son of God."

When it became apparent that Elizabeth wasn't going to join the House of David, Vernon tried a bolder approach. He knocked on her door at night when she was in bed and asked to come in. Elizabeth's response: "That depends on what you want." Vernon left.

Finally, in frustration Elizabeth was dumped from the band and Marc Breault put in her place. Vernon's idea was to set Elizabeth and Marc against each other. Even that didn't work.

In June, 1987 Elizabeth's visa ran out and she made plans to return to Australia. When she went to say goodbye to the sex-crazed prophet, he said, "I'm going to miss you. You know, I daydream of making love to you." Elizabeth replied: "Dream on, because that's as close as you're going to get." Vernon gave her a hard look.

While in Australia, Elizabeth was kicked out of the cult after she hung up the phone on Vernon. Although she was allowed back after a short time, she remained in Australia and didn't return to Mount Carmel until April, 1989 on yet another visitor's visa.

By this time Breault had had enough. He told Vernon that he intended to marry Elizabeth. Vernon didn't want to lose his right-hand man and, anyway, his ego could only take so much bruising from one woman. When Elizabeth arrived at Mount Carmel, she was surprised when Vernon announced that she could finally marry the man she loved. After three long years they wasted no time.

The wedding was a simple affair. It was attended by just two other people. Steve Schneider was Marc Breault's best man, while Sherri Jewell was Elizabeth's matron of honor. Elizabeth's bouquet consisted of wildflowers plucked from the fields of Mount Carmel.

They were married on April 28, 1989 by James Collier, a justice of the peace. Almost exactly four years later Collier had another encounter with the cult. He was called upon by the authorities for the grisly task of confirming the deaths of eighty-six men, women and children in the charred rubble of Ranch Apocalypse.

On that day in 1989 James Collier performed a marriage ceremony that lasted about five minutes. The reception was a sumptuous affair. The four cult members, dressed in their wedding clothes, banqueted at Sizzlers. It was better than eating at Mount Carmel, as Marc Breault remembers.

The four of us were starving. I remember Steve thanking us for getting married, just so he could get a decent meal. I told him I'd be glad to go through it all again, for the same reason.

We pigged out. When you were away from Mount Carmel, you almost felt like a normal human being. Sherri was a little nervous, because she knew Koresh would have a fit if he could see how much Steve and

I were putting on our plates. But even she bowed to her hunger pangs.

In the midst of our banquet, we even managed to feel somewhat sorry for those poor people back at the Ranch, who were probably eating a simple lettuce and tomato salad.

We were having fun. Our wedding was so bizarre even we couldn't believe it.

While eating our fried chicken, sweet corn, and rice, Steve and I made jokes. We had to be careful what we said, however, because Sherri was around. In those days she meant well, but she was fanatically loyal to the cult leader.

"Too bad we weren't married in the winter," I said.

"Why?" asked the others.

"Because we'd be wearing our jackets then, and we could cram food into our pockets and sneak it back on to Mount Carmel," I answered. Goodness knows I'd done that enough times in my college days.

But still one thing was missing. Wedding rings. Following the lunchtime feast, the wedding party went to the local mall in Waco and bought two white-gold bands.

When the happy couple returned to Mount Carmel, however, their welcome was anything but cordial. Vernon didn't like the wedding rings, especially since the newly-weds hadn't asked his permission to buy them. After berating them publicly during an eight-hour

Bible study, he ordered them to return the rings.

Tired and disgruntled on what should have been the happiest day of their lives, Marc and Elizabeth retired to the "honeymoon suite," a tool shed crammed full of equipment. There was no bed, only just enough room to squeeze two single sleeping bags on the hard, wooden floor of the loft.

Shortly afterwards Elizabeth had to go back to Australia. She hadn't planned on marrying when she took her four weeks' leave from her job; after only three weeks of wedded bliss she returned home to her job and was once again separated from Marc.

Breault began applying for a migrant's visa so he could join his wife in Melbourne, Australia. He would not see her again for five months.

Chapter Nineteen

Guns and Rosaries

Power tends to corrupt and absolute power corrupts absolutely.

– Baron Acton (1834–1902)

It was mid-1988, 5 a.m., still dark and dead quiet. I was lying in my sleeping bag fully clothed. That was the way our leader told us to sleep. The reason: we had to be ready for action in case we came under attack during the night. Vernon was paranoid about "the authorities," as he called them, raiding Mount Carmel after dark and taking him away. He didn't give a damn about anyone else, but he knew he had a lot of skeletons in the closet and he was absolutely terrified about the prospect of jail.

So that's why we were doing guard duty. Anyway, I was lying there in my sleeping bag and I was thinking about the day ahead . It was going to be a hot one.

Suddenly there was a loud shout from the guard house, which was only about 20 yards from the bus in which I was sleeping. "Halt!" the guard screamed. This was followed immediately by two gunshots.

I flew out of my sleeping bag and rushed outside. I could make out the shadow of the guard levelling his Ruger .223 rifle at a man. Who was this attacker? Who was this man who dared to invade the sanctity of Mount Carmel?

He was the newspaper delivery man. He stood there with his hands in the air, screaming, "Holy Shit! Don't shoot! Please don't shoot!" The poor man was only trying to deliver the morning edition of the Waco Tribune Herald. *It had almost cost him his life.*

Even the guard, Wally Kennett, was shaking like a leaf. Wally kept stammering, "I'm sorry, I'm so sorry." But the newspaper delivery man wasn't waiting around for apologies. He turned on his heel, ran back to his truck and took off down the road as fast as he could.

That was the end of our newspaper deliveries, one of our few remaining links with the outside world. Poor Wally was barely coherent. He was not normally an aggressive man. He was only following orders.

Vernon had given specific instructions to all the guards that if they ever saw anyone suspicious approach the compound they were to shoot to kill. He would then smile and say: "You can always ask questions later."

You'd think that gunshots at 5 a.m. would have everyone rushing from all directions. Incredibly, Marc Breault was the only person who investigated the disturbance. The other cult members slumbered on totally oblivious to the near tragedy. The reason for this is as dramatic as it is simple: everyone had become used to the sound of gun-fire at any hour of the day or night. They just ignored it.

They were also used to the sight of Vernon, rigged out in camouflage trousers, prowling the compound with his AK-47 slung over his shoulder. He loved his AK-47. Breault says he loved it more than his women. "At least my piece doesn't give me lip," Vernon was fond of saying. The AK-47 rarely left his side. At lunch it was propped against the wall behind him. If he was fixing a truck he'd rest it against the bumper. But if he needed to go into town the trusty assault rifle would be stashed under his bed.

You don't go into Waco with an AK-47. No sir. You take a hand gun instead. Vernon was so gun-crazy that he even built a special compartment in the dashboard of his red 1967 Corvette Classic for his .22 pistol. He later outgrew the .22 and graduated to a .357 magnum.

But nothing could match the sensuous feel of that AK-47 for Vernon. After all, the then world ambassador of peace, Henry Kissinger, had said that power is the ultimate aphrodisiac. Vernon liked that.

What he liked even better, though, was blowing small animals to pieces with his AK-47. His preferred targets were rabbits, snakes and rats. Vernon was a crack shot. Like many people brought up on farms, he had handled guns from an early age. He was able to pick off water moccasins as they swam across the ponds on the property. If you were raised in the South like Vernon, you would know that these deadly snakes are almost invisible as they glide silently through the water. Whereas St Patrick cleared Ireland of snakes with his aura of goodness, Vernon cleared Mount Carmel of snakes by blowing them away with his AK-47.

Once, a three-legged pet dog, which was tied up outside one of the houses, became an innocent victim of Vernon's deadly temper. Its crime: it had dared to bite his mother's dog. Bonnie's mean-tempered terrier, Snuggles, had tormented the tethered Buddy for hours. Snuggles was taking great delight in ambushing Buddy from behind and nipping him painfully on the flank. Finally, Buddy bit back.

Vernon's mother witnessed this and flew into a rage. She picked up a shovel and repeatedly beat the wretched Buddy, eventually slicing open his remaining hind leg. Nobody dared intervene.

Bonnie fetched her son. With his trusty AK-47 on his right shoulder, Vernon advanced on the cowering Buddy. By this stage the commotion had attracted a large audience, most of them children, who loved the dog. Vernon declared to the crowd that there were two things he refused to tolerate: unbelievers and troublemakers. Buddy the three-legged dog fell into the latter category.

Vernon grabbed the dog by the scruff of its neck and

dragged it into the middle of a field. With a satisfied smirk, he lifted the muzzle of his gun and calmly shot Buddy twice in the head, at point-blank range. As the dog lay twitching in the grass, the children, and even some of the adults, began to cry. Vernon admonished the children for crying, telling them he was training them to be warriors for the Lord, not sissies.

The death of Buddy was just another episode in a rapidly growing catalogue of crimes committed by Vernon. An hour after he had killed Buddy, he launched into a thirteen-hour Bible study, preaching love, forgiveness, and eternal life. That night, his faithful followers got just two hours' sleep, as Marc Breault remembers.

At 5.15 a.m. we were roused from our beds by Jean Borst ringing a bell. That's the way we were always woken at Mount Carmel. We were all feeling exhausted but there was no way we could get out of this next duty as Vernon had decreed it sacrosanct. We were about to undergo military training, Mount Carmel style.

It happened every morning at this time. We all had our own battle fatigues and at 5.30 a.m. the men assembled by an old shed at the back of the property. Kevin Whitecliff, the former prison guard, took charge as usual. First, we started with a few stretching exercises. Then we set off two at a time to run an obstacle course designed by Vernon. It was approximately 2 miles long and wound through uncultivated fields and over artificial hills created by Vernon using heavy machinery.

A few minutes into the course, the faster runners broke away from the rest. Then came the real test of faith. We had to swim fully clothed across a 30-yard pond. I prayed that morning that Vernon had killed all the water moccasins. One bite and you were history.

On this day, David Jones was where he liked to be, out in front. "Come on, let's pick it up," he screamed at us, like a drill sergeant.

"That's easy for you to say," I shouted back. "You're usually working and you don't have to stay up late at night." David Jones had a rather unusual job for a trained killer – he was the smiling face of the US postal service, a mail man.

The water was slimy and cold. We could feel sunken logs snagging our pants. There was a horrible weed, too, called wrap-around weed, and that was exactly what it did. If you got tangled up in it, it would drag you down. Let me tell you this – it wasn't a lot of fun in the dark.

I didn't mind it so much, because I'm a strong swimmer. But I could hear the usual grumbling as the guys entered the water. But we were spurred on by Vernon's warnings that one day this was all going to be for real, and that we would be fighting for our lives against the authorities. We had to be prepared.

Those of us who were first across the water always

waited for the rest to catch up. This was important. A few weeks before, Brad Borst had nearly drowned when the wrap-around weeds, plus the weight of his fatigues, had got to him. He had started crying out for help in the middle of the pond. But Vernon had forgotten to insist on water-rescue training. Nobody knew what to do. Fortunately, I'm trained in life-saving so I dove back into the water and dragged him out.

As we stood shivering, waiting for the others to negotiate the pond, I couldn't help wishing they'd hurry up. I just wanted to get this over with.

Finally, we started running again, first in pairs and then, as before, the faster ones broke clear.

The course ended where we had started and we were all pretty wacked by now, especially having only had two hours' sleep the night before.

Then it was time to march toward the kitchen. Whitecliff or Jones would lead us. It was early in the morning and we had to have some humor. Someone started up the old chant we all used to say when we were in elementary school.

Left, left, left right left.
You're knees are knockin',
Your pants are tight.
Your balls are swingin'
From left to right.

"Oops," said Wally Kennett, as we passed under Vernon's bedroom window, "we shouldn't say stuff like that so close to here."

"It doesn't matter," said Neil Vaega, "he's probably still asleep anyway."

"And anyway," I can't help putting in, "we might give him ideas."

That was typical of him. While we ran our guts out in military training, he'd be upstairs in his boudoir with one or more of his wives. I'm not sure who was getting the most exercise, but if you believe the tittle-tattle from his wives, it would have been us.

All our joking stopped as we neared the kitchen. We didn't want the women to think we're not serious about training. There was no joking with the women.

The women's exercise program was just as demanding as ours, only more creative. They met at about the same time in front of the kitchen. They would run and march but only on the flat part of the compound – the gravel road, from one end to the other. The distance between the front gate and the back shed was nearly a mile. Their target was to complete two or three miles.

What made their exercises more interesting than ours was the fact that Jaydeen Wendel, an ex-cop from Honolulu, and Sherri Jewell used to compose marine-style cadences. As they ran, they used to sing out cadences like the following.

We're with Cyrus he's our man
Gonna kill his enemies where they stand.
If you have the world's desire,
Gonna throw you in God's holy fire.

The women took great delight in composing these cadences. Vernon would often castigate the men for not being so creative. I think all of us men were a little scared listening to women talking of killing, raping and destroying the bad guys like that.

For some strange reason, the women departed from the standard "left, left, left right left" chant and reversed it making it "right, right, right left right." To them, this set them apart.

The same regimen was repeated in the afternoon. Then, after Bible study, it was time for target practice. It began as a privilege, but soon became a strict requirement for men and women. I should point out here that since birth, I've been afflicted with poor eyesight. No one trusted me with a gun because of my eyesight, although my aim is far better than most people would think. Vernon was not the only crack shot, as was demonstrated when the Federal agents raided the Mount Carmel fortress. David Jones, who had once received distinctions for marksmanship in the United States Air Force, was, in fact, the top gun.

Jaydeen Wendel and David Jones were in charge of weapons training. Jaydeen's aim was very nearly as good as David's. She was not only a fanatic, but when it came to firing weapons, she made most of the guys look second-rate. Vernon's aim was to make everyone at the compound a crack shot.

As I've said before, Vernon feared a confrontation with the authorities. He knew he was on a collision course with the Government, and he'd conditioned us to think the same thing. I mean, we really believed that. And it was one fight we were determined not to lose.

I was usually free to practice my music and I did so to the sound of gun-fire in the background. At around 5 p.m., the women were once again required to exercise. This time they had a choice. They could either do aerobics or they could repeat the now-familiar cadence exercises. Most chose aerobics and, eventually, both forms became required.

Vernon also ordered that his wives, who now numbered seventeen, were to be competent with guns. In the event that any attackers got past the Mighty Men, Vernon's women would provide the last line of defense.

Life wasn't all work and no play, though, at Camp Koresh. At night time, when he wasn't ranting and raving in the chapel, Vernon entertained his troops with music and videos. The music was his favorite rock 'n' roll. And any concert at Mount Carmel opened with Vernon's favorite performer – himself. This is where Vernon put to use the tens of thousands of dollars worth of musical equipment he had collected. If he hadn't made it big in Hollywood, he sure made it big at Mount Carmel, Texas.

Initially Vernon and Marc Breault enjoyed the same music – a Canadian cosmic rock band called Rush, the English band Queen, and flamboyant David Lee Roth. But Vernon went further, adding heavy metal bands Guns & Roses, Megadeth, and Iron Maiden. He really liked bands like these as they personified eveything he believed in – death, destruction, violence and war. When people phoned him, they didn't hear his dulcet tones, they didn't even hear scripture; they got an answering machine with the voice of a little girl accompanied by music played by Guns & Roses.

Vernon's band had three talented members: Koresh, Koresh, and Koresh. He loved to hear himself playing riffs on the guitar. Ad nauseum. Even after the February 1993 bloodbath, Vernon made recordings of his rock music and tormented the surrounding army, the FBI, the ATF, and the Texas Rangers with it. They retaliated with Andy Williams, Nancy Sinatra and the chants of celibate Tibetan monks.

But during our visit to Mount Carmel in January 1992 this God of Love had a special song to play for us up on the stage, next to the armory. It wasn't quite Carnegie Hall, but at least there were free pre-concert drinks, including the Australian favorite, Foster's Lager, for the boys from Downunder.

Vernon didn't hog the stage. He chose a Jewish bass player named Pabel Cohen and a drummer from Miami, Mike Schroeder, to accompany him. Schroeder was later to die in the shoot-out with the ATF. I asked Vernon to play his favorite song. The lyrics are very apt now, especially when you think of the long, tense, frustrating weeks that the American army laid siege with its Bradley Tanks and armored personnel carriers.

Darkness, darkness in the light,
Frantically watching the night.
Up above the armies come
Riding on White horses fearing the night.
Cry of the bird

See the armies sitting round the camp
Wonder who they are.
Save me!

See the armies
Who are they now
In the time we're living
The game we play we don't know how.

If you love your living,
You want, you don't know where you're going
But in the time we live,
The heaven's not for showing.
So darkness.
Save me!

Vernon was certainly an accomplished guitar player and had an acceptable voice. Even the song, after a couple of times, had a catchy beat. But he played that song for 45 minutes. Not bad for a rendition with just two chords!

If Vernon's disciples couldn't choose what type of music they heard – his was the only acceptable form – they also didn't have a choice when it came to other entertainment. Television was only permissible in his presence because the law according to Koresh was that only he had the wisdom to watch TV without being corrupted by it. In short, all programs were evil and eroded the moral fiber of humanity, unless, of course, the program happened to be MTV, his favorite. He watched this 24-hour rock-video station constantly, and especially if Madonna was featured. She was probably the only person in the world who could stop him mid-sentence.

Sport was totally banned. The children could play games such as hop-scotch. Competition was banned too. It didn't matter if it was arm wrestling, baseball, or football. Chess was especially evil because it took too much time to play. All card games were blacklisted because Vernon said they could lead to other vices, such as gambling.

Vernon personally selected movies from the local video store for the cult members to watch. At first he permitted just three movies, and he forced his followers to watch them again and again. On numerous occasions these soldiers of misfortune had to endure a marathon of violent Vietnam War movies – *Hamburger Hill*, *Platoon*, and *Full Metal Jacket*. The movies were shown on a large-screen television in the chapel. Vernon gave a running commentary during the battle scenes. "This is what it's going to be like," he told his troops, among whom was Marc Breault. "This is what you've gotta be ready for. You've gotta be tough. You've gotta have balls. You've gotta be ready for war! You've gotta be prepared to defend King Solomon's bed."

This conditioning began at dawn and continued all day until late at night. Vernon never let up. And it was in this atmosphere that his mind-control reached such a pitch that his subjects were putty in his hands.

Now was the perfect time to execute the next stage of his sordid plan. In October 1989 he began having sex with the other men's wives. And although Vernon hated the Roman Catholic Church, they shared a common belief – no contraception. After all, you can't embark on a program to conceive pure-bred children on a mass scale and use birth control at the same time. In fact, Vernon had decreed that the famous Australian Billings method – which teaches a woman to recognize when she is fertile – be used in the reverse. The cult leader directed women to inform him when they had reached the fertile part of their cycle to maximize the chance of pregnancy.

One of the first married women to grace King

The family man: Vernon Wayne Howell, his son Cyrus and his then 16-year-old wife, Rachel. San Bernardino, California, 1986. (Photo: Elizabeth Baranyai)

Jean Smith, Lisa Gent, Sheila Martin, Marc Breault and 12-year-old Michele Jones, Vernon's sister-in-law who was soon to become his third "wife." Palestine, Texas, 1986. (Photo: Elizabeth Baranyai)

Lisa and Bruce Gent, whose daughter, Nicole, was to have two of Vernon's children and whose son, Peter, was to be killed in the February 28, 1993 shoot-out. Melbourne, Australia, 1986. (Photo: Elizabeth Baranyai)

David Jones, Vernon's brother-in-law and the chief Mighty Man. Mount Carmel, Texas, 1992. (Photo: "A Current Affair," Nine Network Australia.)

Steve and Judy Schneider with Mayanah, Vernon and Judy's child. Mount Carmel, Texas, 1992. (Photo: "A Current Affair," Nine Network Australia.)

The rock 'n' roll Messiah. Mount Carmel, Texas, 1992. (Photo: "A Current Affair," Nine Network Australia.)

The preacher of the Seven Seals secretly wore seven waist-length plaits. Mount Carmel, Texas, 1992. (Photo: "A Current Affair," Nine Network Australia.)

The 1987 raid by Vernon against Branch Davidian leader George B. Roden (left) led to a court trial. Vernon and his commandos were acquitted and their guns were returned (below). (Photos: Rod Aydelotte, *Waco Tribune Herald*.)

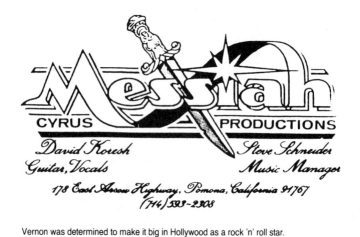

MESSIAH
CYRUS PRODUCTIONS

David Koresh
Guitar, Vocals

Steve Schneider
Music Manager

178 East Arrow Highway, Pomona, California 91767
(714) 593-2308

Vernon was determined to make it big in Hollywood as a rock 'n' roll star.
Steve Schneider was his manager. Pomona, California, 1988.

April 28, 1989: Marc and Elizabeth's wedding day. Steve Schneider, Marc
Breault, Elizabeth Baranyai and Sherri Jewell in the office of Judge James
Collier. Mart, Texas, 1989. (Photo: Elizabeth Baranyai)

"The guy's tough. He's got more than guns. He's got God!" Vernon Howell, aka David Koresh, talking to journalist Martin King. Mount Carmel, Texas, 1992. (Photo: "A Current Affair," Nine Network Australia.)

Bible study. Mike Schroeder, front right, was killed in the February 28, 1993 shoot-out. Mount Carmel, Texas, 1992. (Photo: "A Current Affair," Nine Network Australia.)

A reconnaissance photograph following the February 28, 1993 shoot-out.
Mount Carmel, Texas, 1993. (Photo: Bobby Sanchez, *Waco Tribune Herald*.)

April 19, 1993. Ranch Apocalypse exploded as the world looked on. Mount
Carmel, Texas. (Photo: Rod Aydelotte, *Waco Tribune Herald*.)

Solomon's bed was Judy Schneider. That same October Vernon had sent her husband, Steve, to England on a recruiting drive. For ten years Steve and Judy had desperately wanted a baby. Finally, Judy fell pregnant but it wasn't Judy who gave Steve the wonderful news. It was David Koresh. He told him in January 1990, when Schneider had linked up with the cult leader in Australia for their third Downunder recruiting drive. Steve was shattered by the news.

Vernon and Schneider returned to Mount Carmel in February and March, respectively. Steve later confided to Marc Breault that he had seriously considered killing Vernon at that time. But he had feared that Vernon would have harmed the woman he still loved, should he have failed.

The cult leader had deliberately targeted Judy Schneider because of Steve's influence in the group. If he could bed Steve's wife, he thought, the rest of the married women would fall like a house of cards and, like all but two of the single girls, join the House of David. And that's exactly what happened. One by one, the married women of Mount Carmel capitulated to the cult leader and joined him in unholy matrimony, as Marc Breault recalls.

I had never felt so sorry for a man in my life. Judy had even changed her name to Judy Schneider-Koresh. To make sure that Steve didn't cause too much trouble,

Vernon kept him so busy his feet didn't touch the ground. He sent him all over the United States and basically kept him away from his wife as much as possible.

Amazingly, when the baby girl, named Mayanah by Vernon, was born, Steve grew to love her. You have to understand that Vernon treated baby girls like garbage. He wanted boy babies for his army. So Steve felt sorry for the neglected child.

That's how much Steve loved Judy, difficult as it must be to understand. That's why I felt so sorry for him. This is the thing I hated Vernon for the most, that and the way he beat young Cyrus.

And just what did this Messiah promise his devotees, in exchange for their wives? He told them that if they remained faithful, God would one day return and take them to Heaven in his spaceship. He even claimed to have seen this divine starship. He told his stunned Bible class that he could draw it for them, whereupon he went to a whiteboard and sketched its outline – an erect penis. "That's God's spaceship," he said. The class laughed. Vernon, smirking, said, "It really is."

Mount Carmel was like an army base now, and the women and men were totally segregated. The wives slept in one dormitory with their children, while the men slept in another. Vernon forbade the children from having any contact with their natural fathers. He then claimed all the children as his own. The men walked around like zombies. They'd lost their wives, they'd lost their children, *and they'd been totally stripped of their self-respect.*

Vernon compensated the men for the loss of their families by relaxing one of his strictest rules: he allowed them to drown their sorrows in the demon drink. He gave them as much beer as they could drink.

Vernon knew that the men were angry and resentful, and that emotions were starting to get out of control. So he programmed them to channel all their hatred towards the authorities. Simply, he told them that God had told him to do all this to stun the world into taking notice of the Great Koresh.

That was his logic, not mine.

What actually happened inside Mount Carmel and what Koresh was prepared to say on television were two different things, as the FBI later found, to its chagrin. In January 1992 our interview was well on the way. This time he and I were sitting next to the road that lead to the front gate of the compound. The light was fading fast and so was my patience as Koresh continuously refuted the mountain of evidence against him. This man was amazing. He just loved the camera.

KING How many wives do you have?
KORESH *One.*
KING One wife?
KORESH *One wife. I've always had . . .*
KING Have you committed . . .

KORESH *Have I committed adultery? Is that what you're fixin' to ask me?*

KING Have you committed adultery?

KORESH *[laughing] No I don't commit adultery.*

KING Are you telling me the truth?

KORESH *I am telling you the truth. I don't commit adultery.*

Vernon didn't answer the questions like a man in the firing line. It was as though he was on a stage and he was giving an Oscar-winning performance.

KING Are you a sinner?

KORESH *Yeah, I'm a sinner.*

KING How do you sin?

KORESH *Thoughts, attitudes, feelings, emotions, breathing the air. You know, some people say I'm a sinner because I drink a beer.*

Koresh had begun to lose that smug veneer and he was getting irritated. He continually looked at the Mighty Men, and they edged closer. It was time to bite the bullet.

KING Are you the only man here who can procreate?

KORESH *No, I'm not the only man here who can pro-create. You saw that. You've already been here, you know. I know you're only asking*

these questions for the sake of the record,
but no.

I tell him, for the record, I'm not asking him for the record,
I'm asking him for the truth.

KING She [Robyn Bunds] says you've got seventeen wives.

KORESH *Seventeen wives?*

KING Seventeen women you've slept with who
then became your wives.

KORESH *And how does she know all that? Why is it*
that these individuals are making all these
accusations?

KING I don't know, you tell me.

KORESH *The thing of it is, there is a doctrine, there is*
a truth, they don't want me to be the Son of
God, and they need to attack me on the Seven
Seals and not according to sticks and stones
can break my bones, but there are Seven
Seals, and the one that can reveal the Seven
Seals is the one that is going to set people free.

KING I'm not testing your faith in the Bible, I'm
testing your morality.

KORESH *Yeah . . . I'm not a saint but I know some-*
thing that no one else knows and I want to
share it. Free.

KING How do you describe these allegations?

KORESH *Like I said before, there are Seven Seals.*

KING Is it bullshit?

KORESH *What they're saying? If you want to use that terminology, yes, they're bull dung, OK?*

If the God of love wouldn't give us the gospel truth, would a Mighty Man? Not just any Mighty Man, but the chief Mighty Man, David Jones, the same Mighty Man who threatened me on our arrival.

JONES *Use your eyes and your brains . . . What would I do for him? I love him as a brother.*

KING All right, these allegations. Is there any substance to these allegations?

JONES *What . . .*

KING That he's sleeping with the women here, taking other men's wives, that he's had babies too . . .

JONES *He hasn't taken my wife and I've been married thirteen years. I have three beautiful children . . . If they're talking about David [Koresh] they're talking about me 'cause I know what David does and he knows what I do and David doesn't do these things, and I don't do these things. The important thing is you need to know what the Seven Seals are. Christ said when he returns he's going to lift the Seven Seals*

off that book and no man can look on
that book . . . what is religion doing out
there showing everybody the book . . .
this is a challenge to the world. That's
what's important, the book, and not
what everybody wants to garbage up
things and say things. All it does is hurt
me, man. That's why I can talk to you
right now. It hurts me, man.

KING Makes you angry?

JONES *Yeah, it makes me angry.*

Graeme Craddock is a quietly spoken science and mathematics teacher from Melbourne, Australia. Before he left home he had purchased a paperback entitled *Fox's Book of Martyrs* and a poster depicting the Four Horsemen of the Apocalypse, which he proudly pasted on his bedroom wall. I spoke to him at Mount Carmel.

KING Do you think he's [Koresh] the Son of God?

CRADDOCK *Yeah . . .*

KING Is he the Lamb of God?

CRADDOCK *That's up to people to decide for themselves.*

KING What do you think? I'm asking you.

CRADDOCK *Well, he can do everything a Lamb can do, put it that way.*

KING So you believe in him?

CRADDOCK *I believe in what he says, yes. I can't argue against what he says. If someone else comes to show me something else maybe I'd have to follow . . . listen to them.*

The bearded, bespectacled Graeme Craddock was perhaps the quietest member of this cult I met at Mount Carmel. Even he admitted he was a loner. But when it came to following this Lamb of God, Craddock possessed the faith of a lion.

KING How would you describe this guy?

CRADDOCK *He is everything to all people.*

But what of the women? Margarida Vaega, with Judy Schneider, was one of the first married women to enter the House of David. She was a slightly built woman of Asian descent, with an open, friendly face, and one of the few people at Mount Carmel I ever saw smile.

KING What do you think of David [Koresh]?

VAEGA *I think he's great.*

KING Why do you think he's great?

VAEGA *Well, you should hear what he has to say. The truth is always great, right?*

KING Do you believe he's the Son of God?

VAEGA *I hope he is.*

Margarida is sitting in a battered pick-up with Misty, a white teenage girl, and a black woman. Kathy Schroeder sits in the back of the pick-up with three other women. Vernon hovers in the background, and doesn't miss a word. He looks edgy.

KING [gesturing to Koresh] The man behind me, what do you think of him?

SCHROEDER *Well, he teaches the Bible and he seems to know what he's talking about, so I listen to him. He's pretty nice, yeah.*

Before the conversation can continue, Koresh intervenes.

KORESH *I'm mean.*

SCHROEDER *Don't listen to him.*

KORESH *I'm mean. I'm the Boss. They call me the Boss.*

KING You a tough boss?

KORESH *Yeah. See what I get them to do?*

Koresh jerks his head towards the men building the second story of the fortress.

KING Does he lose his temper?

SCHROEDER *I have never seen him lose his temper.*

We were outside the same fortress where, just over a year later, David Koresh really lost his temper. Where four ATF agents died, and sixteen were wounded. Where six cult members died and many were injured. Where Koresh's time bomb finally exploded.

Chapter Twenty

The End is Nigh

It's 8 o'clock on a sweltering central Texas summer's night in July 1989 and the heat is driving me mad. It's 104 degrees and it's been like this, day and night, for the past ten days. It's so hot even the bugs seem to have disappeared. I wish I could.

Twilight. There's no breeze and no activity. Everyone is dog-tired. We've gone through yet another day of running that damn obstacle course and I'm seriously thinking about running straight back into the ponds. I'm so hot I'll even risk the water moccasins, if Koresh has missed a couple.

I'm sitting in a little downstairs office right below Koresh's bedroom, writing a letter to my mother. Koresh doesn't like people writing to their families, but he's upstairs cleaning his AK-47 so what he doesn't know won't hurt him. Besides, if God wants to tell him, my trying to hide what I'm doing won't make any difference anyway.

I'm seriously beginning to doubt whether God has ever

talked to this guy. That's a long way from where I was in the beginning.

Little Aisha Gyarfas comes through the office door. She walks right past me and goes to the other door that opens up to a wooden staircase that leads directly up to Koresh's room. I hope she's not doing what I think she is.

Ah, who am I kidding. This little 13-year-old is going up there to make love to David. I can't deny this stuff any more. But there's something inside me that says I have to make sure. I've followed Koresh for so many years. I have to know he's making out with a 13-year-old.

The only way little Aisha can leave his room is the same way she came in. If I stay here and work on my computer all night, I can see when she comes out. I have to do this.

I finish my letter and settle down for a long night of computer games. If I'm going to be here all night, I might as well have fun. Koresh doesn't know about these computer games. He's computer illiterate. The kids love me because I let them play the games sometimes when he's not around. It's our little secret.

I'm there for nine hours solid, playing a Star Trek game. Man, I've wiped out a lot of Klingons by now and they've wasted me pretty bad too. Still no Aisha. This is making me sick.

Finally, at 5 a.m. she comes out with tousled hair. She hasn't slept much and she has some clothes wrapped in a towel slung over her right shoulder. She didn't have that *bundle of clothes when she went in. She must have already had a change of clothes up there in his room. She spies me sitting there in the dark. Dawn is only a few minutes away. She doesn't look at all happy to see me.*

"Good morning," I say as cheerfully as I can, although I'm boiling inside.

"What are you doing here?" the little 13-year-old says imperiously, like she's the Queen of England.

"None of your business," I counter. "I'm just doing some work." I'd heard her creaking down the stairs and had got out of my game and quickly put up a document on the word processor.

She glances at the computer screen and appears satisfied I'm telling the truth. Without another word, she ran to the house where her parents were staying. I realize with disgust that she is trying to get there before the rest of the people wake up.

For four years Marc Breault had been a silent witness to the crimes of Vernon Wayne Howell, aka David Koresh. For four years he'd watched the man he'd looked upon as the Messiah shatter all but one of the Ten Commandments. And Marc Breault was determined he wouldn't be around when that one fell: *Thou shalt not kill.*

It was then, on that stifling Texas dawn, the right-hand man made the decision to leave the cult. Leaving, though, simply wasn't a matter of packing his bags and calling a cab. You don't just leave a cult, you have to escape. But you just don't escape, either. You have to plan that escape, and plan it very, very carefully. In a cult like this one, one wrong move could mean a bullet through the brain.

First, I had to get out of Mount Carmel. Then I had to get out of Waco. Then I had to get to California. Then, finally, I had to get to Australia where my wife was waiting.

My plan was simple. I would convince Koresh that we needed to return to Hollywood for a short visit to buy some new musical equipment. My keyboard mixer was old and ready to break down at any time, so what better place to get a new one than Hollywood.

If there was one mecca he couldn't resist, it was Hollywood. Koresh bought the story and he and I drove out to California. I left everything behind except for my portable computer and my wallet.

Vernon might have had his pistols and his AK-47, but Breault had a weapon too – the computer. That Compaq portable contained a regular diary of four years of life inside the Branch Davidian cult – names, addresses, dates, telephone numbers, birth records of children who had never been recorded officially, secret locations of cult properties, a detailed catalogue of the cult's guns, and, in particular, a blow-by-blow account of the depravity of David Koresh.

The cult leader and Breault set off for California two days later on August 1 in the red Camaro. Sitting in the back was none other than the new Princess of Mount Carmel, little Aisha, the girl who had finally triggered Marc Breault's escape. Vernon was driving. His .22 hand gun was hidden under his seat, and, just in case, his AK-47 was wrapped in a towel in the trunk. What Vernon didn't know during that 1700-mile journey was that the contents of Marc Breault's computer were just as dangerous as his weapons. In time the contents of that computer would be the end of him.

Two days later they arrived at the cult house in Pomona, California. Breault had to be careful. Extra careful. He had to organize a visa and money from his wife, Elizabeth, in Australia. Like most other cult members, Breault was in a perpetual state of poverty as Vernon insisted on controlling the purse strings. Any money received by cult members was generally spent on improving the fortress.

But that was the least of Breault's worries on that first day in Pomona. At this stage he wasn't even sure whether he could trust his own wife. After all, she had followed this Messiah for four years. Would her fear of a vengeful God overcome her love for her husband? Breault's escape plan could come to a sudden halt if Elizabeth gave him up. He needed her to send him money for the air fare to Australia. Should he ask her? Would she give him up? After two days of agonizing, the fugitive from Mount Carmel knew he had no alternative. He had to trust somebody. It might as well be the woman he loved.

The telephone at the cult house was closely monitored by Vernon and fanatical members of the cult. Breault was forced to sneak out of the house and walk to a nearby Target department store where he used a US Sprint phone-card to call Elizabeth and the Australian Consulate in Los Angeles.

Down in Australia, Elizabeth wondered if the whole thing was a set-up initiated by Vernon. She was racked by confusion and doubt. She knew only too well how close the two men were and feared that Marc would do what Vernon was now demanding: surrender his wife to the House of David. And it was with this fear that she wrote the following letter to her husband in California.

Dearest Marc

Today is the day you dropped the latest bombshell on me, when you called so early in the morning. When you told me the news I just wanted to die rather than give you up. I still feel that way. You are my only love, the love of my life, and I don't believe I will be able to go through what is being asked. If I thought that it was possible, then I would have become part of the House of David rather than marry you in the first place. And believe me, I did think long and hard about it.

I don't like Vernon in the least. Every time that he touches me I feel ill. The thought that we might never be allowed to be together again makes my mind want to explode. I don't think that I'd want to live any more. Please God don't let it be like that. Don't take my love away from me just when I've found him. Don't be so cruel. I suppose my prayer should be, "Let thy will be done," only I'm too afraid to pray that one now.

I don't know what to say or do any more. Marc I'm really scared. I don't want to disobey the Lord but I can't do what is being asked. I feel very lost at the moment.

With all my Love
Elizabeth
XXXXXXXXXX

Elizabeth agreed to send Marc $900. But getting money from Australia wasn't easy as Vernon monitored all incoming mail closely. If he was at all suspicious of a letter he would open it and examine the contents. Even letters from mothers were treated with distrust.

For the next two weeks Marc Breault made sure that he was there when the postman called. As luck would have it, he was able to fetch the mail the very day his wife's letter, with the $900 inside, arrived. So far, so good.

But the next day Marc wasn't so lucky.

I had to go to downtown LA to submit some final papers for my visa. What could be easier? I told Koresh I was going to check out that mixer for my keyboards. Luckily he didn't want to come with me!

I was standing on Broadway waiting for my next bus to the consulate when a black 250 cc Honda motor bike roared next to me. I got the fright of my life. Holy shit, I thought, how did they find me here? It was Steve Schneider and his wife, Judy. I couldn't believe it. In a country of 270 million people, I had to run into them in the final stages of my escape.

Steve was startled to see me at first, then I could see he was getting really suspicious. His eyes narrowed and I could tell what he was thinking. Oh well, I'd got this far, it wasn't bad for my first effort. I only hoped the Mighty Men wouldn't beat me too hard.

Then an amazing thing happened. Steve said: "Oh well, gotta rush. Judy's got an appointment," and they zoomed off. To this day, I can't believe my luck. Maybe God was on my side that day instead of Koresh's.

Schneider and his wife weren't the only problem. The Branch Davidian cult was run like the Gestapo. Members spied on other members and reported back to the führer, and that's what happened now. Greg Summers was a high-ranking Mighty Man. He became suspicious of the way Breault was acting and told Vernon that he doubted his loyalty. He said he believed

Breault had an attitude problem.

Vernon saw red, and gave instructions to the Mighty Men that if they witnessed disloyalty of any kind Marc was to be taken away from the cult house in Pomona and beaten to a pulp. He wanted Breault cowed. But by then Marc had secretly booked a one-way economy ticket to Australia on Continental Airlines.

The escaping cult member decided to toe the line and act the contrite, submissive acolyte, as was expected of all Vernon's followers. Now it was a waiting game. Then out of the blue Koresh confronted Marc.

It came suddenly. I thought I was doing all the right things and saying all the right words. But Koresh was always paranoid. He had to control things directly. It wasn't good enough for him to rely solely on orders given to other people.

"What's this I hear about your attitude?" he yelled at me.

"Where did you hear it from?"

"That's none of your business!"

"It is my business when someone talks about me behind my back."

"You'd better humble yourself. You'd better lick the dust. You don't have any experience. You have never suffered but have been spoon-fed."

Koresh was screaming so loudly his voice was hoarse. Even though I was almost free of this man I just couldn't bring myself to take any more of his garbage. I lost my cool. I told him what I thought of his so-called suffering and that he should get his facts straight before he accused me of anything. Koresh wasn't used to people talking to him like that. He was so surprised he didn't say anything. Then, a godsend. He told me to pack my bags and go back to Texas. I was to receive my punishment there.

Breault did as he was ordered and packed his bags. But he never did find out what that punishment was. That night, September 29, 1989, Marc Breault passed through immigration at Los Angeles International Airport and caught Continental Flight 1 to Melbourne, Australia.

Chapter Twenty One

Desertion

As the days went by it dawned on the increasingly ·
irrational Vernon Howell that his longtime confidant
Marc Breault wasn't coming home to Ranch Apocalypse.
An emergency summit with the top Mighty Men was
called. The object of the summit was to get Breault back
into the cult. Failing that, they considered two options:
first, they could intimidate other cult members so that
they shunned Marc Breault, and, second, they could shut
him up on a more permanent basis. But before they
could do anything at all they had to find him.

The manhunt was on.

Breault kept a low profile for three months. Apart from
his wife, Elizabeth, the only people he had contact with
were cult members in Melbourne – but only by mail or
telephone.

By now, the entire Gent family – Bruce and Lisa; their
now 21-year-old twins, Nicole and Peter; Lisa's daughter
Michelle and her musician husband, James Tom; and
Lisa's son Ian Manning and his wife Allison – were back

in Australia. Nicole, who was five months pregnant to Vernon, had been sent back in March by the cult leader to have the baby in Melbourne. He was worried about his foreign wives having babies in America because of possible complications with the authorities. As their US visas expired, the rest of the Gent family returned to Australia, the last of them – Ian and Allison – having arrived in August.

The adults returned to work as soon as they could so that they could save the money needed to return to Mount Carmel, Texas. To conserve their funds, all eight adults lived in Lisa and Bruce's home in the eastern suburbs of Melbourne.

Marc Breault put his time in seclusion to good use. For twelve weeks he and Elizabeth purged themselves of Vernon's poison. Together they confronted the ghosts of the past and planned a new future. Breault, who has a Master of Arts degree in Religion from Loma Linda University, California, turned his professional theology training on himself and his wife.

The hardest thing to get used to in my new life was making decisions for myself. I was so used to having Koresh plan out my life for me that I had to get back into the habit of thinking for myself.

In those days I would think about how my relationship with Koresh – who had then been Vernon Howell – had begun. He had been a good friend. Things had been so exciting back in those days. We were a movement of destiny, ready to change the world.

But how things had changed. Now, Elizabeth and I were on the run. We were always looking behind our shoulders afraid that one of the Mighty Men would be following us.

Elizabeth had nightmares continually. "I had another bad dream," she would say, waking me out of my sleep. "I dreamed that Vernon was chasing us. He had a gun."

Once I was in a mall and I thought I saw Nicole Gent. I nearly had a heart attack. The mere fact she was a follower frightened me.

We tried to live as normal a life as possible. We got a new set of friends and sometimes – rarely – I almost forgot I was a wanted man. But behind our facade of normalcy was our real situation. We did a lot of planning. Not planning for our retirement or for our next house, but planning escape routes to take should someone come after us. We installed a burglar alarm. We even devised secret codes to let each other know we were in danger should we become separated.

After three months we'd beaten the curse of Koresh. Now it was time to exorcize the demon from the others. Our immediate target was the Gent circle. First, we genuinely wanted to help them. They were lovely people and, anyway, they had been Elizabeth's friends before all this. We couldn't bear the thought of James and Michelle's little girl, Tarah, being subjected to the cruelty *of Koresh. And, if we could free the Gents from Koresh, there would be fewer people who could act as agents for him here in Australia.*

But Nicole Gent was one less person Marc Breault had to worry about. Remarkably, it took Vernon until mid-October to realise that Marc was in Australia. After having her baby boy, Dayland, Nicole returned to Mount Carmel on Vernon's instructions. He was worried that she would be subverted by Breault. Vernon was only too well aware of the persuasive talents of his former top recruiter.

Marc Breault decided to use the talents developed at Mount Carmel to save as many cult members as he could. He became a cultbuster. He committed his life to righting the wrongs of the past and, more importantly, to putting a stop to Vernon Howell before he could destroy too many more lives.

Marc devised a brilliant strategy. He would become a prophet himself, and beat Vernon at his own game. He wrote the following letter to Lisa Gent on January 16, 1990.

Since I am here in Australia at the Lord's direction God has seen fit to reveal much new light so as to put to shame those who think they know the Scriptures because of all the "wonderful new light" they are getting from the United States. And of course Elizabeth benefits as well through Bible study.

I am instructed to invite any Branches who will give ear to attend very important studies. This is so Psalm 74 can begin to meet its fulfilment. Those who have an ear, let them hear what the Spirit saith. Those who do not, let them dwell in darkness.

Since I don't know Ian and Allison's . . . new address, I leave it in your hands to contact them. You might try contacting Mrs Smith, and the others as well since I'm not certain whether I can communicate with them in time. Then if any wish to hear the word of the Lord, get back to me and arrange a meeting as soon as possible. But keep in mind that one should not delay to fulfil the Lord's commandments.

This letter sent shock waves right across the Pacific to Mount Carmel, Texas. The fact that the disaffected Marc Breault was now claiming to be a rival prophet sent Vernon into an apoplectic fit. Here was another George Roden, another challenger to the throne at Mount Carmel.

Vernon was in a pickle. If he told his followers to ignore the new prophet on the block, they might wonder what he was afraid of. But if he allowed them to listen, he might lose them. In the end, Vernon's reaction was the same as that exhibited during the 1993 stand-off with the FBI. It was war, or nothing.

We met on a Saturday night. Elizabeth and I walked into

the room and the Australian Branch Davidians were
staring at us. It was us against them. I knew that Koresh
could preach for hours so I had to do the same. I went
at it for five solid hours without a pause. It was 13 against
2, and they got tired first.

I simply showed them that Jesus Christ was the true
Lamb of God. Koresh was a pretender and a false
prophet. I showed them basic biblical passages out of the
four gospels, passages known to Christians all over the
world.

By the time I was finished, the Australian followers
were in total confusion. In their eyes, I had done what
only Koresh himself could do – I had taught them the
Bible. They no longer knew what to think.

The next morning Koresh called the Gents from America, to gloat over his assumed victory. He got the shock of his life. They told him that they weren't so sure they wanted to listen to him any more. Marc had told them things, they said, that made them question their previous beliefs.

Koresh was livid, and the fight was on in earnest.

The news reached Mount Carmel fast. People there were amazed that just one Bible study could make followers doubt that their Messiah was the only one capable of teaching biblical truth. Vernon hit the panic button. He and the new right-hand man, Steve Schneider, flew to Australia to quell the rebellion. Vernon began his counter-offensive with a chilling phone call to Breault. He did his talking through Schneider. Unbeknownst to both of them, Marc Breault recorded the conversation on his computer the minute he got off the phone.

SCHNEIDER *You know this is really serious, Marc. I can't tell you how serious.*

BREAULT *I know it's serious Steve, but I just can't agree with Vernon's teachings.*

SCHNEIDER *You know he's changed his name to David?*

BREAULT *Steve, you know why I don't call him David. Like it or not, I refuse to acknowledge him as the Messiah.*

SCHNEIDER *But you used to –*

BREAULT *I know that, but I've changed my mind. I was wrong to follow him. I wish you'd reconsider too.*

SCHNEIDER *But Marc, the Bible studies are so awesome. I can tell you the truth. I have never in all my life and with all my education seen anyone who can reveal the book like this man.*

BREAULT *That's your opinion. I say investigate the alternative, Steve. Don't just look at one side of the coin. Look at –*

SCHNEIDER *Well I'd – Wait, David is saying some-*

thing, hold on. [slight pause] OK. David
says you shouldn't lose your salvation
and follow Elizabeth into Hell.

I can hear Koresh in the background telling Steve what
to say.

BREAULT *I'm not following Elizabeth. My stand is*
based on the Bible and –

SCHNEIDER *Wait, Marc. Listen to what David has to*
say. He's saying that Elizabeth is his
enemy and that he's going to destroy
her. [Koresh can be heard in the back-
ground.] Marc! Did you hear that?
Imagine that, she's a pronounced
enemy. Come on, Marc! Come on – this
is serious!

BREAULT *Does Vernon really expect me to listen*
to someone who calls me up and threat-
ens to kill my wife? You tell Vernon that
I won't tolerate that kind of thing. You
tell him that now.

This wasn't the only death threat Vernon made when he
was in Australia. Incredible as it sounds, he began
teaching his disciples that he was the very incarnation
of death. "Do you know what Koresh means?" he'd ask
them repeatedly. "The scholars say it means Cyrus, but

it means something more. It means death, that's what it means. Just as YHWH [the most sacred name of God in the Old Testament and pronounced "Yahweh"] is the name of God that means life, Koresh is the name of God that means death. God's real name is YHWH Koresh. He's the God of life and death. My name is David Koresh. In other words, David Death." This is how Koresh signed his correspondence to the FBI during the stand-off at Mount Carmel in early 1993. Vernon also said that he, Koresh, was the fourth horseman of the apocalypse, the rider on the pale horse.

> And I looked, and behold a pale horse: and his name that sat on him was Death, and Hell followed with him. And power was given unto them over the fourth part of the earth, to kill with sword, and with hunger, and with death, and with the beasts of the earth.
>
> – Revelation 6:8

The war with Breault became a game of religious chess, except that the pawns were human beings, and the stakes were their lives. Vernon sent those who were loyal to him to spy on Marc and Elizabeth in order to learn who they were talking to. At one stage he even had their residence staked out at 2 o'clock in the morning. Sometimes cult members would secretly visit Breault in the middle of the night because they feared reprisals from Vernon. At the end of the opening gambit, victory went to the pretend prophet. In January 1990 James and Michelle Tom were won over by Breault. Lisa and Bruce Gent soon followed.

In a final bid to intimidate James and Michelle Tom, Vernon told Michelle that he would smash her children's heads open in front of her very eyes. Vernon didn't like the Tom children. As they well knew, it was no idle threat.

Once in early 1989 at Mount Carmel, when their then 8-month-old daughter Tarah had refused to sit on Vernon's knee when ordered, he had spanked the baby for forty minutes. By the end of this horrific assault, witnessed by James and Michelle, baby Tarah was hysterical and her bottom bleeding and covered in welts. Vernon had been flanked by some of his Mighty Men so the Toms couldn't intervene.

James Tom, too, knows what it was like to suffer the wrath of Vernon. He once made disparaging remarks about the cult leader and was reported by Nicole Gent. His punishment: one of the Mighty Men tore a plank from a fence and beat him with it.

It didn't take a lot of convincing for James and Michelle Tom to abandon the cult.

Vernon had to do something and do it fast. In the style of George Roden, Vernon challenged Marc Breault to a Bible study shoot-out. Gun control laws are a lot stricter in Australia. Breault picked up the gauntlet and the date was set for mid-February. The battle might have been on Australian soil, but the contest was American versus American.

In my four years following Koresh I had seen him get worked up. I had seen him rant and rave for hours. But none of that was like the David Koresh I saw now. His eyes were maniacal. He looked possessed. He was dressed in a tank top and jeans. We started talking about biblical doctrines.

Elizabeth and I scored early when we showed he had misquoted the Bible. Then we scored again by making some of his doctrines look stupid. Some were laughing at Koresh by now and he went berserk. I mean, he totally lost it.

He got down on his knees. "I remember when Judas betrayed me," he cried. "I remember how much it hurt me then. The pain! The pain! And now it's happening again. I don't know if I can take this! Marc, who showed you the book? Who showed you these things?"

He turned his face up toward the heavens, palms upward. He acted like Christ on the cross.

"I'm being crucified all over again," he kept saying.

Koresh mesmerized most of the twenty-five people in the room. It was frightening to watch. He was putting on the performance of his life. But this was no time to back down. Elizabeth and I weren't about to let theatrics ruin the lives of our friends. But it soon became apparent that Koresh was beyond reason. We got up and left.

Elizabeth had made a deal with her brother, John. If we weren't back home by 10 p.m., he was to call the police. As luck would have it, we were so intent on our task that we forgot all about the deadline.

At 10 o'clock sharp, the police were called. Elizabeth's brother and her mother, Erna, raced to the house where the showdown was taking place. They beat the police there, and John pounded on the door.

"I called the cops and they're coming," he said.

Those few words struck terror into the this self-styled King of kings and Lord of lords. He raced out the back door, grabbed a bicycle and pedaled down the street for all he was worth. He caught the next plane out of Australia.

Chapter Twenty Two
Cultbusting

It began in late June 1990 in a small house in Waco that was barely large enough to accommodate David and Debbie Bunds and their two little girls, Jennifer and Megan. The Bunds had arrived home from shopping to discover their house had been ransacked. Strangely, nothing had been taken.

It was the first in a series of frightening warnings. Two days later the phone rang. David Bunds, brother of Robyn, picked it up and a male voice rasped: "Watch out for your wife and children." Click.

David and Debbie Bunds had been members of Vernon Howell's Branch Davidian cult. Living in this shack-like house was part of their punishment for committing a crime against God. While living at Mount Carmel, Vernon had discovered they had doughnuts and potato chips in their kitchen.

The Bunds had been living in one of the small cottages near the main fortress on the property. During a routine inspection the cult leader found the offending food. He ransacked the house and emptied the refrigerator. As a message to the blasphemous family he smeared food throughout the house, including over their bed, furnishings and the walls.

Then Vernon expelled them from the cult and threw them out of Mount Carmel. David had since been in contact with the cultbusting American, Marc Breault, now Vernon's nemesis. Breault had heard that Bunds wanted to get back into the cult, and had tried to dissuade him. Word traveled fast around Waco, and even faster around Mount Carmel.

When Koresh heard that his cultbusting enemy was trying to convert the banished Bunds, he did an about face, but by then it was too late. Breault had struck and Bunds had begun trying to rescue the rest of his family – Robyn and her child to Vernon, Wisdom; and his father and mother, Don and Jeannine.

But when David Bunds heard that threatening male voice on the telephone, he wasn't about to take any chances, especially with his wife and children. The entire family packed immediately and fled to California without telling anyone where they were.

By mid-1990 Robyn was having serious thoughts about her commitment to Vernon. Robyn, now 21, had suffered nearly four years of his authoritarian rule. She'd been his teenage lover, she'd had his child, she'd endured the taunts and insults about her weight, and she'd experienced the heartache of being dumped in favor of his latest acquisition. But what she couldn't accept was his latest lover – her mother, Jeannine.

Robyn was disgusted at the thought of sharing the same lover with her mother. To add insult to injury, Vernon had banished Robyn from Mount Carmel to the cult house at La Verne in California.

In the White House, in a quiet, expensive suburb, women were herded together like cattle. When Vernon deigned to visit, he occupied the master bedroom, while his women slept in dormitory-style bunks. Privacy was non-existent. Even though they lived on the outskirts of one of the world's biggest cities, the women were so isolated that Robyn Bunds had no idea where her own brother, David, was.

Robyn wanted out, so she turned to an ex-boyfriend for help. The plot was uncovered. In true Gestapo fashion, she was reported by one of Vernon's Secret Police, one of his other "wives."

Vernon had always been a jealous lover. He knew that there was no better way to get back at an ungrateful young mother than to separate her from her child. And that's exactly what he did. Little Wisdom was shipped back to Mount Carmel. His mother had no say in the matter.

Robyn, desperate now, escaped from the house and moved in with a former high-school friend. By an incredible quirk of fate, Robyn's friend chanced upon Robyn's brother, David, in a Los Angeles street.

It was their first encounter in four years.

Finally, the brother and sister were together again after two years apart. Robyn was a nervous wreck. She was worried about her son, whom Vernon had mistreated in the past. On the other hand, she still believed her former lover was the Son of God. In October 1990 David Bunds convinced his sister to contact Marc Breault for help.

It was 3.30 in the morning when the phone rang. Elizabeth picked it up as usual and I could hear the hysterical sobbing even from the other side of the bed. It was Robyn.

"I want my baby!" she cried. "David [Koresh] has my baby and he won't give him back to me. I don't know what to do. I've heard that he's talking about sacrificing children! My God, what if he tries to kill Wisdom!"

I should explain here that it was about this time James Tom received a call from Koresh in which he was asked which of his children he was willing to sacrifice to God. We were worried that Koresh might be thinking about human sacrifices. We didn't know for sure, but Koresh was unstable enough to make even our darkest nightmares seem possible.

There wasn't much I could do for Robyn directly. I tried to convince her to go to the police. For an ex-follower, this was a big step. Going to the police was the ultimate act of betrayal, the final act that forever severed one's link with Koresh. From that point on, there was no turning back.

Elizabeth and I sent a message to Mount Carmel, strongly suggesting that Koresh give back Robyn's son. Of course, Wisdom was just as much Koresh's son as he was Robyn's. But Koresh could not openly admit this, since that would expose what he was really doing with all the women. Koresh had no choice but to back down. I must admit I derived great satisfaction in pushing this dictator into a corner.

Two days later, Wisdom was back in his mother's arms.

But Vernon did not give ground easily. He had resources of his own. All the cult members' money was now controlled by him. He had so much money that he had to buy a special safe to hold it all. Because he had trouble remembering the combination, he had a bracelet made with the combination written underneath.

This seducer of women decided charm was the order of the day. He invited Robyn back to Mount Carmel for one last chance at reconciliation. Her plane fare, of course, was on him.

Robyn Bunds accepted the invitation. When she arrived in late 1990 the cult leader took her aside and did everything he could to convince her that he loved her. He sang to her. He took her out to dinner. And, when it became apparent that Robyn wasn't about to melt into his arms, Koresh offered her $3000 with promises of more to come.

Although Robyn did not return to the cult, she was influenced by Koresh's hush money. After all, she was a single mother trying to make it in a hard world. David Bunds, along with Marc and Elizabeth in Australia, watched helplessly as Robyn began to slowly shift her allegiance back to Vernon.

Robyn Bunds had become a pivotal player in this chess game. Koresh knew that as well as we did. The only one who seemed unaware of her pawn status was Robyn herself. It was at this time that we made one of the hardest decisions of our lives. Instead of applying direct pressure on Robyn, in an attempt to free her from Koresh's influence once and for all, we decided to do nothing.

We reasoned that Robyn had left because she was sick and tired of life under the Koresh dictatorship. Direct pressure on our part could have a negative effect. What Robyn needed was time to herself. Elizabeth and I had had our three months; Robyn now needed hers.

We stepped back and left her alone.

Vernon applied the same reasoning. He had tried intimidation, then charisma, and still Robyn wavered. Both sides began playing a tense waiting game.

In early 1991 Robyn decided against Vernon. She had simply suffered too much at the hands of the cult leader. She no longer wanted to be manipulated. She told her story publicly for the first time when we interviewed her early in 1992.

Breault hadn't been concentrating all his efforts on Robyn, though. In February 1990 he had also been busy in New Zealand. Leslie and Poia Vaega, who had joined the cult in 1987 after having been recruited by Leslie's brother, Neil, had been forced to return to New Zealand when their visas ran out. They were still under Vernon's spell. After Breault's success in Australia, Vernon sent Neil Vaega, a loyal follower from Texas, to New Zealand to prevent his Kiwi adherents from listening to his arch rival.

Money was no object for Vernon. He was loaded, and he was prepared to spend whatever it took to maintain power. By this time there were up to twenty-five people working outside the cult. Their money was handed to Vernon on payday. At a conservative estimate, he was raking in half a million dollars a year, and that didn't include Paul Fatta's millions, proceeds from the sales of followers' properties, and the turnovers of at least three businesses run by cult members – a mechanics shop in Waco, a law practice, and, most important of all, Magbag, a Waco gun store.

But no matter how much Vernon was willing to spend, Leslie and Poia Vaega refused to be told what to do. Marc's wife, Elizabeth Baranyai, was a good friend of the couple and she arranged for her husband to meet them in their Auckland home without letting Vernon's watchdog, Neil Vaega, know their plan, even though he shared their house.

Breault arrived in New Zealand late on that February 1990 night. The couple invited him to stay. On seeing Marc, Neil Vaega immediately called Vernon, who was back at Mount Carmel. Koresh ordered that Breault be thrown out immediately. But Leslie Vaega wasn't so sure he wanted any more orders from this Texan tyrant.

The phone conversation lasted five hours. Elizabeth, who remained behind in Australia, became unsure of her husband's fate. Because Vernon tied up the phone, she was unable to get through to New Zealand.

Furthermore, Vernon was so confident of success that he ordered Steve Schneider to inform Elizabeth that her husband had been thrown out on the streets of Auckland in the middle of the night.

After five hours of listening to Vernon on the telephone, the Vaega family decided to compromise. They asked Breault to leave. But instead of throwing him out on the street, they put him up in a hotel. Breault was able to conceal his whereabouts from Vernon and his minions. Finally, at 4.30 a.m. he got his chance to convince Leslie and Poia that Vernon was a fake. In the end, the cult leader lost all but one of his New Zealand followers.

Of Vernon's twenty-two followers in Australia, only seven remained loyal to the cult: Peter and Nicole Gent; Oliver and Elizabeth Gyarfas and their two children,

Oliver Jr and Aisha; and Graeme Craddock.

Breault's next targets were England and the United States. He contacted Newbold College to apprise them of the situation. But the college refused to cooperate even though Breault had the backing of high-ranking officials in the Australian Seventh-day Adventist Church. Newbold College refused to provide Breault with the names and addresses of family members who had relatives in the cult. Of all of the English followers, only Mike Shimechero and his family broke from Vernon. But that one family would later contribute much in the effort to bring the cult leader to justice.

In the United States, David and Debbie Bunds, along with Robyn, broke from the cult. Also escaping was big Joel Jones, still smarting from being bashed by Koresh as he slept through Bible study at Mount Carmel. In time Joel and the Bunds family were among Vernon's staunchest opponents.

In Australia and New Zealand, Vernon was hampered by distance. But in his own backyard, the United States, his victims were much more easily intimidated. He was closing ranks. It was time to unite, and re-inforce the Message. The enforcers were Steve Schneider, Perry Jones, Greg Summers, David Jones and Paul Fatta. Their job was to establish a barrier around the followers so the cultbusting Breault couldn't influence them.

Vernon's elite guard severed all connections between cult members and their families around the globe. On the rare occasion that Vernon allowed contact, the letters were censored and the phone calls monitored. The telephone in the La Verne house became unlisted and changed constantly. At Pomona an answering machine was installed. At Mount Carmel, the phone was guarded.

Bruce and Lisa Gent know only too well the tactics employed by the cult to keep the enemy away. They tried to contact Nicole and Peter on several occasions over 1990–91. "What happens is people pick up the phone . . . as soon as they know who it is they say, 'Oh, I'm not sure where they are.' They'll leave you hanging on the phone for five, ten, fifteen, twenty minutes. So what do you do? It's an overseas call. You hang up," Bruce Gent says. Bruce also remembers a time when Perry Jones answered the phone. "And he was saying, "the line is breaking up, I can't hear you.' And he hung up. Another time, Mary Bell, his wife . . . I spoke to her. She said Nicole wasn't there. I said, 'If Nicole isn't there I'd like to speak to Peter.' And she said, 'Peter, who's Peter?' I said, 'You know who Peter is, Peter Gent.' And she said, 'I don't know who Peter Gent is.' "

Marc Breault even tried reaching cult members at Mount Carmel by mail.

I wrote literally dozens of letters to a number of people. The only response I ever received came about only because Koresh wanted to lure me to Mount Carmel and kill me. Trying to phone was completely useless. No one ever returned our calls.

The situation was so bad I even tried to send people letters disguised as junk mail. That was the only way I could break through. And when people did get my letters, they were never allowed to read them in private.

Of the ten or so letters I sent to Steve Schneider, he only knew about one or two of them. He even admitted that to me.

If Vernon ever discovered a letter I'd written, he would post it on a bulletin board so people could make fun of it.

In September 1990 the breakaways from Australia, New Zealand, England and the United States, led by Marc Breault and his wife, Elizabeth Baranyai, conferred and decided that it was time to up the ante. Vernon was dangerous and needed to be stopped. What better way than to contact law enforcement authorities. They had the evidence, they had the numbers, and they also had the motive.

Chapter Twenty Three

The Brick Wall
of Frustration

*Wherefore I gave them also statutes [that were] not
good, and judgments whereby they should not live; And
I polluted them in their own gifts, in that they caused
to pass through [the fire] all that openeth the womb,
that I might make them desolate, to the end that they
might know that I [am] the LORD.*

– Ezekiel 20:25–26

Breault's story was so bizarre that he was afraid no
outsider would believe him. After all, how many Jones-
towns could there be? Fortunately, Bruce Gent had a
friend who could refer the breakaways to one of the top
private investigators in Australia. His name was Geoffrey
Hossack.

At first Hossack was skeptical, and agreed to see Bruce
Gent as a favor to their mutual friend. He scheduled a
short appointment. Five hours later, Geoffrey Hossack
was convinced that something had to be done, and done

quickly. But now the spectre that was to haunt the law enforcement agencies on four continents raised its ugly head. Who could be trusted?

Even though many people had parted company from Vernon Howell, the possibility still existed that they might have second thoughts. Approaching such an ex-member could prove disastrous because they might suddenly develop a guilty conscience and inform Vernon. Hossack asked Breault to determine who was strong, and who might buckle under pressure.

In August 1990 the cultbusting American called a meeting of all the breakaways in Australia.

I wanted to get their attention, so I decided to shock them. I told them that Koresh was thinking about sacrificing children. I knew there were a number of passages in the Bible that Koresh was misusing to teach this doctrine. But I also had another reason for my fears.

Once Steve Schneider had confided to me that Koresh had said some especially horrifying things. According to Steve, God was going to demand that Koresh do with his son Cyrus what Abraham of old was commanded to do with Isaac.

I was shocked. According to the book of Genesis God told Abraham to sacrifice his son Isaac as proof of his loyalty. Only at the last minute did God intervene to tell Abraham it was only a test of faith.

After my short Bible study on human sacrifices many

of the Australians became outraged. They couldn't comprehend how anyone could kill their own children, or somebody else's. Even though these people had experienced unbelievable treatment at the hands of Koresh, they still could not believe that the madman of Mount Carmel would actually kill someone.

They accused me of deliberately making up lies in order to put Koresh behind bars. Some even stormed out of the meeting and immediately called Koresh in Texas to tell him that I was making up stories about him.

Once I had weeded out those I couldn't trust, the rest of us got to work.

Acting upon Geoffrey Hossack's advice, eight Australians, along with Marc Breault, wrote affidavits that were signed and sealed at the American Consulate in Melbourne, Australia. These documents contained highly sensitive and explosive information about Vernon Howell and his organization, and included details about the following incidents.

- Statutory rape
- Assault with a deadly weapon
- Tax fraud
- Massive immigration violations
- Failure to register the births of children
- Possession and carrying of concealed weapons
- Food and water deprivation

- Child abuse
- Failure to enrol children at school
- Plans to engage authorities in a gun battle
- Fears of child sacrifices
- Exposing children to explicit episodes of sex and violence

Rembember that this was 1990, and two-and-a-half years before the ATF shoot-out on February 28, 1993.

The Australians did not stop there. They helped Hossack create detailed flow charts describing who the cult members were, where they were, and who they were related to. They also turned over very damaging tapes made by Vernon, fragments of which appear in this book. Armed with this evidence, and numerous photographs, Geoffrey Hossack flew to the United States to confront the Texas authorities. He was confident that someone would take notice.

Time passed and, incredibly, the Australians received no word from the authorities. Even after Robyn Bunds began to tell her story in 1991 the authorities did not respond. Hossack couldn't believe that the Texas authorities would ignore a top investigator, with credentials in both Australia and the United States, not to mention the mountain of evidence he had. He approached the Texas Department of Public Safety, the Department of Immigration and Naturalization, the Internal Revenue Service, the McLennan County Sheriff's Department in Waco, and the La Verne Police Department in California. None of his efforts yielded any results.

For his part, Vernon was determined to act, and act quickly. It seemed that Breault's massive letter-writing campaign to convince cult members in the United States to leave had failed. No one had responded. Suddenly all that changed. Vernon declared that he wanted a summit of the two super-prophets. This summit was to be held at Mount Carmel during Yom Kippur, the holiest day of the Branch Davidian year. Steve Schneider and Sherri Jewell wrote and telephoned Breault repeatedly, asking him to attend the talks.

I wanted to attend Koresh's summit because I thought I might be able to convince some to leave. On the other hand, however, I didn't trust Koresh. For all I knew, he could be out to kill me.

Koresh had already prophesied, for some time, that I would suffer a terrible judgment from God. He further stated that I would die an horrific death.

Much as I hated to admit it, Koresh had backed me into a corner. If I refused the summit, I would be seen as a coward. Koresh would emerge as the true biblical champion and any hope of reaching the Americans would be lost. If I accepted, I might be killed.

While I was at work, still unsure of my course of action, I received a call from Bruce Gent. Bruce had been in touch with people in Waco. I didn't quite know who they were – they were very secretive. They asked Bruce to send me an urgent message not to attend the Bible showdown.

"They can't tell me how they know," Bruce told me, "but they're pretty sure Vernon plans on slipping something into your drink so that you'll drop dead on the spot."

Well, there was that horrific death Koresh had prophesied. How simple. I'd be spouting anti-Koresh heresy and then, right in the middle of it all, I'd drop dead. You couldn't ask for more perfect divine retribution than that.

I declined Koresh's offer.

Frustrated with the Texas authorities' seeming indifference, Marc Breault and his wife, Elizabeth, flew to Los Angeles, California in June 1991 with several objectives in mind: contact Ruth Mosher, grandmother of Kiri Jewell, a 10-year-old cult member who was destined for the House of David; contact the La Verne Police Department; attempt to see Nicole and Dayland on behalf of Bruce Gent; and contact the McLennan County Sheriff's Department.

Kiri Jewell's mother, Sherri, was fanatically loyal to David Koresh. This loyalty even extended to preparing her own daughter to be one of Vernon's brides. The child had already been selected as a prime candidate.

Kiri's father, David Jewell, who had been divorced

from Sherri for a number of years, had never been a member of the cult. Despite their best efforts, Breault and his wife were unable to locate David Jewell. Instead they decided to appeal to the child's maternal grandmother, Ruth. Marc sent a letter that began with a warning, and contained the following eyewitness statement and conclusion.

I have strong reason to believe that your granddaughter, Kiri, is in extreme danger

"He [Koresh] was saying things like, Rachel [Sylvia] and Kiri were just sluts and that if he did not take them they would end up going to bed with some other guy and that would be wrong. In other words he was trying to say that he would be doing it for their own good."

Please take seriously what I am trying to tell you. I am not asking for your daughter and grand-daughter to leave Vernon's group only to follow me. I am not interested in any following, and never have been. Sherri will probably hate me for writing this letter to you, but I must do so anyway for the good of them both. Maybe, some day, they will understand.

May the Lord guide and bless you in this matter.

Marc Breault

The eyewitness account in this letter was from none other than Robyn Bunds. Robyn first alerted the breakaways that Kiri Jewell was a prime candidate for life in the House of David.

Upon reading this letter Ruth Mosher immediately began her own investigation and within weeks arranged for a meeting between herself, her daughter Sherri and Marc and Elizabeth, who would fly to California especially. The meeting would take place in her house in Anaheim Hills, California.

Sherri Jewell was incensed that someone would try to take her daughter from her. When Marc and Elizabeth arrived, they were met by Ruth and Sherri, as well as one of Sherri's friends, cult member and ex-cop Jaydeen Wendel. Marc Breault recalls the meeting.

It was a tense situation. Jaydeen kept threatening us with lawsuits for slander and libel. She also insisted our conversation be taped. Ruth concurred. When Sherri and I retired to Ruth's private study, we talked for nearly four hours.

Sherri Jewell, who had been one of my best friends in the cult, had changed. When I last saw her she was a concerned, caring, lovely woman. Now she was hard as nails. If looks could kill, I would have died a thousand times over. All this anger and hatred from a petite 5'2" woman.

We started by talking about the Bible but I soon moved

the conversation to Kiri. Sherri denied all of my accusations. But I had two weapons to employ. The first were the Australian affidavits, which I modified to disguise their legal significance from Sherri. If Koresh knew we had gone as far as submitting legal documents to authorities he might have panicked and ordered our executions.

By the time Ruth Mosher read through some, she was in shock. Sherri was in even worse shape. She tried to get Ruth to allow Jaydeen in to help her, but Ruth wanted the interview to remain the way it was.

Then I moved the conversation to education. Ruth was a retired school teacher. My intent was to fool Sherri into describing Kiri's good education at Mount Carmel, then attack on a different front. That is precisely what happened. The conversation was so startling that I wrote it down in our Holiday Inn hotel room. I didn't want to forget it.

Breault included that conversation in a comprehensive report to the La Verne Police Department.

BREAULT *One of the reasons I'm doing this is that I'm afraid that children will suffer for the rest of their lives. After all, they don't have the power to choose. One of the things I don't agree with is that they're pulled out of school.*

SHERRI *The kids aren't pulled out of school. They went while you were there.*

RUTH *Yes, I know Kiri was going to school while she was living in Waco.*

BREAULT *That's true she was. Many of the kids were bussed to school like Shari Doyle, Brad [I name others]. But they were pulled out of school.*

SHERRI *Yes, but we taught them ourselves. I taught Kiri myself. She was so much more advanced than the other kids who went to normal school that she skipped a grade.*

BREAULT *It helps being a school teacher Sherri. That is good. But my point is that Michele Jones didn't go to school. I believe Michele stopped going to school after the sixth grade or somewhere around there. My point is, she did not go to school while the other kids were.*

RUTH *How old is Michele?*

SHERRI *[by this time she is very wary] I don't know.*

BREAULT *Michele Jones was born on July 4, 1974.*

When Sherri was teaching Kiri it was 1989. Ruth knew that so she would have known that, at the time in question, Michele was only 14 years of age.

237

RUTH *And she was pulled out of school?*

BREAULT *Yes, she was. She was pulled out of school because she was pregnant. I know because I was there. Michele Jones did not go to school with the other kids because she was pregnant.*

RUTH *[indignant] Were her parents there?*

BREAULT *Yes, they were. Michele was definitely pregnant and I saw the child myself.*

RUTH: *And they condoned it?*

BREAULT *Yes, they did.*

RUTH: *Who was the father of the child?*

BREAULT *Vernon was. People were not supposed to know about it.*

RUTH *[to Sherri] Did you know she was pregnant?*

SHERRI *Well, I noticed her tummy was a bit pouchy.*

RUTH *[to Sherri] Oh come on. You knew she was pregnant.*

SHERRI *Yes, she was.*

For the first time, Breault had obtained evidence in front of a neutral witness. After viewing his report, the La Verne Police Department promised to investigate the matter further. But that was not all Breault had to tell the La Verne police. While in California he was met by none other than Joel Jones, who was then a member of the

238

National Guard Reserve. When he found out Breault was in the United States, he went AWOL in order to see his best friend.

Joel had always been somewhat of a loner. Breault was the only one who had really befriended him in the cult. With part of his family at Mount Carmel, and the rest relatively indifferent, Joel turned to the friend he hadn't seen in years. Breault took down the big man's story in his hotel room and forwarded it to the La Verne Police Department. He urged the La Verne police to contact Joel and obtain an official statement.

Joel's story was a dramatic one. He had left the group in October 1989, but wanted to return soon afterwards, partly out of fear that Vernon might really be the Son of God and partly because he had nowhere else to stay. Vernon decided to wait before determining whether Big Joel, who had been raised a Branch Davidian, would be allowed back into the fold. While waiting, Joel's money was stolen, his mail was intercepted, and he was carefully watched, especially by Paul Fatta. After a few weeks, Vernon finally decided to accept Joel back into the fold, but only on one condition: that he receive a beating from fifteen of his Mighty Men.

Joel made a bee-line towards the National Guard armory, pursued by the Mighty Men. If a police car hadn't come by the consequences for Joel could have been very serious. When the Mighty Men saw the police, however, they decided to avoid the long arm of the law and left

Joel alone. The National Guard armory was closed, so Joel spent the night behind a dumpster. The next morning, he caught a bus to Washington State, never to return to the cult of his childhood.

Big Joel and Breault tried to obtain birth certificates for Serenity Sea, Michele Jones's child to Vernon. Michele, Joel's sister, had been raped when only 12 years old. Joel wanted to prove to the authorities that Vernon was having sex with minors. Even though he was Michele's brother, Joel was unable to obtain the certificates required. He was told that he needed letters from his sister – the child's mother – requesting the certificates.

Breault then phoned McLennan County Sheriff, Gene Barber, who had spoken to Hossack. Barber told Marc that the DA's office had closed the investigation against Vernon Howell because of lack of probable cause. When Breault pressed him about the meaning of the term "probable cause," Barber refused to elaborate. Barber also said that no Federal investigation existed. He then asked Breault if he would fly to Texas to make a statement. Breault responded that he was financially unable to do that, but that he would be glad to make official complaints at the American Consulate in Melbourne. (He had been advised by the Consulate that such an action was possible.) In frustration, Breault wrote the following letter on July 4, 1991, to Gene Barber when he returned to Australia.

Dear Mr Barber

I am the person who called you from California regarding the Branch Davidian Seventh-day Adventist movement currently headquartered at Mount Carmel center or Rodenville. Because there is sufficient dispute as to whether this is truly the Branch Davidian Seventh-day Adventist movement, I prefer to call this group the Vernonites. For the record, I am not disputing the Branch Davidian claim and neither am I starting up a rival organization. There are other sects scattered throughout the US which claim to be true Branch Davidians etc.

I am enclosing a summary of a meeting I had with Sherri Jewell, a Vernonite, and her mother, Ruth Mosher, who is not a Vernonite. The matter revolved around whether Sherri's 11 or 12 year old daughter Kiri Jewell, was in danger of being sexually molested by Vernon (now David Koresh).

Some of this material dealt with specific actions done in your county. For your purpose, #1 below is especially important since Michele Jones became pregnant by Vernon Howell in Texas. She was only 14 years old at the time. Sherri Jewel (aged 41) was forced to admit, in front of her mother, that Michele Jones was indeed pregnant at that time.

That may not be much, but maybe it is something. I am also enclosing a summary of Joel Jones' story with respect to his involvement with the Vernonites. If you wish to confirm any of that, you can contact Mr. Jones at the following address [address omitted to preserve privacy].

Now if you would, I would appreciate if you could answer (by letter) a number of questions for my benefit, and for the benefit of the other Australians who still live under the shadow of Vernon's threats. Before listing these questions, however, I would like to point out that I am an American citizen and I would very much like to be treated as one. While there is probably no real obligation for you to answer to Australians, and perhaps there is no real obligation for you to answer to me either, I was under the impression American citizens had at least some benefits.

1. *Just what does the term "probable cause" mean? You used that term while speaking to me on the phone and it took me a while to realize I really did not know what that term meant.*

2. *I understood you to mean by "probable cause" that it meant a sufficient probability of wrong action to take immediate measures, like obtaining a search warrant etc. Is that correct? If this understanding is correct, then why has the written, sworn testimony of*

eight *adult Australians and one adult American, along with the confirming testimony of at least four other Americans, two New Zealanders and a reputable private investigation firm, not been seen as enough evidence to establish probable cause? To add to this evidence, there is the following.*

a. *Children such as Michele Jones were not in school from a very early age. This is verifiable from school records.*

b. *The physical existence of a child, whose mother is a minor.*

c. *Vernon had not filed income tax from at least 1981 to, if not the present, at least to 1989. This is also verifiable.*

d. *A number of American citizens, all belonging to the same group, suddenly marry foreigners. This is also verifiable.*

e. *Vernon has never been acquitted for the Rodenville incident of 1987.*

f. *The existence of numerous birth certificates of young children, whose parents belong to this organization, whose father's names are left out of the certificates.*

g. *The tape of Vernon's "Bible study" in which he blatantly and clearly threatens to kill, and admits to being inside a number of "girls." You should have that tape. If not, I will be happy to send it.*

b. The fact that warrants were issued against Vernon in the state of California, some of which were for statutory rape.

i. The presence of the Hell's angels.

Now I find it very hard to believe that this is not enough evidence to have probable cause. Exactly what does it take anyway?

3. I have seen some things take place in Texas to which I am willing to testify in court, if necessary. Unfortunately, I am not financially able to fly to Texas to make my statement in your presence. Is there any way I can give my testimony (I do not mean courtwise because I'd have to be there in person for that) in order to help establish probable cause?

4. Just how much weight does the written sworn statements provided have?

5. If things came down to a court case, what would be necessary for those of us here to be witnesses?

I realize that I have quite a lot of questions and I would very much appreciate you answering them. I am sorry for whatever inconvenience this may cause you but I would really like to have this explained to me.

Finally,——— (I don't know her married name),
who was raped by Vernon [in your county], and had
a loaded gun pointed at her head . . . is still frightened
of going to court to testify. After all, she is pregnant and
her parents still follow Vernon. However she is coming
to realize the need for that testimony and is willing, at
this time, to provide a written sworn statement. She does
not now reside in Texas. I believe you need to know what
she has to say. What are her options if any?

Sincerely

Marc A. Breault

This letter received no response. All subsequent efforts
to communicate with the McLennan County Sheriff's
Department resulted in the same lack of response.
When later asked by *Waco Tribune Herald* reporter
Mark England why this was so, Gene Barber responded
that, in his judgment, Breault's complaints, along with
the others, stemmed from "sour grapes."

While in California, Marc and Elizabeth tried to reach
the Immigration and Naturalization Service. Spring fever
had struck at Ranch Apocalypse. Vernon's American
followers seemed unable to resist foreigners of the
opposite sex. American Robyn Bunds had married
English artist Cliff Sellors. When Bunds left the cult, she
told INS that she had been involved in a sham marriage.

But she was not alone. Australian Nicole Gent married American Jeff Little. American Jimmy Riddle fell for Canadian Ruth Ottman. Canadian Novelette Sinclair wedded American Peter Hipsman, while Australian Aisha Gyarfas fell head over heals for American Greg Summers.

Breault felt certain that INS would look suspiciously at this incredible string of blatant violations of the law. After all, Nicole Gent, Ruth Ottman, and Aisha Gyarfas were definitely Vernon's "wives," while Novelette was very likely one by then. But Marc and his wife were not only unable to make any headway with the INS, they were denied a chance to make a statement.

But Vernon did not limit his marriage fraud to foreigners. He also needed to disguise his secret babies as belonging to someone else. He was so afraid that someone would discover Michele Jones that he married her off to drummer David Thibodeau. And so the truth surrounding Michele's children (by then she had also given birth to twin girls) remained a secret from the world.

But Michele Jones's child, Serenity, was one of the lucky ones. People at least knew of her existence. Vernon fathered a number of children who were never registered. These children were born at Ranch Apocalypse, Mount Carmel, where two women, Mary Bell Jones and Jeannine Bunds, were qualified midwives. Jeannine herself delivered at least fourteen children there, most of whom belonged to the cult leader. (By the time of the shoot-out on February 28, 1993 Vernon had fathered no fewer than twenty-two children.)

While Breault was desperately trying to attract attention to Vernon's atrocities, this Texas Hitler added other positions to his hierarchy. There were three people directly under him: David Jones, the chief Mighty Man; lawyer Douglas Wayne Martin, who handled all legal responsibilities; and Steve Schneider, the chief evangelist and spokesman. Steve Schneider also had another distinction. He was David Koresh's High Priest. Not content with godhood, Vernon required homage. As High Priest, Schneider was responsible for ensuring that homage.

"You know the old sayin' that familiarity breeds contempt?" Koresh once asked Breault. "Well, people know me too much so they don't respect who I am. Maybe I should be like one of them oriental god-kings, you know, the kind that surround themselves with mystery. Maybe I should make it so the people can't get to me so easily. Maybe then they'll respect God's anointed." What Breault had at first thought to be nothing more than another raving fantasy, turned into a reality. Vernon was determined to turn his dreams, or nightmares, into reality, no matter what the cost.

When Marc and Elizabeth tried to see Nicole Gent, and her son Dayland, as they'd promised Bruce and Lisa Gent they would, they only got as close as her husband, Jeff Little. Little refused to allow Marc and Elizabeth to see

Nicole. Instead, he arrived at the front lobby of the Holiday Inn in Anaheim, accompanied by Jaydeen Wendel, who immediately repeated threats of lawsuits. Breault countered with a reminder that one DNA test could expose Little's charade. The fight was on in earnest, right there in the front lobby.

Talking to Jaydeen was like talking to a brick wall with legs. My DNA reminder really frightened Jeff Little, however, and I think we almost persuaded him to leave Koresh that night. He asked to meet me alone, so the two of us separated. We spoke for around four hours. Jeff's first words to me were: "Marc, I don't want to go to jail."

Jeff Little got into trouble with the cult after speaking to me alone. I'm not sure he was ever really trusted again. Jeff seemed sincerely shaken and tired of the whole cult business. But I just couldn't break him free in the one meeting. It was frustrating to come so close, yet remain so far. I also learned from Little that he hadn't been given letters and messages I directed specifically to him.

In June 1991 the final degradation occurred at Mount Carmel. A 29-year-old woman, who had developed mental problems under Vernon's tyrannical rule, was singled out for brutality after she began hearing voices. The cult leader feared that she might be perceived by other members as a rival prophet. There's only one direct line to God at Mount Carmel.

Vernon's idea of rehabilitation was to imprison her for four months in one of the many small cottages on the property. This woman was considered such a threat that he imposed a 24-hour guard – one of the Mighty Men. Vernon instructed the muscular guard: "If she gives you any trouble, fuck her." And for the next four months, that was the fate that befell her. The wretched woman was repeatedly raped and bashed by the guard, and beaten by a succession of others, including her noble leader.

When her "treatment" was complete, Vernon allowed her to leave. A week later police found her wandering the streets of San Francisco, and she was committed to a mental asylum. Reports were filed to police in both San Francisco and Texas, but, as usual, no action was taken. The woman never again came under the cult's influence, and is today living a normal life.

By now, at least six law enforcement agencies had been contacted, covering Texas and California. No positive action was forthcoming.

The only time the authorities are going to do something is when there's a pile of bodies . . . and then they're going to go in and find them and then it's all over. It'll be another Jonestown. And he has said that the world will know about this. And that's what he's working towards.

– Bruce Gent, April 1992

My gut feeling is that if nothing is done there will be a lot of dead people. Our sources tell us he has enough ammunition and firearms to field a 100-man army.

– Marc Breault, April 1992

He asked, "are you prepared to die for me?" And they would all gladly die for him. I know that. When I was there, yes I would have . . . We just think, well, this is the end. The kids haven't got a chance any more now. He's planning to exit.

– Lisa Gent, April 1992

He always said the authorities would never take the children away from him. He'd rather kill them before giving them up.

– Elizabeth Baranyai, April 1992

By the end of 1991 Vernon was confident. He had not only survived the loss of a number of followers, he had also survived attempts to initiate both state and Federal investigations against him. The mad man of Mount Carmel seemed invincible. It was time for a hit list.

Marc Breault and his wife Elizabeth graced the top slots, followed closely by the Gents, the Toms, the Mannings, and the Bunds. Breault discovered the list's existence from frightened ex-members with whom he came in contact. At the same time, he was receiving letters containing intelligence such as this example from

David Bunds, dated January 1, 1992. David's mother, Jeannine, had fled the cult in September 1991.

Trickles of information keep coming through my sister from my mother. Here it goes:

1. *Right before my mother left, Vernon told her that she shouldn't leave because everything that he has been striving for would be finished in sixth months. He told her this in August. My mother also got the impression of mass suicide or homicide, she was not really sure.*
2. *Tell Bruce that Nicole has had another child. We do not know the sex. This cannot get back to Nicole because Vernon will know that my mother told and that should be avoided.*
3. *Vernon now urinates in public, in full view of the people and continues to speak and give the study while doing so.*
4. *———— has had another baby. The child (according to my mother) has a heart murmur and Vernon will not even allow a visit to the doctor to evaluate this condition.*
5. *Aisha Gyarfas was due to give birth in October.*
6. *Shari Doyle was due in December.*
7. *Kathy Andrade (Paul Fatta's convert) is pregnant.*
8. *———— (one of Vernon's wives) has some kind of venereal disease.*
9. *Vernon has moved Perry, Michele Jones and her children, Aisha and hers, Cyrus and maybe other*

*favorites to Palestine to protect them so they cannot
be taken away from him. He has surrounded them
with an arsenal of weapons.*

The situation was intolerable. Koresh just had to be
stopped. Breault had to find another way.

*For the most part, my methods had been direct. I did try
a few underhanded tricks like sending letters in junk
mail envelopes so that they could penetrate the Koresh
censor. But I had generally tried the direct approach.*

*Now it was time for something a little more subtle. In
terms of my physical safety, it was good that Koresh felt
confident. I became, or so he bragged, a mosquito that
was only an annoyance rather than a major threat.*

*To my mind, however, Koresh seemed too confident.
Steve Schneider started wagging that silver tongue of his
just a little too freely. I began to wonder if Koresh had
a more sinister source for his confidence. He seemed to
know, for example, that there were no warrants against
him in California. He also seemed to know what we were
telling the Sheriff's department.*

*When the child protection people came onto the
compound in Waco, they found no evidence of child
abuse. I was happy for the children, but I knew better.
Koresh had a number of properties he could use to secrete
anyone who could harm him, either directly or indirectly.*

There seemed to be no chink in Koresh's armor. I had

grown up respecting the justice system. Now I was beginning to wonder if law enforcement agents were worth the metal used for their badges.

Then we hit upon the obvious solution to our quandary.

Breault and the others would not acquiesce, despite their past frustrations. Vernon had two weaknesses of which he was unaware. The first was the media. The second, little Kiri Jewell, whom Vernon thought forever safe in her mother's arms, and his.

When Marc and Elizabeth found Kiri's father, David, the final countdown to Armageddon began.

Chapter Twenty Four

The Rescue of Kiri Jewell and the Aborted Armageddon

Up until late 1991 David Jewell and his new wife, Heather, had never heard of Marc Breault. But they soon would though, and it would change their lives. It was October 31, 1991. Halloween. But the phone call at 7.30 a.m. was no trick or treat. The male voice at the other end of the line said he was from Australia.

The Jewell's were skeptical. Why would an American call them from Australia? "I've got something to tell you," Marc Breault warned. "And you're not going to like it. It's about your daughter, Kiri, and I have reason to believe she's in extreme danger."

Kiri, then aged ten, was David Jewell's daughter from a previous marriage. He knew that his daughter and ex-wife, Sherri, were involved in a strange religion. He even knew that there were guns involved, having heard of the November 3, 1987 shoot-out with George Roden.

But nothing could have prepared him for Marc Breault's bombshell.

I didn't know if David Jewell would believe me. For all he knew, I could be some nut case trying to cause a sensation. I had to tell David things that were so disturbing that I was afraid he would simply go into denial. I don't know who was more nervous, David Jewell or myself.

I called David simply to tell him that I was sending him a package with all the proof and evidence I could get my hands on. I didn't ask him for anything, not even information. I just wanted him to read my material before making a judgment.

Of course I couldn't see David Jewell's reaction over the phone, but you could tell he was in shock. He was too dazed to take it all in.

David asked us to Federal Express our package and said that we could charge it to him.

Breault and the child's father worked closely for the next four months. He and Jewell decided to tap into CompuServe, a world-wide computer network that gives each user an electronic mail box (E-mail), allowing them to send and receive huge quantities of information quickly, cheaply and, more importantly, without fear of prying eyes.

David Jewell's older sister Lois had been agonizing over the child's plight for years. She, like her brother, was aware that Kiri belonged to a bizarre and possibly dangerous religion. Within minutes of Breault's phone call she came to her brother's aid. Together they ploughed through the mountains of documentation and sent a series of questions to Breault via E-mail.

After seeing the irrefutable evidence Jewell engaged an attorney. He and Breault faced two major hurdles. First, they needed to ensure that neither Vernon, nor Sherri, discovered their plans until the last possible moment. Second, they knew that Vernon's financial reserves could get him the best lawyers who could make it nearly impossible for David Jewell to secure custody. There was also a more sinister ploy available to Vernon: Kiri could simply disappear. So while Jewell went down the legal road in November 1991, engaging one of the area's top attorneys, Victor McFadden, Breault had to find a way to distract Vernon so that he wouldn't uncover the rescue bid. When McFadden realized the danger posed to young Kiri, he took the case without charge.

In the meantime, Marc Breault had given up on the authorities, so he went to the American media. This would not only expose the cult leader's wickedness to the world, but it would also provide a valuable insurance policy. If Vernon knew that Breault had gone public, he'd think twice about trying to kill him again. But, amazingly, Marc couldn't get the American media interested in this devil in their midst. Then he turned to Australian television.

On October 24 Breault furnished the National Nine Network in Melbourne, Australia with the same extensive documentation he had attempted to show law enforcement agencies, and the media, in America. The network knew a good story when it saw one. As a reporter for "A Current Affair" (Australia) I took up a challenge that was to dominate my life for the next two years.

But how would we convince Vernon to be a willing participant in a television report, the secret agenda of which was to expose him as a sex-crazed despot? He was contacted, purposely, by a female researcher, Neheda Barakat. Breault advised Channel Nine that Vernon believed women were inferior and would grant an interview if the reporter was a female, and a seductive-sounding one. It was never, however, the Network's intention to send a woman into Ranch Apocalypse – and Vernon's clutches.

The supposedly all-seeing, all-knowing Son of God immediately fell for Neheda and the story she told about wanting to do a feature documentary about him. He granted the world's first and only face-to-face interview at Mount Carmel. Unbeknownst to Vernon, I was on my way to Texas. Step one accomplished. Step two was agreeing on a date. Vernon chose New Year's Day, and we had no choice but to accept. Then, a major complication: Marc Breault asked us to change the date of our visit to the cult headquarters so he and David Jewell could initiate court action to prevent Kiri's return to Waco.

It was a real dilemma for us at Channel Nine. We had

spent months investigating the cult and had already interviewed nine former cult members. We risked losing the lot, plus a world-exclusive interview, by messing up Vernon's schedule. But if we didn't, little Kiri Jewell might not be saved. We didn't have a choice.

Vernon wasn't happy. He said he was busy but to come anyway, and he'd see how he felt. We thought we might have blown it. And Vernon was still to discover that his interviewer was indeed a male, and not the seductive female he'd been promised.

On January 4, 1992, we met Vernon for the first time. He was dressed in black jeans, a crumpled shirt and those sneakers. He asked where the female reporter was. Told Ms Barakat had been sent on another assignment, he was crestfallen, and not a little peeved. It was a worrying few moments for us as he consulted with his minders. But the lure of the limelight proved irresistible and he gave us his blessing to spend as long as we wished at Mount Carmel, with one restriction: we were never to go anywhere alone. We could only pray that Breault's secret rescue mission would remain just that – secret.

So far, so good. Vernon and Sherri Jewell had sent the 10-year-old to her father in Michigan shortly after Christmas, 1991. Although the Branch Davidians do not celebrate the Christmas holiday, Kiri seemed all too eager to do so with her family. Sherri had not sent Kiri away empty handed. In her jacket pocket was a note containing instructions on how she should treat her father, beginning with "Give him Hell" and listing the ways to accomplish this. But it was David Jewell who was to give his ex-wife and her Messianic lover all the Hell they could handle.

The Michigan state court granted Jewell temporary custody of his daughter, pending a full hearing. Both David and Lois were thrilled. In yet another E-mail message, they said to Marc Breault: "We all wish we could be there with you to celebrate. What we have done already, even though temporary, is still a major victory against Vernon. We can now pull out all the stops and run at them with swords blazing!!!! (OK, perhaps that's a little dramatic but that's how I feel.)"

For her part, Kiri had mixed emotions. She was happy about the decision but she was also frightened at the prospect of her natural mother and Vernon finding out. She'd wanted to leave the cult for a long time but was terrified of Vernon and the divine retribution he would send. "Some day, you kids might be taken away from me," Koresh used to tell the children. "The unbelievers might ask you a lot of questions about me and what I do. But you have to be strong. Don't tell them shit-kickers anything, or God'll throw you in the fire."

The Jewell family decided to be honest with Kiri. After the temporary court order was granted, they told her that they knew all about the sinister activities of the cult. The child was both shocked and relieved at the same time and burst into tears.

259

The decoy had worked. Kiri's father had won temporary custody and we left Mount Carmel with a world-exclusive. The very next day Sherri Jewell received a court order to go to Michigan to fight for custody of her daughter. She was livid, but not as livid as her lover, David Koresh.

If the court order upset him, imagine his reaction when he discovered that the Australian television crew had worked in with his arch rival Marc Breault to rescue Kiri. And when Vernon saw the finished program, depicting him as a sex-deranged lunatic preparing to lead his followers into Hell, he threatened dire vengeance.

Steve Schneider repeatedly threatened producer Craig Walsh and I with terrible retribution. According to Schneider, Vernon was so upset that he vowed never to speak to the media again. He ordered Sherri Jewell to call her daughter and instil defiance in her. He also instructed Kiri to spy on her father, to learn what she could. Ironically, she was told to be his little FBI. But when Sherri called she was greeted with chilling words from her daughter – "Mom, they know everything. There's nothing they don't know."

Vernon was in trouble. Kiri Jewell was a minor. And like so many other minors in his perverted regime, she had been abused. Kiri Jewell could do damage! So began a frantic effort to influence the mind of this innocent child.

Sherri called her daughter repeatedly, telling her that her eternal soul hung in the balance. Both David Jewell and his sister Lois taped those phone calls. The tapes contain highly sensitive information that cannot appear in this publication for reasons of privacy. Suffice to say, however, that if the Jewells had been shocked at Breault's allegations, they were horrified at Sherri's treatment of her own daughter. The law allowed Sherri to have access to her daughter, but each minute was an agony.

Transcripts were made of the taped conversations and sent to Breault. Sherri often passed information to her daughter in code. She sent veiled messages in the same manner. Breault was able to crack her scriptural codes. It was through this method that Bruce and Lisa Gent learned they had a second grandchild, as Marc Breault recalls.

It was terrible learning about Nicole's second child that way. We felt we couldn't simply call the Gents. We had to visit them personally. When we told Bruce, he had to leave the room for a time. It was bad enough his daughter was Koresh's lover. But the worst part about it was the fact that the Gents had to learn of their new grand-daughter from a friend who had just cracked a code from a taped phone conversation half a world away. I almost cried myself.

Sherri strongly suspected she was being taped, of course. That's why she used codes. She told Kiri, for example, that someone was coming with her. When Kiri asked who it was, Sherri was reluctant to answer directly. Instead, she referred to two scriptures: Zechariah 3, and Revelation 11. Those passages were designed to tell Kiri who was helping her.

I don't know whether Kiri understood her mother, but I certainly did. Those two scriptures spoke volumes. Steve Schneider was about to visit Michigan.

Elizabeth and I worked feverishly for hours every night compiling evidence. A new set of affidavits needed to be made. Cult properties where Sherri and Kiri might have stayed had to be found. Unlisted phone numbers had to be traced. Detailed chronologies covering the time of Sherri Jewell's involvement had to be ascertained. Cult beliefs and practices were chronicled in detail.

The Jewells had a mountain of evidence, but Sherri had witnesses. While Steve Schneider was designated to help Sherri, she also knew that she could call on nearly a hundred people who would tell the court that Vernon was as nice as Mother Teresa. Marc and Elizabeth feared that personal testimony would outweigh written evidence, so they decided to fly to Michigan and testify in person.

Jean Smith, an Australian woman who had been a Branch Davidian for years but had left the cult in June 1990 after returning to Australia in April that year, decided to accompany these cultbusters from Downunder on their third trip to America in as many years.

As he had done throughout his ordeal, Marc Breault kept a diary on that portable Compaq.

Thursday, February 20, 1992
David [Jewell] . . . gave us a big hug and said he was glad we were here . . . He pulled out a sheet of paper. It was the latest message from David Bunds via E-mail. He told us that Dorothy [not her real name] had left the group because Vernon was wrong. According to David Bunds, she said that she was never going back. She left with her two children and was on her way to her parents' home. Dorothy had contacted Jeannine Bunds about getting copies of birth certificates for her children. That was all the message said.

Elizabeth jumped up and down for joy right there in the airport. Dorothy had been one of Elizabeth's best friends in the cult. They'd shared a little shack while living in Palestine, Texas.

I, however, was already wondering if there was a way to get her testimony. Oh well, at a time like this, you cannot allow one's emotions to cloud your perspective. David Jewell was, of course, thinking along the same lines.

I found out later, after meeting with the Jewells, that even though they didn't know most of the Vernonites, they have been pulling for them. When we arrived at Lois's place, Lois said that this was the best news she had heard in a while. She was really happy and she's never met Dorothy.

David and Lois are very close. It had been decided that Kiri would stay with her aunt Lois thus leaving David free to handle all the preparations necessary for the court case. It didn't take me long to learn that Kiri couldn't possibly have been in better hands. Lois was like Kiri's second mother – Sherri should take notes from Lois.

At David's house . . . David called Lois to see if it was safe for us to arrive. You see, we didn't want to spook Kiri.

It was not. Kiri had been talking to her mother Sherri. Sherri had really put the pressure on Kiri, telling her that I was on my way and that I would grill her and try to make her talk. She did a lot of other things, including trying to lay on a heavy guilt trip. The poor girl was so upset after she got off the phone she cried and cried in Lois's arms. Up until then, she didn't know we were going to stay there.

Apparently, Sherri talked to Lois and bragged that Kiri would leave if I came. Another wrong prediction. Kiri was having trouble getting to sleep, and she had to go to school the next morning.

Kiri was so upset, she asked Lois if she could take some sleeping pills to get to sleep. At one point she sobbed to

Lois: "I wish you were my mommy." Eventually, at approximately 11.15 p.m., Kiri went to sleep and it was safe to come. So we did.

Lois's house is huge and it took me a while to get used to the idea that we could talk in normal conversational tones without being heard upstairs . . . Lois was absolutely disgusted with Sherri's tactics. She was, at first, all for banning communication between Sherri and Kiri. However, David Jewell correctly pointed out that this would be illegal and that they had come this far, so far, because they had played by the book.

We showed them Martin King's report on the cult and people were suitably horrified. The phone rang often enough with people wondering whether we had arrived etc. We talked for a long time. It was good to have friends and we had yet another late night, despite having been on the road for over nineteen hours.

Friday, February 21, 1992
We spent most of today in Victor McFadden's office, preparing for the upcoming hearing. Vic, as he likes to be called, is a nice guy. His desk is chaos, much like mine. He's always being interrupted and he keeps misplacing his pens. But he also inspires confidence. I won't say he's exactly like Columbo, he dresses better, but the thought has crossed my mind.

Tonight we met Mike Shimechero and his wife and daughter. Mike had been recruited from England but had left the group after realizing Vernon was wrong. It was good to see him again.

We only talked about old times for a while. Then, Mike came up with an idea. It was an idea I had considered, but dreaded. He wanted to let Steve Schneider's family know everything. Steve's family live in Wisconsin, only one state over. They could come and talk to us and then speak with Steve.

I had tried to recruit the Schneider family in 1986. Thank God they didn't join. But I guess Vernon had more to do with that than I did. They liked me but were turned off by him. I wondered whether they would even speak to me after getting their son involved in something like this.

The minimum benefit from telling Steve's family was that they could come and distract Steve from helping Sherri. The maximum, of course, was that his parents and three sisters could persuade him to leave the cult. We especially hoped Pat Schneider, Steve's mother, could influence him.

We agreed to put the plan into action the next day.

Mike drove us home and, I don't mean to be paranoid, but I think we were followed. I borrowed a trick from a Robert Ludlum book and had Elizabeth take out her compact. We used that mirror to make sure. Yes, the car was following, but turned off as we approached the Jewell's place. Coincidence or reality?

Saturday, February 22, 1992

If Lois Jewell were in a locked room alone with Vernon, I'd put my money on Lois. She does more with her brain than Vernon could ever hope to accomplish with his guns. Today Sherri gave Kiri her phone number. Lois traced it down and found Sherri's hotel. Working on the assumption that Steve was staying in the same hotel, she managed to find his room as well.

Great! Now we could tell where the Schneiders could go to meet their son, if they came.

We thought that one of Steve's old teachers, the one who had married Steve and Judy, should approach the Schneiders first. Doug Waterhouse was trusted by the whole family.

While Sherri was visiting Kiri, we spoke to Doug Waterhouse around 3.30 p.m. He was horrified. He was in shock. He kept saying "How can anyone follow Vernon" and then apologized for repeating himself. He was a very nice guy and seemed concerned. We showed him Martin King's story so he could get up to speed quickly. Waterhouse promised to contact the Schneiders on our behalf.

We stayed at Mike's [Schimechero's] place for several hours. We were just stepping out the door when the phone rang. This was some time later after Doug's visit. It turned out to be Sue Johnson, Steve's oldest sister. That family goes Sue, Steve, Shelley and Sidnee.

Sue wanted to speak to me. I was nervous because,

after what Waterhouse told her, I didn't know whether Sue would hate me or not. I was responsible for getting Steve into this mess in the first place.

It turned out that Sue wanted to get a hold of me. Sue told me that Steve had made contact with his family about two weeks earlier and warned them that I might be trying to get in contact with them and that I had left Vernon's group. He admonished them not to believe my "lies."

Steve's family, on the other hand, wanted to see me after this warning. They knew Vernon and distrusted him intensely. They reasoned that if I had left the group, and was trying to get in contact with them, I'd probably be telling them the truth.

Sue told me something that really alarmed me. She said that Steve had called them to say goodbye. He said that he would probably have to do something which would cause him to die, but that he would be resurrected shortly thereafter and fulfil Isaiah 13 and Joel 2.

That was really scary stuff. Steve was basically saying goodbye and that he was planning to die shortly. He sounded suicidal. The something which would cause him to die was termed "the end." This was not something limited entirely to Steve himself, but concerned the whole group.

When I told Sue the rest of what was going on, she started to panic and well she should. It was then that phase two of Mike's Schneider plan began to take shape.

Since the Schneiders lived relatively close to where we were staying, I asked them to come up and we would explain everything to them and let them see the videos and read various affidavits.

We left it at that hoping they would arrive tomorrow.

Sunday, February 23, 1992

Well the Schneiders drove all night to get to here early. Apparently, they couldn't sleep so they figured they might as well not waste time. It was nice seeing them again. I have fond memories of that family. I felt so sorry for Pat because, being Steve's mother, she was naturally upset. She hugged me and said she was glad I was out of Vernon's group. I apologized for involving Steve but they said it was okay. After all, people are responsible for their own actions at some point.

It turns out they already suspected what was going on so they weren't too shocked when I told them about Judy's child really being Koresh's. They already knew that Steve couldn't have children; at least Sue did. Steve and Sue were closest. They were, of course, shocked at seeing the videos and learning (officially) what was really going on. They wanted to see Steve right away.

It turned out, though, that they had to wait. Steve wasn't there. In fact, he was visiting with Doug Water-house. Steve had no idea his family was coming.

Eventually, Steve did show up at the hotel and that's when his family struck. They knocked on the door and, according to them, Steve turned pale when he saw his father, mother, and sisters standing there.

Steve said, "Oh no, how am I going to deal with you." The family wasn't taking any denials. They showed up just when Sherri was on the phone with Kiri. Sherri heard a knock on the door and it was Steve, asking her to come help him out. That was unfortunate.

Sidnee told me that things got very heated in there and Steve was putting up a front. Mike called me up because he was waiting at the front of the hotel. Apparently, things weren't going well at all as Steve was so angry he was threatening to throw them out. Steve was saying no one could refute Vernon.

The Schneiders asked me to come up there and rebut Vernon. I figured, however, Steve would be too angry to listen. Besides, what he needed was an hysterical mother sobbing her eyes out begging him not to remain in the cult. I hated to do it to Pat but her emotions could speak louder than any theology.

So here we are, very troubled. Things aren't going well with Steve but he is being distracted from the Jewell case, which was the minimum gain from all this anyway. Maybe Steve will feel bad about treating his family this way and try to smooth things over tomorrow, alone, and without Sherri. After all, Sherri will probably have to deal with her attorney.

Monday, February 24, 1992

Well Steve did feel bad. I talked to Sidnee this morning and she told me that things didn't go well but that Steve would be spending the day with them, alone. I explained that Steve needed his family and Sidnee agreed. She said that Sherri was virtually useless in there with Steve. Every time she would try to say something Steve would cut her off. In fact, Sherri was annoying the whole family and she didn't have any right being there.

At 5 p.m. I called the Schneiders. I didn't want to antagonize Steve so I just talked to Sidnee and Sue. Sue clarified what Steve had said. Both said Steve was doing a lot better today and that they were having a pleasant time together. They were going over the "good old times" and Steve didn't seem to be denying everything. He said that he was tired of Vernon's group but that the book compelled him.

Tuesday, February 25, 1992

Today the court case began at 9 a.m. All the principles were, of course, early. Sherri and Steve were there and Steve was very polite, saying hello to everyone. Sherri introduced him to the Jewells whom, of course, he wouldn't have known.

As I said, Steve was very polite and wanted to know how we were getting along. Steve knew, of course, that I was behind his family's sudden visitation. Yet he showed no trace of anger. I think he might have been relieved that his family knew everything.

Sherri, however, was another matter. She didn't say one word to us. She had her hair tied up in a severe bun, and she had one of those burgundy leather briefcases. She looked professional on the surface, but one could tell she was under a lot of stress. I mean, not only was Sherri having to deal with Kiri, she was having to answer to Koresh too, and that ain't easy. Sherri didn't bother trying to appear civil. She just ignored us.

The hearing started pretty much on time. Sherri's attorney was one Paul Jancha. We were cast in the role of the plaintiff or prosecution, while Sherri was the defendant.

Sherri's attorney immediately made a motion to sequester the witnesses. This meant that we couldn't be in the court room except while we were testifying. This prevented us from modifying our testimony to suit the occasion.

The only witnesses allowed to participate full time were David Jewell and Sherri herself. Our side's witnesses were myself, Elizabeth, Jean Smith and Lois Jewell. Sherri had Steve.

Outside the court room, Steve sat with Lois and the three of us. At first the atmosphere was somewhat tense but pretty soon we began talking. We weren't allowed to talk about the case. Steve did express his lack of desire to be there.

At around 10.30 a.m. the court recessed. Elizabeth saw

Sherri whispering something to Steve. According to Sherri (later), she was asking where the water fountain was. But since when do you whisper when asking for the location of a water fountain? Victor, our attorney, caught on to this . . . Sherri was not supposed to discuss the case with Steve [and her] attorney Paul had to warn Sherri to cut it out. She wasn't too pleased.

I was called in following an afternoon recess. I was sworn in and Vic began asking me questions.

That was when the real shock set in. The judge was totally blown away. I had to go into graphic details about Vernon's sexual practices and teachings, especially as relating to Sherri. I had no mercy. I was like a sledge-hammer pounding Sherri into the ground. I didn't like doing it, but it had to be done.

Our attorney was methodical and thorough. He took his time and missed nothing. No detail was too insignificant. He reminded me of a scientist, carefully dissecting a specimen. Sherri Jewell was that specimen.

All the while Sherri sat there, madly taking down everything that was said in shorthand. Why? She wanted to report back to Vernon. The court proceedings were videotaped, so Sherri didn't need to write anything down. It was weird watching a woman more concerned with reporting to Vernon, than fighting for her own daughter.

Sherri was so engrossed in her task, that her own attorney had trouble conferring with her. On a couple of occasions, he became visibly annoyed.

Sherri's contention was that the state of Michigan had no jurisdiction over this case. In other words, they wanted to move things to California. We needed to keep this matter in Michigan so we had to prove that a state of emergency existed.

It was an open court session and David had many family and friends there for support. They were horrified upon learning what was really going on. As I said, I spared no one and kept nothing back. I had to try to convince the judge that Kiri was in a hazardous situation.

Before the trial, David's stepfather had thought we were exaggerating things. After about ninety minutes, the judge had to call a recess, with me still on the stand. David's stepfather looked like he'd been hit by a truck.

When we resumed, Victor continued to ask questions and I continued to answer them. I didn't find it difficult in any way whatsoever. Some people thought I was brave. But I had nothing to scare me. It simply had to be done and that was that. The real "bravery" will come in the cross-examination.

At one point I told the court how Vernon publicly, and in front of Kiri, described Sherri's genitalia, differentiating it from that of other women. Sherri's attorney couldn't take any more. He stood up and objected, spluttering that Sherri would deny everything I said. The judge, however, assured him that Sherri would get her chance. Poor Jancha looked like he didn't know what bit him. I almost felt sorry for the guy. I'm sure Sherri hadn't told him what I would say and he was totally unprepared.

When the court recessed for the day, I was tired. The audience was stunned. Round one was over and we had the enemy on the ropes. Hopefully, the KO will come tomorrow.

That evening, Sherri was supposed to see Kiri so we stayed in our room while she was there. I think Sherri wanted to vent her rage at us by day's end and I think it frustrated her that we wouldn't accommodate her.

Kiri was still afraid of us. Sherri and Steve were trying to get Kiri to testify and say she wanted her mommy. But Kiri was terrified. She was so scared of testifying, in fact, that she couldn't sleep at night. She spent a lot of time sobbing in David's arms . . . We were letting Kiri decide whether she'd testify, but if she didn't, we didn't want to see her forced to do so.

My only consolation in all this, so far, was that Vernon was just as nervous and tense as we were. I hoped his ulcer was growing!

As soon as Sherri got back to her hotel she called Kiri. David Jewell watched. Suddenly, the child's expression and demeanor changed. She seemed stilted and tense. David suspected Sherri had put Steve on the phone. He asked Kiri if that was the case and she nodded. David took the phone from his daughter and told Steve that it was not appropriate for him to talk to his daughter.

Steve was surprised and said he was just saying hello. But Steve was actually quoting Psalm 8 to Kiri. Psalm 8 is one of Vernon's favorites, as he used this to teach that he will sire his master race.

I couldn't sleep. I kept thinking about what Sue had told me. Steve believed the end was near. I could not stop thinking of my best friend blowing his brains out, or taking cyanide, or getting shot in a gun-fight with the authorities. What's wrong with you Steve!

I cried for the first time in a long while.

Wednesday, February 26, 1992

The first thing David did when he saw Victor was tell him about Steve's talking to Kiri last night. Victor promptly conferred with the other attorney. They went off privately and later I saw Jancha admonishing Sherri and Steve.

Round two began with Vic finishing his questioning. When it was over, it was time for the cross-examination to begin.

Jancha wanted blood. He didn't bother to disguise his hostile intentions. This attorney had been forced to listen to me completely trash Sherri for hours. He wanted my guts, and he wanted them now!

He began by attacking my eyesight. Since I had lost my reading glasses, he almost scored. Indeed, he had me on the ropes there for a while. His contention was that my poor eyesight invalidated my testimony, since I could not have possibly seen all the things I said I'd seen.

But eventually it became apparent that I could see well enough and he had to back down.

Then, Jancha accused me of being a rival prophet, making up allegations solely to take over Mount Carmel from Vernon. For the first time I explained my deprogramming ploy in the presence of a Vernonite. I told Jancha I only acted like a prophet in order to get people to listen to me. I did not wish, in any way, for anyone to think that I saw myself as a prophet like Vernon.

Sherri was in total, absolute shock. She was so angry I thought she might charge me then and there. But she held her ground and did a good job of recovering. She even stopped taking shorthand for a time. Her attorney eventually ran out of steam and handed me back over to Vic.

At one point, Vic asked me a leading question out of the scope of the cross-examination. Jancha rightly objected and both were summoned to the bench. The judge basically told Jancha that his cross-examination was tangential and admonished Vic not to follow in his footsteps. That was when I realized we had won. The main part of Jancha's steam was spent and I began to relax. It appeared that all the planning had been well ordered and successful.

Elizabeth took the stand about twenty minutes before lunch. Elizabeth told the judge she thought Sherri was a good mother who believed she was doing the right thing by Kiri. But Elizabeth also stated that she felt Sherri was misguided because of her religious beliefs. The judged nodded his agreement. Sherri's attorney wasn't nearly as hostile towards Elizabeth as he was toward me.

Kiri ended up talking to a "friend of the court" and it was determined that she should not testify.

Jean followed Elizabeth on the stand. What can I say? Who's going to dispute a 72-year-old woman who flies half-way around the world just to testify? She was a big hit with the judge.

Round two also belonged to us. So far, we were ahead on points.

During the time Elizabeth and Jean spent on the stand, I talked with Steve. Poor Steve was a tired man. He told me he had just been seriously ill. He admitted to me that he wanted out of Vernon's group, but that the book compelled him to continue. I tried to talk him around but, frankly, Steve appeared too tired to even care. The poor guy could hardly concentrate any more. He was a shell of the man I once knew.

In the light of what Steve told me I honestly thought Steve wanted to die. I think he had nothing else to live for.

Sherri came over to see Kiri and we once again retreated to our rooms. We had packing to do anyway. Elizabeth did run into Sherri accidentally, however, and Sherri thanked Elizabeth for what she had said about her while she was on the stand. Sherri even hugged her.

Elizabeth cried because of what she had had to do to her friend.

I hate to leave without seeing the final outcome but such is life. So tomorrow we're out of here and I'll miss the Jewells. They are a neat bunch of people.

Finally, tonight, there is talk of concession. It looks like Vernon has had enough so we're past the two-minute warning now. In a way, I would have liked all the evidence to be heard. But, for Kiri's sake, it's better that Sherri "Get out of Dodge," as David puts it. It is difficult to describe in a diary the flavor of this fight but it hasn't been pretty. The Vernonites went for whatever they could find to discredit us. That's okay; I had to be ruthless too. I don't feel malevolent, of course. This is just something that has to be done, no matter how painful the experience to Sherri, Kiri, or even David Jewell. At least David understands; too bad Sherri doesn't.

Maybe some day Kiri will, when she's older, look back and realize that we had only her welfare in mind. Maybe she'll even understand. I'll be curious to know what she thinks ten years down the track. For now, however, she is a very hurt, vulnerable, yet bright 11-year-old girl. I wish you well Kiri.

On February 28, 1992, exactly one year to the day before the ATF raid on Mount Carmel, David Jewell won sole custody of his daughter. He won by a technical knockout – Vernon gave the order to surrender. The judge said it was the worst case of abuse and neglect he had ever heard.

Sherri Jewell retained some visitation rights. These rights, however, were granted on the condition that they took place only at the residence of the child's maternal grandmother, Ruth Mosher, and that the child not have contact – physically, by phone, or otherwise – with any cult members.

Sherri Jewell never exercised her visitation rights. David Koresh told her that Kiri had been a traitor because she hadn't remained loyal to him. Sherri believed her lover. She never saw her daughter again.

One year later, in March 1993, little Kiri stunned millions of televison viewers around the world when she revealed on "Donahue" that Vernon had instructed the children in the best ways to commit suicide: "You were supposed to stick a gun in your mouth, because if you stuck it to your head you'd . . . there would be a chance you could survive." She also confirmed that Koresh had cyanide, and they'd been taught how to use that as well. She had no doubt in her mind that the group would kill themselves rather than sur- render to authorities.

She was in a position to know.

Vernon Howell feared that the damaging court testi- mony would bring down the wrath of law enforcement. Believing the end was nigh, cult members from all around the world abandoned property, money, and other assets.

Don Bunds, a long time follower of Vernon, was so convinced he would die that, he gave his wife, Jeannine, who had left Vernon in September 1991, control over the cult house in Pomona. When she went to claim it, she and her two children, David and Robyn, found credit cards, titles to vehicles and property, keys, and other valuables simply lying around. Vernon's followers had left them behind expecting never to return.

Steve Schneider almost left the cult. Instead of returning to Mount Carmel from Michigan, he went home with his family to Wisconsin. Eventually, however, Judy Schneider called her husband and told him Vernon wanted him back immediately. Tragically, Steve obeyed.

Cult members phoned relatives to say goodbye. Frantic efforts were made by former members to convince the FBI that something needed to be done. Letters were written to Congress.

Vernon Howell began to divest himself of assets. He wanted cash, and he wanted it fast. He tried to sell his four properties in California, Texas and Florida. He wanted to make sure he'd be ready for whatever the law enforcement agencies threw at him.

But nothing happened. The FBI assured Congress that they had the situation well under control. Nobody went to arrest Vernon Howell. No one investigated him. They left him alone.

It was April 1992 and Armageddon was put on hold, leaving Vernon free to prepare for his ultimate bid for glory – a military-style offensive against the innocent inhabitants of Waco, Texas.

Chapter Twenty Five

David Koresh and Waco, Texas

Slay utterly old [and] young, both maids, and little children, and women . . . And he said unto them, Defile the house, and fill the courts with the slain: go ye forth. And they went forth, and slew in the city.

– Ezekiel 9: 6–7

There are some who would say that Vernon Howell and Waco deserved one another. After all, both had a love of guns, both were religion crazy, and both changed their names: Vernon Wayne Howell became David Koresh, and Waco was once known as Six-shooter Junction.

Until Vernon arrived in Waco in 1981, the town was somewhat of an enigma. Unlike Ireland and Lebanon, it was one of the few places in the world where God and guns co-existed in relative peace. After all, in Waco, population 103,000, guns are a way of life.

Indeed, in Texas guns are seen not only as a biblical right, but as a constitutional right. To prove the point, 17 million Texans own a staggering 68 million guns.

That's a lot of guns, and there are a lot of preachers too. And not too many people find it so surprising that Vernon claimed to have a direct line to God. Here, deep in the heart of Texas, one local reckons that saying "God spoke to me" is like saying the Avon lady called last week.

Naturally, if you've got a lot of preachers, you've got a whole bunch of churches too. In Waco, which is 95 per cent Baptist, there are more than two hundred churches, from the Freeway Church of God to the First Church of Miracles.

The people of Waco, at first, didn't spend too much time thinking about the skinny, long-haired fellow who had moved into George Roden's joint 9 miles from the edge of town. It was a strange relationship, really, between Howell and the locals. As the years rolled by, most people thought him eccentric but harmless. But the 1987 shoot-out with George Roden changed a lot of folks' minds. They wondered if it could happen again.

But what they didn't know couldn't hurt them, so the people in this college town pretty much ignored Mount Carmel and its prophet. Vernon, though, wasn't a man to be dismissed easily. He wanted to make his mark on this town, but first he had to be accepted. And what better way to do that than through music. He began frequenting music stores, bars and nightclubs. He was never shy about sharing his beliefs. In fact, in 1990 Vernon claimed that the entire city knew of his cult, and were interested in learning the Bible from his inspired lips.

At that time, Vernon finally got a chance to perform his brand of rock 'n' roll in front of a live audience. It was in a nightclub called Cue Stick. At first, Vernon had a good relationship with the management. He even stored some of his musical gear there. Cue Stick provided an ideal recruiting ground.

But things soon went sour when the management felt that biblical preaching was not conducive to the atmosphere they wished to create. Vernon was told to leave. He was so upset that he began preparing for his revenge. God would bring terrible judgment on that establishment, he said, as well as the rest of Waco. But the people of Waco weren't as interested in him as he believed.

"When God's ready," said Vernon, "I'm gonna show 'em God's judgment. They're fixin' to get their dicks cut off for what they've done to me." This was an oft-repeated threat.

Beaten but unbowed, the cult leader turned to an unlikely group of people to convert – a gang of bikies. As the 3-mile-long Santa Fe trains blasted their mournful early morning whistles across Waco, Vernon and his beloved bikies drank beer, played rock music, and prattled about prophecy. The gang was even permitted to stay overnight at Ranch Apocalypse.

For their part, the bikies appreciated this isolated stop-off. It didn't even bother them that Vernon continuously Bible-bashed them. He dreamed of a network of motorcycle gangs stretching from New York to California. Instead of Hell's Angels, though, Vernon wanted to call his gangs The Children of Light. They were his children, and he was the Light.

As anyone knows, a bikie will give you his money, his beer, and the shirt off his back. He might even give you a ride on his motorcycle. But there's one thing a bikie just won't share – and that's his woman.

Small wonder, then, that Vernon's new-found bikie friends rode off into the sunset after he tried to add their girlfriends to the House of David, which, incidentally, was bursting at the seams with more than thirty Brides of Christ. Vernon was left with his dream and revenge on his mind. For years he had taught that the slaughter described in the ninth chapter of the biblical book of Ezekiel would take place in Waco, Texas.

"The Davidians have been here for years," Vernon often said to Bible study classes. "Waco has the most light of anybody," he said, referring to the decades of Davidian preaching in the city. He said Waco had had enough time to learn the Truth about God, but that they were bad listeners. "God's fixin' to judge them 'cause they rejected truth for so many years. God's gonna execute the slaughter of Ezekiel 9 on 'em." According to Vernon, God was going to annihilate the wicked who had rejected what Vernon believed was the only interpretation of the Bible.

From God, this Prophet of Doom turned to guns. What

the good people of Waco didn't know was that there were a lot of guns out at Mount Carmel. A whole mess of guns. And Vernon's army of mighty warriors were primed, and ready to massacre. Military-style training had become the main focus at the cult headquarters.

The locals might have thought the Branch Davidians were just another bunch of religious crazies out on the prairie, living in a funny-looking wooden building. But that funny-looking wooden building contained enough fire-power to wipe out a small town.

In the sixteen months from October 1991 to February 1993 Vernon and his Mighty Men spent more than $200,000 readying themselves for war. Their shopping list – and it only includes what could be traced – leaves no doubt that the cult leader was preparing to wreak his vengeance.

- 104 AR-15-M-16 upper receiver parts (when this part is added to an AR-15 rifle it becomes a fully automatic weapon, and is illegal in the United States).
- 8100 rounds of 9 mm and .223 calibre ammunition for AR-15-M-16s.
- 260 AR-15-M-16 magazines.
- One M-76 grenade launcher and grenades.
- 26 assorted hand guns and rifles.
- Mortar shells.
- A 50-calibre machine-gun.
- Approximately a million rounds of ammunition.

Chapter Twenty Six
The Connection

If the American authorities had ignored the warnings from eyewitnesses like Marc Breault, why should they listen to a journalist from Australia? It was worth a try, anyway.

We went to the McLennan County Sheriff's Department, which rules the roost out Mount Carmel way, and told them we were about to expose Vernon Howell for the criminal that he was. For people who had come such a long way, we received a very short audience. Not in person, mind you. We didn't even get that far.

The Sheriff's Department told us over the phone, and none too politely, that they knew all about the allegations but refused to discuss what action, if any, they planned to take. In a nutshell, we got the cold shoulder. Now we had some idea of how frustrating it must have been for Marc Breault, the man who'd seen it all but couldn't get anybody to listen.

And all the while cult leader Koresh remained at large,

unleashing physical and emotional havoc on hundreds of lives – adult cult members, their children and the families they'd left behind. Thirteen months before the ATF bloodbath on February 28, 1993 I sat with Vernon next to the pond near the main road that leads to Mount Carmel.

KING Why you? Why do you do this?

KORESH *Because I can, that's what I was born for, that's why I do it . . . Christ did what he did because he was born to do that. He can, so I can do this. That's why I do it.*

KING You were chosen to do this?

KORESH *Well, it looks that way doesn't it.*

KING Are you a fighter or a lover?

KORESH *No, not a fighter. Do I look like a fighter?*

KING You're a lover?

KORESH *[laughs] Do I look like a lover? Do I? Do I look like a fighter? What difference does it make what I look like? Did Jesus look like the Son of God?*

On March 23, 1992 Marc Breault, still determined to bring down this self-professed Son of God, wrote to Congress. Breault chose David Jewell's representative in Michigan, Fred Upton.

Dear Representative Upton

A few days ago you received a letter from Mr. David Jewell. This letter outlined a desperate situation regarding a cult known as the Branch Davidian Seventh-day Adventists. While the cult's headquarters falls in the Waco, Texas area, and while its other major property is in Southern California, the only official evidence against this group was lodged in a court room in St. Joseph Michigan. I believe Mr. Jewell explained that to you in his letter. It is for this reason that I am writing to you now.

*The situation with respect to this cult is **desperate** as the cult leader, one Vernon Wayne Howell, is planning a mass suicide somewhere around April 18th of this year. This fact has been confirmed by a number of sources including an ex-member who has just recently (within the last month) fled the group.*

My difficulty is simply defined. I have not been able to speak to the FBI or any other proper agency. This is not a case in which I have given evidence to the authorities and they have not acted. Rather, it is a case in which I have not been able to talk to, or give evidence to, the authorities directly. Every time I attempt to, I am told to wait, or I am passed around from one department to another.

I should point out that I am an American citizen currently residing in Australia. I was a high-ranking member of the cult until 1989. Even in 1989 the cult was heading down the road of a Jonestown. I have tried for two years now to alert the authorities to the child abuse, child sexual abuse, illegal weapons, sham marriages, and even kidnapping taking place in the group.

The situation has become so acute, that three ex-members, including my wife and I, traveled from Australia to Niles, Michigan to help Mr. Jewell rescue his 11-year-old daughter from the hands of the cult. Mr. Jewell's ex-wife is a member of the cult. We made the trip at our own expense.

Time is fast running out and I **need** *to talk to the FBI or someone who can do something. If this does not happen, I believe that over 200 persons will be massacred next month. Please take action and set the wheels in motion. Each day nothing is done, children are being abused, either physically or sexually. Each day brings us closer to another Jonestown. I look forward to your reply.*

If you wish to reach me, you can go through Mr. David Jewell and he will get your message to me. We have a computer link set up using CompuServe so our communications are very rapid. If you have access to

CompuServe, my ID number is ———. Please act
quickly before it is too late.

Sincerely
Marc A. Breault
P.S. Evidence gathered includes:

1. *Court testimony.*
2. *Two media stories which are on video.*
3. *Audio tapes of the cult leader in which he actually describes sexual activities with under-aged girls.*
4. *At least nine affidavits.*
5. *Raw footage from the media, containing uncut versions of the material pertaining to this case.*
6. *Written histories of the organization.*

The evidence is overwhelming and I sincerely hope someone acts on it quickly.

Congressman Upton never responded to Breault's letter.
Another congressman, however, responded to a similar
letter written by David Jewell. Senator Dan Reigle contacted the FBI and was told that, by law, they couldn't
disclose the existence or status of any investigation. The
first time the FBI contacted Breault was on March 1, 1993,
the day *after* four ATF agents were shot and killed and
sixteen were wounded. The day *after* six cult members

were shot dead, and many others were wounded.

The grim irony is that the Bureau of Alcohol, Tobacco and Firearms was the only United States law enforcement agency that took Marc Breault seriously.

Chapter Twenty Seven

The Build-up to
The Big Bang

The ringing phone jars Marc Breault from a deep sleep. But it's his wife, Elizabeth, who reaches over and picks up the receiver. "It's for you," she says. "Some guy in America who says he's with the ATF. What's the ATF?"

It's just before dawn in Marc and Elizabeth's home in Melbourne, Australia. To Elizabeth, an Australian, the ATF means nothing. But Breault, an American citizen, is only too familiar with the organization. And he knows the call is crucial.

Breault covers the mouthpiece with his hand. "You know The Untouchables?" he asks. "You remember Elliott Ness? They're the guys who brought down Al Capone."

It was December 1992, ten weeks before the abortive raid on Vernon Howell's Mount Carmel headquarters. The caller was Special Agent Derek Anderson (not his real name) with the Bureau of Alcohol, Tobacco and

Firearms, a branch of the US Treasury Department. Marc Breault and Elizabeth Baranyai breathed a sigh of relief. After all their efforts, someone was finally prepared to listen. And act.

It was to be the first of many – almost daily – phone calls between Breault and senior officials of the United States Government, which included the ATF, the FBI, Congress, the State Department, and the Texas Rangers. It was those dozens of highly confidential trans-Pacific telephone calls that helped authorities bring Vernon Howell's ten-year Reich to an end. A Reich in which child beatings, child sex, rape, violence, cruelty, mind control, food and water deprivation, enforced isolation, guns and terrorism were endemic.

Here, then, is Marc Breault's exclusive, behind-the-scenes account of the build up to the end of the evil Messiah.

Special Agent Derek Anderson got straight to the point: "We need your help. I've read everything you've written. I've been working on this case for months and I've found all the stuff you've put together on David Koresh. We're impressed and we need more information."

I asked him about the specifics of his investigation. I wanted to know if he was looking into drugs or firearms. He told me that the ATF had started their investigation when neighbors had reported hearing automatic gun-fire on the compound. They had reported it to the

Sheriff's Department and they, in turn, had turned the case over to the ATF.

"When I started, I didn't know about your stuff. I didn't know you and others had been trying to get the authorities to stop Koresh for so long. I had never heard of Koresh. Then I find out all this other stuff."

I was incredulous. Not only had the ATF never heard of the cult, no one had told them until May, 1992. After years of trying to draw the authorities' attention to this disaster waiting to happen, no one knew about it? Derek said he didn't understand it either. I liked him immediately, because he seemed so honest and down-to-earth.

Elizabeth and I had tried to get the authorities to listen to us for so long that we were ready to talk to anyone by now. We would have talked to the Tooth Fairy if she'd have listened.

Our introductions were short. It was time to get to work.

I knew Vernon had guns. I knew he had a lot of guns. I didn't know he had the kinds of weapons Derek described: grenades, automatics, and 50-calibre guns capable of piercing light armor.

Even I, despite all my knowledge of Koresh, was in shock. "My God," I thought, "Vernon's Armageddon is just around the corner."

The ATF knew Koresh was dangerous. They knew he should have been behind bars. They were amazed that nothing had been done for years. But they needed to

convince a Federal judge that Koresh had illegal firearms. They needed a search warrant.

I'm sure most readers will think that talking to ex-
members was an obvious beginning. But with a cult like
the Branch Davidians such a strategy could backfire.
People who have spent years worshipping a man might
not easily betray him. Koresh taught that talking to the
authorities, especially Federal authorities, made one the
ultimate Judas, the antichrist, the beast from the bottom-
less pit. Some ex-members, if confronted, might not be
able to betray the Son of God. They might get doubts. They
might get a guilty conscience. They might run to Koresh
to tell all.

One phone call to Koresh would blow the whole
investigation. The last thing the ATF wanted was to alert
Vernon. So they had to be extremely selective in whom
they confided. They basically trusted David, Debbie and
Robyn Bunds, along with Elizabeth and me. Later, the
Jewells would be included. We were asked to tell no one
of these proceedings. It was a request we honored. Lives
were at stake.

So gathering evidence would be difficult. The ATF,
however, had another problem. Once they obtained
warrants to conduct raids, how were they to proceed?
The Branch Davidians were not an ordinary group of
criminals. They were religious zealots who would think
nothing of dying for their leader. In many respects, they
were like terrorists.

The ATF required psychological profiles on everyone. They needed to know who was with Koresh, who his most trusted people were, where they were, and how much military training they had had.

They needed to know everything about the man who called himself the Messiah.

Using our computer, Elizabeth and I spent scores of hours compiling a comprehensive database on the cult. We had to glean information from people without letting them know we were working with the ATF. From Australia, we tapped into huge databases in America that contained property and phone numbers of every person listed in every phone book of the United States. We tapped into other resources as well to find information. We even had to spy on some of our best friends, and that was really painful. But it just had to be done.

Marc Breault and Elizabeth Baranyai kept a diary of everything that happened during this extraordinary investigation.

Monday, December 14, 1992
Sue Johnson, Steve Schneider's oldest sister, called us at 2.30 in the morning . . . Sue was concerned about a sudden interest on Steve and Judy's part to contact them. Sue had been Vernon's sworn enemy for years. Vernon is paranoid of Sue. Why would Vernon order Steve and Judy to start "saving Sue's soul" as she put

it? Could it be that Steve and Judy are having second thoughts? I hope so.

Sue said that Steve seemed very unhappy. Steve even went so far as to admit to her that he hated the Message and, if it weren't for the awesome biblical truth, he would have left long ago.

That jolted me when Sue told me that. Steve knows I am in contact with Sue. Steve knows we exchange information. Steve knows that I told his family what was really happening in the cult. I even told them that Judy's baby wasn't his but Vernon's.

Why would Steve be admitting to his sister, who is in contact with Vernon's arch enemy – me – that he hates the Message? Is he trying to send me some sort of help signal, or is it a trap? Is Vernon using Steve as a sort of marker or decoy, to trick us into showing our hands?

Man, I hate questions without answers. At least in a Robert Ludlum novel you eventually know what's happening in the minds of the characters. Here, we're the characters. We're the ones worrying about double agents and spies. What are Steve and Vernon up to?

Tuesday, December 15, 1992

Derek Anderson seems sincere. He asked us a few questions and expressed thanks and appreciation for all the background material we've been providing. Anderson said that he felt Vernon was a lunatic and needed to be put away. He said that while he had circumstantial evidence he could not do anything because he lacked direct evidence.

Anderson was also very interested in any information we had on Perry Jones's brother, Paul. They had tracked him down to Redding, California. We knew that Paul was a hard core survivalist and that Vernon had been in close contact with him to find out about weapons, explosives and survival techniques. Paul was very friendly toward Vernon, which was a worry.

Derek asked us to supply him with any birth date information or social security information.

Friday, December 18, 1992

Derek Anderson called at 2.30 in the morning (I guess he miscalculated, too). He asked us if we could supply him with information regarding any military service undertaken by any group member. Anderson said that he wanted to know what they were up against.

We spoke for some time about guns and I mentioned that Vernon was trying to build up the guns slowly while I was there. Derek assured us, however (Elizabeth was on the other line), that the slow build-up had turned into a fast escalation.

Later that morning, I sent him a fax with the military history of cult members. Several people had been in the air force and army, and some had been distinguished for their marksmanship. David Jones, Vernon's brother-in-law and chief Mighty Man, is the biggest danger. He's a real crack shot, and has taught the others a lot.

Thursday, December 24, 1992

Derek Anderson called us again and asked if we could provide him with an update of who's in and who's out. He said he had the flow chart private investigator Hossack took over, but he wanted to update it. Anderson also mentioned the possibility of coming out to Australia to interview us.

Thursday, December 31, 1992

The ATF is becoming increasingly paranoid about the media. They know we're in almost daily contact with Mark England [Waco Tribune Herald]. Derek begged me to let him know if Mark asked any questions at all even remotely hinting of any knowledge of an investigation.

"He can't know about this," he said. "That's very important. I'm sure Mark England is a good guy, but he's got a job to do. If he confronts Koresh with any story of a Federal investigation, everything we've done for the past seven months will go down the tubes."

Derek also wanted to know if I could come to California at their expense. He said they wanted to interview me and go over some maps and pictures. We asked if Elizabeth could come too but he said he didn't know and would get back to us. We'll be thinking about it.

Elizabeth says I shouldn't go without her. We are

starting to argue about this now. This is our biggest opportunity to date to put Vernon away. I'd hate to blow it, just because they can't afford to fly two of us to California.

Elizabeth says, though, that she can see the reconnaissance pictures better than I can. Besides, she says, "The Feds have plenty of money. They're just being bureaucrats."

Elizabeth stressed to me, and she was right, that she had been a cult member, too. She had helped me compile all the information we sent out to the Feds.

Friday, January 1, 1993

Well they don't want to pay for both Elizabeth and me but I've said I would go. Derek said the interview would only take a few hours and I could be there one day, gone the next. Elizabeth was very upset, and that is putting it mildly.

We're under a lot of stress. I'm sick of it. This has gone on for years and it's about time it ended. Elizabeth is really adamant. She doesn't want me to go alone.

"How do I know it's not a trap from Vernon? How do I know these are real Federal agents? How do I know that Vernon isn't trying to lure you to America to kill you like he's done before? You'll be there all alone and I'll be here in Australia not knowing what will happen to you."

Wednesday, January 6, 1993

Derek called today and asked if I could leave for California tomorrow. Elizabeth had been hoping the trip would be off . . . I'm getting really hyped-up now. I'm getting closer to finally nailing Vernon. I wonder what the ATF will do when I finally meet them.

Elizabeth refused to take me to the airport.

My biggest fear is that Vernon will find out what I'm up to and murder my parents . . . First, Vernon has a fantastic intelligence network, and second, he knows where my parents live.

I know he's blackmailed families before. He's even held children hostage to get back at their parents. If there was one thing I discovered in my four years with Vernon, nothing is beyond him.

Thursday, January 7, 1993

After some problems with the travel agent, I left Melbourne at about 1.30 p.m. I arrived in Ontario, California on the same day of course. The flight was long but I slept well.

I went to the United counter at the Ontario airport and met Derek. He had another agent with him named Bradley Waters [not his real name] and I liked them at once. They did their best to put me at ease. Derek showed me his ID right at the start.

The first thing Bradley said to me was: "I don't mean to be rude in asking you this right away, but how did

you get such detailed property listings and phone infor-
mation on all those people? I'd like to be able to do that."

I was amazed. I had always thought the Feds were like
Big Brother, able to find out anything about anyone. I
told him about CompuServe's huge database of phone
numbers, addresses, and property listings. This included
more than 80 million white page entries, not to mention
untold thousands of business entries. All this, from the
convenience of your own home.

The ATF agents were flabbergasted. They couldn't
believe that anyone, from almost anywhere in the world,
could gain access to this much information.

We got to the hotel and they asked me a few questions
regarding Vernon . . . Derek told me that Bradley was
on the case with him because he had worked on another
cult case in 1985.

"It's really difficult to prosecute such groups," Bradley
said. "On the one hand you've got the First Amendment
that guarantees freedom of religion. But on the other,
you've got almost unbelievable violations of the law from
groups like this. If you try to go after them, the media
and fundamentalist groups cry foul."

Friday, January 8, 1993
Well they had a lot of questions. They had folders with
hundreds of pictures of every conceivable weapon
ranging from simple hand guns to rocket launchers.
They wanted me to go through each and every picture

and identify what I knew Vernon had. I was able to identify the AK-47 (of which there are many different varieties) and some . 223s.

I was also able to tell them that Vernon probably had a lot of explosives. When I was just leaving the cult, Vernon had been desperately trying to get a hold of a book called The Anarchist's Cookbook. *"My God!" they said, and immediately began writing frantically. They told me that this book is one of the most dangerous books ever written. It gives detailed explanations on how to make all kinds of explosives. It is banned in the United States.*

One of the first things I [had done] upon leaving the cult was find out how easily this banned book could be obtained. It only took me three days to find someone willing to photocopy it for me. If it only took me three days, Vernon had to have a copy.

The ATF agents were really concerned now. They asked questions regarding Vernon's psychological make up and how he would react if he was subpoenaed or summoned.

ATF *If surrounded, would Vernon allow women and children to leave the compound so they wouldn't be hurt in a firefight?*

BREAULT *No way. He would use them as hostages. Vernon always said that if the authorities*

	ever came to take the children, they wouldn't take them alive.
ATF	*If Vernon were away, who would he leave in charge?*
BREAULT	*If Vernon were expecting trouble, Jaydeen [Wendel], or someone with equivalent training like David Jones. If Vernon were not expecting something, he might leave someone like Novelette [Sinclair] in charge.*
ATF	*Who are the fanatics?*
BREAULT	*Jaydeen Wendel, Mark Wendel, Peter and Nicole Gent, Kathy Andrade, Peter Hipsman, Stan Sylvia , Floyd Houtman, Greg Summers and, of course, David Jones and his father, Perry.*
ATF	*If Vernon received a summons to answer questions put to him by the Department of Social Services, would he show up? The intent is to draw him away from the camp.*
BREAULT	*Yes, I think he would because Vernon feels he has beaten that rap. Vernon feels he can handle Social Services.*
ATF	*If Vernon received a summons to answer questions regarding firearms, would he show up?*
BREAULT	*No way.*

ATF *If the good guys came with a search warrant, would Vernon allow it?*

BREAULT *If Vernon were not expecting it, no. If Vernon had prior warning, yes. He'd have time to shift all the firearms.*

ATF *Vernon used to teach that he would go to Israel, die, and be resurrected. The killing afterward would be a supernatural one. Does this still apply or is there a chance Vernon will start his war beforehand?*

BREAULT *There is a considerable amount of danger because Vernon feels that since he is Jesus Christ, he has already died. Therefore he can skip that phase of things. Since he does not have to die, there is no resurrection and therefore he may well feel he can start shooting beforehand.*

ATF *What does Vernon fear the most?*

BREAULT *Going to prison. I think that Vernon is essentially a coward and does not want to die. However, if faced with a certainty of going to prison, Vernon might well opt for the easy way out. First, however, he would try to disappear and leave his followers to cover for him.*

ATF *If Steve Schneider were in charge and the camp surrounded, would Steve, after a while, see reason and give up?*

BREAULT *Believe it or not, Steve might. For this reason, I don't think Vernon trusts Steve when it comes to killing.*

ATF *Are any of the followers able to kill when it comes down to it?*

BREAULT *Several would kill without thinking about it. Jimmy Riddle is one such person. I consider Jimmy very dangerous. He's got a screw loose somewhere. Others, like Wally, might not be able to when the time comes, but that is a very subjective opinion. David Jones is a certainty, and so is the Australian Peter Gent. They're both fanatics.*

ATF *Is Vernon mainly offensive now or defensive (in your opinion)?*

BREAULT *At this stage, I would say defensive, but that is a very uncertain guess. When Vernon feels confident (for instance he may feel we've tried with the authorities and failed), Vernon would probably be offensive. That is my worry. I believe Vernon feels we've tried all we could and have failed.*

ATF *Does Vernon really believe all this religious stuff he's teaching or is he just a con man?*

BREAULT *I think a little of both. Vernon gets a craving. Then he finds the theology to justify that craving. When others buy into his doctrine, he starts believing it himself.*

ATF *Does he really believe he's the Son of God?*

BREAULT *Definitely.*

ATF *How much control does that give him over his followers?*

BREAULT *Absolute control. I know it's hard for you to understand this. But just imagine you believe someone is Jesus Christ. He can tell you anything. If you argue, you go to Hell. He's the Son of God. Who wants to fight against God?*

ATF *Is Vernon good with a gun?*

BREAULT *Very good. This guy can shoot water moccasins from a distance.*

ATF *You're kidding.*

BREAULT *No, I'm not. I've seen him do it.*

ATF *You've mentioned Vernon and David Jones as being good shots. Anyone else a good shot?*

BREAULT *With all the target practise they have, they're probably all good shots by now.*

ATF *You told us once about an underground firing range. What about that?*

BREAULT *Mark England* [Waco Tribune Herald] *flew over the property just a few days ago. He said he could see what appeared to resemble an underground firing range.*

ATF *He flew over in a chopper?*

BREAULT *Yes. I think it was a weather chopper.*

The interrogation lasted for hours. Afterwards, we drove down to the La Verne Police Department and met John Hackworth. Hackworth is a real character and I got on well with him He likes Shakespeare and poetry, something one wouldn't normally expect in a cop.

Hackworth didn't like Vernon. In 1990 he had participated in a raid on the cult's property in La Verne. He said Vernon was slime all over. When the cops came he was all trembling and scared. "No Son of God here," he said. "He was all oh yes sir, no sir, anything sir. That little weed was so frightened he hardly knew what to do," [said Hackworth].

John Hackworth hates paedophiles with a passion. He couldn't refer to Vernon by name. He called him things like: "That blasphemous little insect." Hackworth wanted to get Vernon for years, but most of Howell's felony-type offences had occurred in the deep isolation of the compound in Texas. He had tried to get the Texas authorities to do something but without much success . . .

We had two things to do at the police station. The first was to track down a cult member who had only recently fled Vernon's reign of terror. He was Dennis Black [not his real name], a handsome honey-blond-haired man from California in his mid-thirties. I knew him well. All we knew, though, was that his family had hired a professional cultbuster who had managed to deprogram him. But none of them were talking. We didn't even know where they were, let alone Dennis himself.

Dennis was in hiding. We had been trying to find him for months. Ironically, Steve Schneider had inadvertently put us on his trail. Schneider had made an off-hand comment to his sister Sue. He had mentioned that he had been trying to get a hold of a friend, but that friend's brother would not let him talk to him. Sue and I began trying to find who that "friend" was. After a couple of months, we finally deduced it was Dennis, and the hunt was on.

Here, in the La Verne police station, we managed to narrow down the possible locations where he could be hiding. We believed he was somewhere in California.

Dennis had contacted the [Waco Tribune Herald] *newspaper reporter Mark England, and the ATF asked me to get whatever information I could out of Mark, without making him suspicious that I was working for the Federal authorities. We tried calling Mark but he wasn't in his office.*

The second thing we had to do was to look over reconnaissance photographs . . . These pictures were taken over several months and showed quite a lot of detail. One picture showed an entire school bus buried underground. It was by the kitchen. I wouldn't have believed it unless I saw it with my own eyes. What the heck was that for? When I first saw it I exclaimed: "What the hell is that!" Everyone in the room laughed.

And then there was the compound. I'm not good at

judging size but David Bunds, who had also seen the pictures, believed it was around the size of a city block. It dominated the property and resembled a fortress. The windows were staggered. They were not all in rows. They looked like gun emplacements. Maybe Vernon wanted them at different levels. A flag waved in the breeze on top of the compound.

There seemed to be a main room near the top of the building. It was probably Vernon's bedroom since he liked to be up high. I think that there were a series of escape tunnels or passages connected to it.

A satellite dish on the top. I wonder if Vernon saw Martin King's television report on the cult using that dish? I always wondered how he got to see the story so quickly. Boy, did Vernon hate that story, and boy did he hate Martin King too. If there's one thing a con-man hates it's being exposed.

Apart from the fortress there was not much else on Mount Carmel. I could see a huge swimming pool next to it. The water seemed a little green to me. All the houses were gone and the compound was the only structure on the place, from what I could tell.

This meant that Vernon had them all sleeping and living in the one central place. There couldn't be any real privacy for anyone. Man it must [have been] Hell in there.

There also appeared to be a collection of All Terrain Vehicles around the place. I couldn't quite tell how many *there were. David Bunds seemed to think there were around ten.*

Finally, it was time for me to leave for the airport. I managed to get on the plane and I began the long flight home to Australia. Both Derek and Bradley decided to go through security with me. You should have seen the look on the airport security staff's faces when two armed men came up to them. But they showed their identification and, after a security check, they were allowed to pass. We parted company on friendly terms, drinking Budweiser beer at the airport bar.

Things are moving now.

Saturday, January 9, 1993

The ATF wants detailed diagrams of every possible property Vernon has access to. Not only do they want to raid Mount Carmel, they want to raid all the properties simultaneously so that Vernon won't be able to hide weapons anywhere.

It is time to let Lisa and Bruce Gent in on all the details. Bruce, a builder, can supply highly detailed plans of Palestine, including the large steel reinforced cellar just underneath the kitchen. If Vernon is going to hide weapons anywhere, it will be there.

Bruce helped build that cellar, and he knows it better than anyone.

Lisa and I need to draw the floor plan of David Jones's trailer house, the one about 2 miles away from Mount

Carmel. In 1987 Vernon stored guns there before. He's probably got some there now.

I have never seen the mechanic shop, but I did manage to find the address for the ATF. The mechanic shop is also in Waco. The ATF has that place monitored too.

So far, however, no warrants. I wonder if we'll be able to get them.

Elizabeth and I almost went to the divorce court. She is still livid that I went [to the States] without her. I am trying to calm her down, but I suppose she is right too. I'll try to make sure that doesn't happen again.

Monday, January 11, 1993

Mark England called today to find out whether anything was happening, whether I had heard anything. He said he heard a rumor that something was up, but knew nothing else. I told him I hadn't heard anything significant, which was unfortunately a lie. Oh well, it was an ethical one at least.

Mark England has no idea that I was recently in America. I needed to get information about Dennis from him, so I simply asked, in an off-hand way, whether he knew who Dennis's deprogrammer was.

Mark England is a really nice guy. He told me at once. I don't know what Mark England knows, but I don't think it is much yet. Dennis's deprogrammer is Rick Ross who is based in Phoenix. I immediately faxed this information to Anderson. I also fax Sue Johnson.

Sue has detailed information on cult awareness groups and cultbusters. Maybe she has some info on file regarding Rick Ross. I tell Sue that I would like to talk to Ross to get some information.

This is scary stuff, trying to get information without letting anyone know something major is brewing. This is something right out of James Bond. The only thing missing is the firefight. Oh well, if things go wrong, that will become a reality.

Tuesday, January 12, 1993
Received a fax from Tom Johnson, Steve [Schneider's] brother-in-law, today. Tom said Sue saw Rick Ross on TV in Florida (not related to this case). Apparently, Rick Ross is a well-known deprogrammer. I received this fax at work so I immediately transcribed it into my computer. Good thing we have a shredder. Vernon could send Oliver Gyarfas [Aisha's father] around to spy. Man, what's happening to me? I'm getting paranoid now.

Lisa Gent came over and . . . we managed to sketch out the trailer belonging to David Jones.

Monday, January 18, 1993
The Gents are grandparents again. Ian and Allison had another daughter. Everyone is happy. But behind the happiness is the knowledge that this is just one more person Vernon might kill some day. I wish this would end soon.

Thursday, January 21, 1993

Received a call from Mark England today . . . Mark said that they were going to ask Vernon if he would be willing to be interviewed. He said they would ask him next week. Vernon has not yet been contacted. Mark wanted to clarify a few things with me including when Vernon first told me about him being Cyrus. Mark also wanted to talk to James and Michelle [Tom] about when Vernon took off due to the police [Australia, 1990].

Finally, Mark said that they had already lined up a lab company to perform a DNA test between Vernon and Robyn's child Shaun [formerly called Wisdom]. They are going to ask Vernon next week whether he will back up his boast and submit to a DNA test. Man, Vernon will be one pissed off dude when the Tribune Herald challenges him. Good for you, Robyn.

Vernon had told Martin King that he would be willing to take a blood test to prove that he wasn't Shaun's father. Mark asked me why Vernon would make such a boast to a reporter when he knew full well he really was the father of Robyn's child. I said I didn't know, although perhaps Vernon felt that he could say that on Australian television. Australia is a long way from America.

And the Waco Tribune Herald also has birth certificates that Vernon doesn't want anyone to see. Mark and his colleague Darlene McCormick are thorough. Vernon is going to hit the roof!

Tuesday, February 16, 1993

It's been a while since I wrote in this diary. You can feel the tension mounting. It's like a powder keg waiting to explode.

Sue Johnson has talked to Rick Ross. Rick told Sue something was about to happen real soon. He urged her to hire him to deprogram Steve. Rick has Sue all scared now. The Schneider family doesn't know what to do. Rick didn't tell them what was about to happen, but he said that they should get Steve out as soon as possible.

I know that Rick has talked to the ATF. What is Rick trying to do? As much as I love Steve, deprogramming him at this stage is risky. If it isn't done right, Vernon could start the Apocalypse without waiting for any Federal intervention.

I stressed to Sue that if Steve were suddenly kidnapped and deprogrammed, Vernon would not only use Judy as a hostage – not to mention Judy's child – but Vernon might also freak out. He might hurt others. "It's bad enough for Vernon that I'm against him," I told her. "He won't be able to tolerate Steve opposing him as well."

Thursday, February 18, 1993

A bombshell!!! Steve told Sue that Vernon is worried about the arms he has and what the Government might do about them. I asked Sue whether Steve mentioned illegal weapons. She assured me that Steve did not mention illegal weapons, but only arms in general.

Steve also said Vernon is searching Reuters and the AP news services to find out anything about Government involvement in arms cases. Vernon has joined the computer age. My guess is he is using CompuServe, much as I do. Steve said Vernon is particularly interested in the Randy Weaver case, some guy who shot it out with the Feds somewhere in Ohio, I think, although I could have the place wrong.

Now the real question. **Why is Steve saying all this!!!!** *What does Vernon know? Does Vernon suspect? Has someone tipped Vernon off? What the Hell is going on? If Vernon knows Steve is talking, he'd shoot him on the spot.*

So far, there aren't any warrants that I'm aware of. I don't like the sound of this.

Thursday, February 25, 1993
We learnt [today] that the ATF believes there might be a connection between Vernon and the McLennan County Sheriff's Department. They are bypassing the local authorities. Maybe that explains why Vernon always seems to know what we are doing with respect to the authorities.

When will they move against Vernon? They must be getting close to getting those warrants by now.

That weekend the warrants came through. The ATF intended to lure Vernon away from the compound in order to avoid involving the women and children in any confrontation. But then they learnt that Vernon had been tipped off. They had to act – and immediately.

Sunday, February 28, 1993
It's 9.55 a.m. in Waco, Texas. The time bomb has been detonated.

Chapter Twenty Eight
Armageddon Begins

David Michael Jones, chief Mighty Man, was the first to know. Mount Carmel was about to be raided by more than a hundred armed ATF agents searching for illegal weapons.

When the Mighty Man heard the news – and we still don't know his source – he didn't waste any time getting to cult headquarters to despatch the news to his Supreme Leader.

David Jones wasn't the only one to beat the hapless ATF to the punch. A television crew rolled up, along with reporters and a photographer from the *Waco Tribune Herald*. Again, the media lead the way.

At 9.55 a.m., when the ATF arrived, the place was primed. Reporters waited expectantly, the TV camera rolled, and inside that funny-looking wooden fortress the mood was very serious indeed.

The rest is history. It was one of the worst casualty rates sustained in law-enforcement history in the United States of America: twenty casualties – four dead and sixteen wounded, some shockingly. Vernon wasn't going to walk out of this one.

The Bureau of Alcohol, Tobacco and Firearms say the cult leader confronted them at the front door of the fortress, clad in black and carrying a rifle, and declared he would not be taken alive. "Neither ATF or the National Guard will ever get me," he was quoted as saying. "They got me once, and they will never get me again. They are coming; the time has come."

And so began a forty-five-minute bloodbath. Vernon, his lawyer, accountant, nurses, computer programmers, a postman, school teachers, and mechanics were on one side; professionally trained Federal agents on the other.

Among the dead was Peter Gent, the 24-year-old twin brother of Nicole and son of Bruce and Lisa Gent. Cult members later released by Vernon claimed that Peter Gent had climbed the water tower to defend the property. The 40-foot steel cylinder stood isolated from the main fortress. It might have provided a good view of invaders, but it also provided no protection. Also killed were Vernon's father-in-law, Perry Jones, Mike Schroeder, Winston Blake, and two others. Judy Schneider was shot in the hand, while Scott Sonobe, the man who ate those hot dogs along with Big Joel, sustained a serious leg wound. By all reports, the chief Mighty Man, David Jones, was shot in the butt.

By now Vernon had definitely excited the interest of the authorities. Now it was time to see who was more powerful – the Son of God or Uncle Sam.

Chapter Twenty Nine
The Gents Return to Waco

On February 28, 1993 I was on assignment in Tasmania, an island state at the bottom of Australia. It was a lovely story, too, about a couple of young sisters aged 11 and 14 who have defied the world recession and have launched a booming business selling their own home-made ice cream.

At 7.30 a.m. I left the hotel for my morning run. Waco was a year behind me, but about to catch up fast. When I returned to my room thirty minutes later, there was an urgent message under the door. Ring work. Urgent.

"God, where have you been?" It's the chief of staff. "Remember your cult story in Waco? There's been a bloodbath."

I caught the first plane back to Melbourne. Five hours later – after interviewing Bruce and Lisa Gent and cutting a story for that night's edition of the Nine Network's "A Current Affair" (which has nothing to do, by the way, with the American show) – I flew to Sydney with the Gents. The next day we leave for Waco, Texas.

The Gents are a mess. Details of the dead and injured haven't been released. At this stage they don't know if Nicole and Peter are dead or alive. Or if their two grand-children have survived. They can only hope.

I looked at Bruce and Lisa on the Qantas flight to Los Angeles and I felt sick for them. I'd never met Peter or Nicole, but after months of investigations, and so many interviews, it was as though I knew them well. The closest I'd got to them was a color photo-graph. I thought of our story fourteen months before, warning the world that Vernon was a power-hungry, psychopathic, child-molesting religious loony who was ever-so-systematically destroying life after life on a daily basis.

I thought of the innocent children we'd captured on film. The little old ladies and the young men who were building the fortress during our visit. And I thought of them all surrounded by the might of the US military. And I felt so sorry for them. Then I thought of the man who led them into this disaster and I wondered how his disciples were feeling about David Koresh now. And I suddenly realized how close to death we'd come ourselves during our stay with the crazed cult leader.

But my immediate thoughts were for Bruce and Lisa and the pain they were enduring. Neither of them had slept during the thirteen-hour flight. After a three-hour lay-over in Los Angeles we caught an American Airlines flight to Dallas-Fort Worth.

By now we were all numb with tiredness but still could talk of nothing else but Peter and Nicole and our hopes for their survival. But Bruce was pessimistic.

"I'm really worried about Peter," he says as we board our third flight. "He's just so gung-ho. He would have been right in it; he'd do anything for that bastard."

Finally, eighteen hours after leaving Australia, we arrive in Waco, and the welcome is anything but friendly. My Channel 9 story was screened across the States last night while we were in the air. The Gents and I are now familiar faces.

Bruce and Lisa are ambushed by a crew from the infamous American tabloid television show "A Current Affair." This quiet, middle-aged couple, exhausted, and grieving over their children and grandchildren, are chased three times in and around the small terminal by a cameraman, a sound man and a producer, who want the exclusive interview with the family that has given three generations to the Koresh cult.

Eventually, airport staff hide the couple in a cargo area where they take cover like common criminals until a taxi comes to the rescue.

But outside the airport, the chase continues, this time at high speed through the streets of Waco. As the pursuing van edges closer, now just a few feet from our rear bumper, Bruce Gent lets out a loud groan, "Martin, I don't need this, really, I don't need this," he says.

"Well, Bruce neither do I, but there's not much I can bloody well do about it." We are starting to crack and we haven't even reached the hotel yet.

"Well I tell ya," chips in the taxi driver, a Waco boy from way back, "there's something I can do," and he grabs his two-way radio.

"Yeah base, I've got a bunch of nuts on my tail coming in on the airport road and my passengers are scared to death." The cabbie tells us he used to race cars around these streets as a teenager. And he says it with a gleam of mischief in his eyes.

As the needle on the speedo edges past 80 miles an hour, Bruce Gent's blood pressure rises accordingly. The taxi begins to shake and rattle; I just hope like Hell it doesn't roll. With the Gents terrified in the back, our cabbie runs a red light and the boys from "A Current Affair" America follow suit. Thankfully this is one facet of journalism we don't have in Australia.

The high-speed chase finishes when three police cars, sirens wailing and lights flashing, emerge from the night.

We watch with amusement from across the street as six officers descend on the rented van. Oh Lord, are those boys desperate for an angle. They are even filming their own citation.

It was the beginning of six days of heart-ache and trauma

for the Gents, whose sole goal was to satisfy themselves that their children were safe, and at the same time satisfy the rapacious appetite of the American mass media.

The next day the Gents made the pilgrimage to David Koresh's cult headquarters, this time, though, as the enemy. Bruce wore the cameraman's baseball cap so the waiting hordes of reporters couldn't recognize him. It worked. The couple were stunned by the carnival of hundreds of television satellite dishes, link vans and other media vehicles, not to mention the Texas Rangers, the FBI and the military.

"It's unbelievable, it's hard to comprehend," Bruce says. "Vernon has accomplished exactly what he's wanted. He's got the world stage." But the closest the Melbourne couple get to their children and grandchildren is an impossible 3 miles.

"I don't know what we can accomplish," Bruce says. "We came to hope against hope that maybe there's a chance . . .," and he bites his lip with emotion. "We might get to see the kids," Lisa says, but it's more a desperate wish than anything else.

The irony isn't lost on any of us. This suburban couple who once entered the bizarre world of this preacher of death to search for truth are now trapped on the outside, hating him for his lies. It's a poignant moment as Bruce and Lisa look over the fields to Mount Carmel hoping for a glimpse of the fortress. But they can't even see that.

Over those fields, and behind the wooden walls, were, we hoped, the twin children whose minds had been poisoned against their parents. "What makes me cry is that you're so close and yet so far," Lisa said, and she cried.

It was five days since the ATF bloodbath and the frustration of simply not knowing pushed Lisa Gent towards breaking point. She even thought about making a run for the compound.

Bruce snaps. "Don't be bloody stupid. What are you thinking of? That's just crazy!"

"I know," she says. I turn away so this brave couple can have some semblance of privacy in what is now a very public place.

It was one of many agonizing moments I shared with the Gents, amid all the emotional and physical exhaustion and the unrelenting pain of a family torn apart by one man's quest for the ultimate glory.

The next few days in Waco were simply a blur of telephone calls, interviews and desperate attempts to wring any drop of information from the authorities about the welfare of their family. For the Gents, the only link with their loved ones would come through the FBI. But even after a secret meeting with two agents in our hotel they were still none the wiser.

After five days in Waco Bruce managed to make contact with a senior ATF agent. It was a phone call made by a desperate father, and to this day I can remember every word.

ATF *At the present time sixteen people have been released, these children [the Gent's grandchildren] are not among those we have. I have their names and your name and should they be released, I will attempt to contact you.*

GENT *Look, I don't know if you've got any kids . . .*

ATF *Yes, sir, I have three.*

GENT *We've flown over from Australia and we're to a stage where I don't know if I have two children or not, whether they've been killed or not. Can you enlighten me there?*

ATF *Sir, we do have information from children who've already got out, and two elderly ladies we removed, that there are casualties inside. Some people are dead. We do not know any names.*

GENT *You don't?*

ATF *No sir, we can't even get an accurate count. I know that doesn't offer you much hope, but I'm sorry for that.*

GENT *Can you give me a number of how many have been killed?*

ATF *No sir, I can't. The children that have been released are quite young and they don't really answer questions well in regard to numbers.*

GENT *Right . . .*

ATF *Let me tell you I am the intelligence officer assigned to this operation.*

GENT *This is a terrible position to be in . . .*

ATF *I understand sir. I understand your concern.*

GENT *I don't know which questions I can ask – I'm sorry – I don't mean to pester you . . .*

ATF *Well, you can ask anything sir. If I can't answer it I won't. I can tell you everything I can . . . Do you have any information regarding an underground escape-tunnel system?*

GENT *No, I'm sorry, I don't.*

Bruce Gent then asks the intelligence officer what will happen should Koresh release more adults.

ATF *They'll be arrested or if they're illegally in the country they'll be deported.*

GENT *Can I ask you, will they be deported straight off? Because the state of their minds, these people, they'll virtually be walking time bombs.*

ATF *Yes sir, I understand that . . .*

GENT *Because, with my two children, if they're deported . . . I don't know who would look after them at the other end, because what we have done, they're liable to kill us, that's the bottom line of the whole situation.*

ATF *You're really that concerned with your own safety?*

GENT *Yes, that's not overdramatizing the situation.*

The ATF intelligence officer then gives Bruce Gent a special telephone number should they need help.

ATF *Maybe something will happen in the meantime and we'll get a peaceful resolution.*

GENT *I really hope so.*

ATF *We do too.*

After nearly one week in Waco, and no news, the devastated couple returned to Australia. On March 7, at 10 a.m., the phone rang in their neat brick home in the eastern suburbs of Melbourne. The caller was a senior official from the Australian Foreign Affairs Department. His message was brief.

Peter Gent was dead. He was one of the first to die in the gun-fight. He was dead – and here was the most terrible of ironies – the entire time we were in Waco. Even worse, the world had watched on television as fellow cult members buried Peter in the dead of night in a shallow grave outside the compound.

Only now can it be revealed that Peter Gent's death was little more than suicide. He'd been told to stand without cover on top of the compound's water tower. Firing wildly at ATF agents he was picked off easily by

331

a marksman. The theory is that he was deliberately placed there by a vengeful David Koresh as a pay-back to Bruce and Lisa for daring to defy him.

Chapter Thirty
The FBI

The FBI has investigated many strange and bizarre cases. They've dealt with serial killers, international terrorists, presidential assassins and countless thousands of violent and deranged criminals.

But the Feds weren't ready for someone like Vernon Howell. When the guns went silent after the February 28 shoot-out, he blasted them with the Bible. For fifty-one days he tormented the FBI with a rambling dissertation of scriptural readings, a crash course in his interpretation of the Seven Seals, and a string of lies and broken promises.

Within hours of the ATF raid, Vernon wanted the world to believe that he was about the meet his Maker. He even left a message on his mother's answering machine: "They shot me and I'm dying . . . but I'll be back real soon, OK?" What's never been publicized until now is that Vernon went even further with his charade. After this brief message, the tape went silent. Seconds went by and then an unidentified voice from within the compound came on the line: "He's dead." Bonnie was hysterical. But it was all a trick.

For a dying man, Vernon conducted a miraculous number of telephone interviews that day. He promised that he and his followers would surrender if a Christian radio station broadcast a sermon that ran for fifty-eight minutes. The FBI kept their end of the bargain. The cult leader didn't.

The very next day Koresh told the Feds he'd had a vision from God telling him to wait. Nearly seven weeks later the world was still waiting on that decision from Heaven.

The next chance for a breakthrough came at Passover. Vernon told his followers that this would be the last Passover they would celebrate together. The FBI hoped this meant a surrender, but the Holy Feast came and went with no end in sight.

Then, in mid-April, 1993 Koresh told the FBI that he would come out when he had finished writing a detailed treatise on the Seven Seals. Thirty pages later, he hadn't made it past the first seal. By now the FBI was openly saying that it was just another stalling tactic.

And during the stand-off this professed Son of God continuously tried to convert the Feds to his Message. After listening to his scriptural onslaught by telephone, the negotiators could empathize with former cult members for what they had gone through.

While Vernon's ravings must have seemed like a

foreign language to the FBI, they wanted to be sure there wasn't a hidden agenda contained in his scriptures. Who better to decipher the words of Koresh than the man who knew them by heart, former confidant Marc Breault.

As soon as the siege began, our house was chaos personified. The media blitz was unbelievable. For the next forty-eight hours, the longest space between calls was three minutes. Reporters from Israel to France, New York to Australia wanted to speak to us.

The FBI tried for hours to contact us, but they simply couldn't get through. They grew so desperate, in fact, that they almost sent the police to drag us to police headquarters. Just before they took that drastic action, however, the negotiators broke through.

The FBI had taken over the Chrysler building in Waco and converted it into their command center. One of the negotiators who had spoken to Koresh asked us for as much information as we could provide.

The first thing he said, after introducing himself was, "can you tell us anything about the Seven Seals." I almost laughed right then and there. I could imagine their confusion.

But the situation was serious. I gave them a quick rundown of the seals according to Koresh, but concentrated especially on the fifth seal. I told the FBI that Koresh believed the fifth seal taught suicide and martyrdom. Koresh further believed that God had ordained a fixed number of martyrs, and that this number was almost complete. The end of the world could only take place once this was done.

The negotiator was very interested in that. He took down extensive notes. I emphasized over and over that a mass suicide posed the greatest danger. I said further that I did not believe Koresh would ever give up.

Then the negotiator asked me about the other people. He wanted to know if any were likely to defy Koresh at any given time. He asked me who the fanatics were. I told him about the detailed profiles I had provided to the ATF. He had no idea of their existence. I found it hard to believe that negotiators were not given this vital material. In all fairness, however, Waco was a madhouse at the time. These poor negotiators had come on this case cold. People were running around everywhere. They simply did not have my profiles because of all the confusion.

I asked the negotiator, then, how many casualties there were. At this stage media reports were so inconclusive that you couldn't gauge anything by them. The negotiator said that he only knew of one casualty, but that the situation was such that they could not possibly obtain accurate figures. He told me that they couldn't get close to any of the bodies. In short, he had no idea.

The FBI contacted us throughout the siege. They showed us Koresh's letters, which were nothing more than scriptural ramblings written down. After reading those *we became more and more convinced that Koresh had no intentions of coming out. We told the FBI as much.*

Towards the end, Koresh's letters indicated to us he was getting desperate. The cult leader had been waiting for a sign from God for over forty days by then. Of course, nothing happened. By now Koresh had negotiated himself into a corner. He turned to his old theology, things he had abandoned years ago. He was grasping at straws. We told the FBI that Koresh was starting to lose his grip and that he would probably end the siege violently.

Even God had deserted him.

Chapter Thirty One

The Holocaust

I was dreaming. David Koresh was standing over me. "Blood to blood, don't take what I'm telling you lightly, for your sake."

A ringing sound. Was I dreaming this? I wasn't sure. Seconds later the haze cleared and I realized it was the phone. It was 3.40 a.m. Australian time, and I sensed trouble. The caller was Marc Breault.

"It's all over. The place has gone up in a fireball. It doesn't look like there are any survivors."

I was fully awake now. I told Marc about the dream. "That doesn't surprise me," he replied. "We've all been eating and sleeping Koresh for months now."

It was hard to comprehend. It seemed surreal, almost as if it was just too terrible to be true. I felt sick in my stomach. This thing was too big to absorb. I told Marc that.

Then I saw the faces. Jesus. All those little kids. Seventeen of Vernon's own. Then I thought of the terror they were going through then. I mean, that place was still burning and I remembered that when the ATF shot it out with Vernon and the Mighty Men the little kids hid under the beds trembling with fear.

Then I hoped Koresh was dead. At least then all the suffering would end and he wouldn't hurt anyone else. Suddenly I saw right through him. This was the man who vehemently denied, on a television program screened around the world, that he really had been contemplating child sacrifices.

Suddenly I felt very alone. I needed someone to talk to. I told Marc I'd be right over.

Elizabeth, Martin and I watched the compound burn to the ground on CNN. We didn't say anything for a while; I think each of us was lost in our own thoughts.

My first thought was that I hoped the children hadn't suffered. What a way to die. Elizabeth was especially sad because she thought we had failed in our efforts to save these people, in particular the children, from Koresh. I hoped he was dead. So did Elizabeth.

As I watched the holocaust, I felt strangely detached. It was like I was somewhere else. Now I know it was shock.

Strangely, I remembered all the little things, both the good times and the bad. I remembered little Cyrus, Koresh's oldest son. I remember holding him in my arms and showing him an elevator for the first time. He was astonished when the door suddenly disappeared in front of him. He kept pointing to it saying: "Ooh, ooh, ooh."

I remembered all the little games I invented for the children: little Rachel Sylvia, Audrey, and Abigail and all the others. We used to play tag in the fields of Mount Carmel, with Rachel's little brother, Joshua, trying to keep up. We used to see who could jump the farthest, and I'd let them win. I remembered them laughing and joking and saying: "This is fun."

Now I'm talking about them in the past tense. At least Joshua made it.

I think of Scott Sonobe eating thirteen hot dogs as punishment. I remember Jeff Little's laugh and how he used to talk in his sleep. Once, he sat bolt upright in bed and practically yelled: "Cause thy mighty ones to come down Oh Lord." Jeff didn't remember a thing, but the rest of us thought it was a big joke. There are no mighty ones for you now, Jeff.

And Sherri. She was one of my best friends. I couldn't think of all the hatred she had toward me, as I wrested her daughter, Kiri, from her. You died Sherri, but at least your daughter has a future. I thought of how I helped you, Sherri, pass your math exam, so you could qualify as a teacher in California. I remembered you teaching me how to make vegetarian fried rice and saying: "I wonder what Vernon would say if he saw us doing this?"

I remembered all the letters I wrote to Sherri, begging her to leave the cult. In one of them I wrote a poem. It was in 1990. A few verses are appropriate here.

The wind howls over the desolate land,
The rusting water tower stands alone,
Except for the old man
Sitting on the hard sun-baked earth
Petting two thin and hungry dogs.

"We had such hope once.
This land was full of children playing,
And ah, how the people were excited
Who knew, and read, and taught.
We thought we would be free soon.
We looked for the day as close.
But now I am alone.
There is none who cares for me.
There is none to help."

The wind howls over the desolate land
And silence is her only companion.
Gray clouds hang low.
The foolish people thought
To rise and meet those clouds.
But alas, they will meet the earth instead.

The wind howls over the desolate land
And silence is her only companion.
Gray clouds hang low,
Waiting for the sun that rises somewhere else.
Alas for Carmel,
Alas for the foolish people.

You never made it out, Steve and Judy. God knows I tried, though. I remember you used to say that sometimes you were in two minds. You had your doubts. But it's too late now, my friends. I remember, Steve, you and me on the beach in Hawaii, before this nightmare began. I remember Judy sobbing her eyes out on the grass, in that park in Pomona. I remember you as my best man at my wedding. Now I choose just to think of the good times. I want to forget about the bad times. You and Judy were my best friends. I want to remember you before Koresh turned you into something else.

I'm writing this book in your memory. You died in that inferno but I'm going to make sure it wasn't in vain. I want to show people what we went through, so they won't make the same mistakes we did, and so the damned ruins of that fortress won't be a monument to anything, except evil. You'd want it that way wouldn't you?

Chapter Thirty Two
The End

So here we are, David Koresh and I, sitting in the flaxen fields of Mount Carmel on a January afternoon in 1992.

Camera set. Boom in place. Rolling. And he's telling me, for the record, that he's going to die. The winter-soft Texas sun is fading fast and it's getting cold. Koresh shivers. "Who will kill you?" I ask.

"Fanatics," he says, deadpan. And for a man who's about to die, he seems awfully relaxed.

"Who are these fanatics?" I ask.

"People that revolve around tradition, that are not going to have their mind unsettled in regards to what they believe or how they feel." He's talking about the authorities.

I ask him how he will die.

"Well, let me say this much," he says pushing his glasses back on his nose. "If the world or the people that I'm contacting, if they hate me, if they don't want to hear what I have to say, there is a multitude of ways, and I

don't want to hear anyone of them. There's a multitude of ways."

In the end, though, it was David Koresh who chose the way out. Death by fire. It was what he always wanted – a blaze of glory.

He was born Vernon Wayne Howell in Houston, Texas on August 17, 1959. He died David Koresh, son of a carpenter, aged 33 – the age Christ was when he died on the Cross – at Ranch Apocalypse on April 19, 1993.

On May 2, 1993 the charred body of the leader of the Branch Davidians was found in the kitchen area of the compound near a number of other bodies. Vernon Howell, aka David Koresh, had died of a gunshot wound to the head.

"And when he had opened the seventh seal there was silence . . ."

Appendix I

A History of the Branch Davidian Seventh-day Adventists

The history of the Branch Davidian movement actually starts in 1831, with a man named William Miller. William Miller was an atheist turned Baptist preacher. He lived in a time when the world was swept by Christian revival. Especially prominent in the revivalist theology of the time was the belief in the soon and literal appearing of Jesus Christ in the clouds of Heaven.

Today many take it for granted that most Christians believe Christ will literally appear a second time. But in the mid-19th century this was not a given belief. In fact, there were many prominent Christian theologians who held that Christ's coming was not literal, and this view extended well into the 20th century.

The emergence of eschatological emphasis – the study of last-day or end-of-the-world events – was also accompanied by an immense interest in the prophetic books of Daniel and Revelation. While Christ was on earth, He pointed to many signs that would indicate His coming was near. Although we could not know the exact day and hour of His appearing, we could, by following the specified signs, know that His coming was near.

Through a study of the Bible William Miller came to the conclusion that Christ would come in the northern spring of 1844. It is sufficient to note here that Miller's 1844 theology was based on the eighth and ninth chapters of the book of Daniel. His theology sparked enough excitement and debate that it occupied prominent positions in many of the newspapers of that time. Indeed, discussions on the book of Daniel were common among both Christians and non-Christians.

When William Miller began preaching his 1844 doctrine in 1833, he and his followers eventually became known as Adventists. And, indeed, they gained quite a following.

Needless to say, Christ did not literally appear in the spring of 1844. William Miller, however, had made a mistake in his calculations and soon revised his date to October 22, 1844.

It may be interpreted from this that William Miller conveniently found a mistake, and conveniently managed to postpone the date. But he had a reputation for honesty and his mistake seems to have been a genuine one. In fact, from the spring to the fall of 1844, his movement gained even more momentum than it had before.

When Christ did not appear on October 22, 1844 the Adventist movement virtually collapsed. William Miller was very disappointed. But from the shattered remnants arose a movement that was to carry on William Miller's theology.

On October 23, 1844 one of the leading Millerite ministers, Hiram Edson, claimed to have had a vision while in a corn field. Edson learnt from this vision that the Millerites had correctly calculated the time prophecies, but had misunderstood the event. Instead of His glorious return in the clouds, Christ began a new phase of his ministry. This vision showed Edson that Christ was beginning a new work in Heaven, one that was later termed "the investigative judgment."

Basically, Edson believed Judgment Day had arrived. On

that date, the books were opened and God was going through them name by name, determining, through investigation, which ones had been righteous and which had not. Edson and his followers eventually came to believe that God was starting with the dead, but that He would some day move to the living. So on October 22, 1844, the investigative judgment began.

Some of the former Millerites were encouraged by Edson's vision because it offered a way to explain their mistake. An event that took place in December of 1844 also encouraged the former Millerites.

This event was the emergence of Ellen Gould Harmon (1827-1915) as a prophet to the Adventists. In December of 1844, Ellen Harmon claimed to have had a very comprehensive vision regarding end-time events. This vision also explained the mistake made on October 22, 1844. This was the first of many visions, and Ellen Harmon's ministry was to result in the large world-wide denomination known today as the Seventh-day Adventist Church. Shortly after her first vision Ellen Harmon married James White and is known today primarily as Ellen G. White.

So now there were, generally speaking, two groups of Millerites: those who were disillusioned, and those who forged a new theology, explaining the mistake of October 22, 1844.

For the purposes of this account, one Millerite belief bears notice. William Miller had made a number of mistakes in his time calculations. The little band of Millerites who clung to their beliefs after the great disappointment of October 22, 1844 had to explain how Miller could have been led by God, and yet be incorrect at the same time.

Since it was unthinkable that God was in error, the Millerites formulated a doctrine of "progressive truth." In essence, this doctrine states that God sometimes hides truth, allowing prophets and messengers to make mistakes. At some point in the future, God allows His people to discover their error. These errors or mistakes are purposely allowed and fostered by God in order to test the faithfulness of His people to the organization.

Ellen G. White wrote of her attempts to explain Miller's mistakes in a work titled *Early Writings* (Review and Herald Publishing Association, Washington D.C., 1945, 1882).

> I saw the people of God joyful in expectation, looking for their Lord. But God designed to prove them. His hand covered a mistake in the reckoning of the prophetic periods. Those who were looking for their Lord did not discover this mistake, and the most learned men who opposed the time also failed to see it. God designed that His people should meet with a disappointment. The time passed, and those who had looked with joyful expectation for their Saviour were sad and disheartened, while those who had not loved the appearing of Jesus, but embraced the message through fear, were pleased that He did not come at the time of expectation . . . I saw the wisdom of God in proving His people and giving them a searching test to discover those who would shrink and turn back in the hour of trial.
>
> Jesus and all the heavenly host looked with sympathy and love upon those who had with sweet expectation longed to see Him whom their souls loved. Angels were hovering around them, to sustain them in the hour of their trail . . . Those faithful, disappointed ones, who could not understand why their Lord did not come, were not left in darkness.

> Again they were led to their Bibles to search the
> prophetic periods. The hand of the Lord was
> removed from the figures and the mistake was
> explained.

The solution adopted by these Millerites was that God was only giving them light a little at a time. William Miller had been right, up to the point God wanted him to be right. But God purposely hid the whole truth from William Miller.

This theology was to be used many times in the future to allow for the present-day prophets to make mistakes. Think of it as a precedent. Lawyers often refer to the case of so and so vs. such and such to bolster their own cases. So if a future prophet was shown to be wrong, he or she could simply say: "William Miller was wrong, but he was still right."

William Miller did not join this sect of his followers and utterly rejected the new investigative judgment theology. This new sect of Millerites also came to believe that Christians should worship God on the seventh day of the week instead of the first. This became a central doctrine, so much so that in 1863 it became part of their official name. This new sect saw two points of theology as crucial: the seventh-day Sabbath, and the soon coming or advent of Christ.

So when they chose their official name, they combined the two and that is how we have Seventh-day Adventists today. Seventh-day Adventists also believe that Revelation 14 shows a progression of messages or truths that God's people would proclaim to the world.

The first "message" is found in Revelation 14:6,7. It proclaims that the hour of God's judgment is near. In the eyes of Seventh-day Adventists, this is essentially what William Miller proclaimed. Thus, William Miller's ministry was the "first angel's message."

Seventh-day Adventists felt that other Christian denominations had fallen from God's grace because they refused to accept the investigative judgment doctrine of October 23, 1844. Because these other denominations had rejected God's "true remnant," they were no longer given divine light. These fallen churches, according to Seventh-day Adventists, comprised the apostate power know in the apocalypse (book of Revelation) as Babylon the Great.

The second message in Revelation 14, found in verse 8, proclaims the fall of Babylon. Now that Adventists knew the identity of Revelation's Babylon, they could proclaim its fall. Because William Miller's message formed the dividing line between the true church and the apostates, William Miller was credited with bringing both the first and second angels' messages to the world.

Finally, Seventh-day Adventists believed that theirs was the "third angel's message" found in Revelation 14:9–12. This message warns against the mark of the beast. Seventh-day Adventists basically defined the beast as the Roman Catholic Church and all of its false theology. Sunday observance was high on the taboo list. In fact, they went so far as to teach that just prior to Christ's second coming, the entire world would be tested on whether they kept the seventh day or the first.

The reader should be able to figure out the rest. The next "prophet" would naturally be ascribed as having the fourth angel's message, the next the fifth, and so on.

Despite Edson's corn-field vision, it was Ellen White who became the central figure of the Seventh-day Adventist movement. In all fairness, Ellen White did a great deal of good, creating schools and health institutes through her ministry.

By the time Ellen White died in 1915, the Seventh-day

Adventist denomination was well established world-wide. In fact, the next time you eat Kellogg's Corn Flakes, you can thank Seventh-day Adventists. Dr Kellogg was a Seventh-day Adventist who began making healthy foods because of his religious beliefs. It is true that, eventually, Kellogg left the church, but his health-food business was started during his Seventh-day Adventist years.

One might not agree with everything Seventh-day Adventists believe or teach. But the Seventh-day Adventist Church is not a dangerous cult, and has no connection whatsoever with Vernon Howell's Branch Davidians. In purely theological terms, some of the doctrines of the Seventh-day Adventist Church differ from Christian orthodoxy. For this reason, many have classified this denomination as a cult. This denomination, however, poses no physical danger to anyone and, in fact, is responsible for a great deal of good, ranging from hospitals and schools, to disaster-relief work.

The Davidian Seventh-day Adventists

In 1930, fifteen years after the death of Ellen G. White, Victor T. Houteff claimed to have the prophetic office. He started preaching his message in the southern California area and caused quite a bit of division within the Seventh-day Adventist denomination. His teachings became known as the Davidian movement, as will be explained.

Victor Houteff was eventually thrown out of the Seventh-day Adventist Church and most of his followers shared the same fate. He then wrote two books entitled *The Shepherd's Rod* (volumes 1 and 2), along with a number of small tracts and published sermons. The Davidian movement became commonly known as the "Shepherd's Rod" movement, or the "Rod" for short.

Seeing himself cast out from the Seventh-day Adventist

Church, Victor Houteff acquired property in Waco, Texas and named it the Mount Carmel Center (this site is not that of the present-day Mount Carmel).

Houteff's doctrines were quite wide-ranging. Essentially, however, he believed that the prophecies spoke of a latter-day King David, who would lead Israel (the church) into the promised kingdom of God. Whoever this King David was, the church was obligated to follow him, as if he were an actual king.

Houteff taught that this modern-day King David would have to be a prophet. In fact, it is highly probable that he thought that he was that David. In terms of our story, Houteff was the one responsible for introducing the idea of an actual religious and temporal king who would rule the church. Houteff taught that the Seventh-day Adventist Church would be purged of all the wicked and that those who were left would march into the glorious land under the leadership of the modern David.

Davidians also believed that God would slaughter all Seventh-day Adventists who refused to accept the Rod message. This slaughter, said Houteff, was depicted in the ninth chapter of the biblical book of Ezekiel. This chapter was to play an extremely prominent role in Davidian and Branch Davidian theology. God's kingdom would only prosper after this slaughter took place. This event was seen as God's way of weeding out the wicked from the church.

Houteff prospered in Waco and ran a number of businesses. He even printed his own currency, which was good on the Mount Carmel property. The Mount Carmel money was required currency on the property, which included a number of stores.

Houteff and his followers really emphasized the antitypical or modern David. Hence, they took on the official name of

Davidian Seventh-day Adventists. Houteff confined his preaching to Seventh-day Adventists but only managed a small minority of converts.

By the time Houteff was in full swing, many Seventh-day Adventists had fallen into the habit of using the writings of Ellen White to prove points of doctrine. While some Seventh-day Adventist scholars tried to stick to the Bible and the Bible only, the use of Ellen White's writings as another source for doctrine became common for the average Seventh-day Adventist.

Victor Houteff was no exception. His writings are full of Ellen White proofs. Indeed, some of his tracts are chiefly comprised of Ellen White quotations. It is noteworthy that Ellen White herself implored people not to use her writings as a basis for proving doctrines.

Let us suppose, for argument's sake, that Ellen White was actually wrong on a given point of doctrine. We will call it doctrine X. Now let us suppose that Victor Houteff wished to prove a new doctrine. We will call this doctrine Y. Now let us suppose that Victor Houteff uses Ellen White's statements concerning doctrine X to build his proof of doctrine Y. It follows logically that Houteff's doctrine Y would be flawed, that is, given that White's doctrine X is fallacious. Many of the Davidian and Branch Davidian strict dietary and dress codes stemmed from strict literal interpretations of Ellen White's writings.

There is also the danger of taking Ellen White's statements out of context, just as there is of taking biblical passages out of context. So not only could Houteff misuse (whether intentionally or unintentionally) biblical passages, but Ellen White's writings as well.

By falling into the habit of using Ellen White for proof, both Adventists and Davidian Seventh-day Adventists took many things for granted. Ellen White was more or less assumed right in whatever she said and many complicated and finally ridiculous chains of doctrinal logic resulted from that assumption.

Upon Ellen White's death, the White Estate was formed. The White Estate is a Seventh-day Adventist-operated organization that controls the publication and distribution of Ellen White's writings. Nothing she wrote can be published or copied without their permission.

Ellen White's writings are kept in a vault. Many of her published works are nothing more than compilations of her writings, put together by the White Estate. These compilations are formed from bits and pieces of her manuscripts. Some of these manuscripts are edited to such a degree that only scattered paragraphs are included, while the rest is left out. This provides a distorted view of what Ellen White actually said because the reader of the final compilation has no way of knowing which part of a manuscript was used and which was not. Text from several manuscripts are often blended together to make them appear as if they came from the same source.

So not only do the Seventh-day Adventists and their various splinter groups endanger themselves by relying too heavily on Ellen White's writings, they rely on a highly distorted view of those writings.

Concerned members of the Adventist church, or various splinter groups, have often smuggled unpublished manuscripts out of the vaults so that the people could see what was actually written. Discovery results in prosecution as the church guards Ellen White's writings jealously. Some of her manuscripts are the best-kept secrets of the church.

On the one hand, Adventists claim that Ellen White was inspired by God. On the other, they guard those writings and exercise absolute control over which portions of "the spirit of prophecy" are fit for the public to see.

Not only do Adventists and their splinter groups fight over varying interpretations of the Bible, but they also fight over varying interpretations of Ellen White's writings.

The Collapse of the Davidian Seventh-day Adventists

Victor Houteff, founder of the Shepherd's Rod, died in 1955. In order to keep the organization cohesive, the leadership role was assumed by Houteff's wife, Florence Houteff.

Prior to Victor Houteff's death, the Shepherd's Rod had drafted a constitution. In this constitution, provision was made for an executive committee consisting of a president, vice president, secretary, and treasurer. While the latter three offices were usually elected by the people, the president had a large say in the filling of these offices.

According to the Rod's constitution, the president had to be directly appointed by God. This worked well enough for the Shepherd's Rod since Victor Houteff had claimed to be appointed a prophet by God. Thus, during his life there was no quarrel as to who should fill the office of Davidian president.

Unfortunately for the Rod, this constitution was rather shortsighted since upon Houteff's death the office of president could only be filled by another prophet. The reason for this shortsightedness was due to the fact that most Rod members, including most probably Victor Houteff himself, believed that he would be the prophet who would see things out to the second coming of Christ. In fact, the Rod's constitution stated that the president's job would be to hand the leadership over to Christ upon his coming. The Davidian constitution provided, however, for the possibility of successive presidents. It must also be pointed out here that the last president, the one present at Christ's second coming, was known among Rod members as the Antitypical David, the king foretold in the prophecies who would hand his kingship over to Christ upon his glorious appearing. The role of Antitypical David plays a prominent role in Rod/Branch History.

Although Florence Houteff assumed the leadership role, she remained as Vice President, leaving the presidency vacant. She believed and taught that Victor Houteff would be resurrected to take up the president's mantle once again. She gave a three-and-a-half-year prophecy that would end in 1959. She stated that at the end of this three-and-a-half-year period, God would execute Ezekiel 9 upon the unbelieving Seventh-day Adventists.

The following is a rough chronological list of Rod eschatology as they understood it at the time.

1. After three-and-a-half years God would execute Ezekiel 9 on the unbelieving (non-Rod) Seventh-day Adventists.
2. Shortly after this slaughter (which was seen also as the destruction of the tares spoken of in Matthew 13), God would exalt the Rod members.
3. God would miraculously transport the faithful to Israel, there to reign in peace and prosperity.
4. Victor Houteff would be resurrected, along with a few other faithful. Houteff would be crowned King in Israel. He would be answerable only to Jesus Christ himself.
5. The city of Jerusalem would be the headquarters from which the loud cry of the third angel would then be given to the world.

It has been alleged that the Rod believed that they themselves would literally carry out the slaughter of Ezekiel 9. From our research on the subject, we believe that Victor

Houteff himself *did not* believe this but that upon his death, this understanding sprang up.

In the years from 1955 to 1959, the Rod proclaimed their message most zealously. In fact, they were probably more zealous during that period than during Houteff's ministry. In 1955 Florence Houteff sold the Old Mount Carmel property. She had seen how much money was involved and did not wish the assets to be so bound up in property. With part of the money she purchased New Mount Carmel. This property also lay in Waco, Texas and consisted of around 400 acres. Eventually, bits and pieces of the 400-acre property were sold off until only the 77 acres, known to the world as the compound, were left. Today, the property that was Old Mount Carmel houses many of the wealthy residents of Waco and the land is worth millions. It has no affiliation with any Davidian organization.

In 1959 more than a thousand Davidians met at New Mount Carmel to await the execution of Ezekiel 9 and their deliverance into God's kingdom. Many of these Davidians gave up their homes, and jobs, in order to be on the property when God wrought his deliverance. There were some Seventh-day Adventist ministers among the crowd as well, who endeavored to show the Davidians the error of their ways, and to persuade them to give up their reckless course.

Also there that day was one Ben L. Roden, who believed that God had called him to warn the Davidians that they were following a foolish course. Roden had arranged matters with the Israeli government so that it gave him (and any who would follow) a grant of land in the northern part of Israel. Therefore Roden informed the Davidians that they were not going to be miraculously delivered on this day in 1959, but that they needed to immigrate to Israel, where they could be present in the holy land itself. He believed that deliverance would come to God's people in 1960. The Davidians declined his invitation to move to Israel, and continued to hope that Florence Houteff's prophecy would come true.

Ben Roden was fully convinced that his ministry would center in Israel. As he was about to move there permanently himself, however, to establish his headquarters, Ben Roden had a vision. In his vision he saw a map of the world, focusing upon the United States. He was living in Texas at the time. In his vision, Ben Roden was about to walk across the map of the world to go to Israel. But then a voice said: "No. Waco." So Ben Roden set his sights on setting up his headquarters in Waco, Texas. It was for this reason that he attempted to obtain the Davidian property.

Florence Houteff's prophecy failed and the organization soon broke apart. Since that time, many splinter groups have emerged. Each splinter group has its own prophet, claiming to be the true president of the Davidian association. The Branch Davidian Seventh-day Adventists formed one of these splinter groups.

Ben Roden and the Branch Davidian Seventh-day Adventists

As shown above, the presidency, according to the Davidian constitution, demanded a prophet or inspired figure. Thus, with these numerous splinter groups came numerous prophets.

One of these, as mentioned, was Ben Roden, who founded the Branch Davidian Seventh-day Adventist organization in 1955. He died in 1978.

Only after the fiasco of 1959 did Roden merit serious consideration among Davidian members. It was under his administration that New Mount Carmel was acquired. Although it was actually Florence Houteff who purchased the

New Mount Carmel property, the courts soon had jurisdiction because the Davidian organization eventually became insolvent. It thus became unclear who had rights to the property. Ben Roden was forced to stake his claim in court. He lost his bid and was told that the only way he could use Mount Carmel as his headquarters was to purchase it from other Davidian members. Roden sent out a plea to all who followed him to contribute in buying out everyone else's shares. This was eventually accomplished at a cost of approximately $75,000. This done, Roden established the property as his headquarters. Only now there were two differences. First, the new headquarters occupied only 77 acres of land. Second, no longer was the organization known as the Davidian Seventh-day Adventists, but the Branch Davidian Seventh-day Adventists.

Why Branch? Ben Roden definitely believed that he was the Messiah. He believed that he was the Elijah spoken of in the Bible and that he would not die, but usher in the kingdom of God.

Ellen White had prophesied in *Testimony to Ministers and Gospel Workers* (Pacific Press Publishing Association, Boise, Idaho, 1923) that someone would come as a modern-day Elijah and that he would be rejected by the church.

> Prophecy must be fulfilled. The Lord says: "Behold, I will send you Elijah the prophet before the coming of the great and dreadful day of the Lord." Somebody is to come in the spirit and power of Elijah, and when he appears, men may say: "You are too earnest, you do not interpret the Scriptures in the proper way. Let me tell you how to teach your message."

In addition to being Elijah, Ben Roden said that he was

the "the man whose name is The BRANCH."

> And speak unto him, saying, Thus speaketh the
> LORD of hosts, saying, Behold the man whose
> name [is] The BRANCH; and he shall grow up
> out of his place, and he shall build the temple
> of the LORD: Even he shall build the temple of
> the LORD; and he shall bear the glory, and shall
> sit and rule upon his throne; and he shall be
> a priest upon his throne: and the counsel of peace
> shall be between them both.
>
> – Zechariah 6: 12–13

The BRANCH was to hold absolute power. As such, Ben
Roden controlled every aspect of both the Branch organization
and its members.

The Davidian Seventh-day Adventists under Victor Houteff
had drafted a constitution consisting of by-laws. This document was for the governing of the body of believers. Ben
Roden published an addendum to that constitution in which
the following statement best illustrates the absolute control
wielded by the Branch president/prophet.

> Therefore as members of the Branch Davidian
> Seventh-day Adventist Association, the membership
> appoints (Hosea 1:11) the president Ben L. Roden,
> as holding in his sole possession all legal, moral,
> and Scriptural ownership and rights of the Associ-
> ation, all its assets and holdings, and to operate
> the same for the furtherance of the Association's
> work at home and abroad: to execute and adminis-
> trate the entire balances of the Association, to judge
> and make final judgment in all matters concerning

> the Association's works, assets, and holdings, and
> to be its chief and sole administrator.

Ben Roden even went so far as to hold a crowning ceremony at Mount Carmel. He called it: "The crowning in the wilderness." At this ceremony, Roden was crowned king.

But despite these incredible claims and boasts, Ben Roden himself appeared the humblest of men. A rather large man, Ben Roden had been a bricklayer by trade. He spoke with a slow Texas drawl that gave him the appearance of being uneducated.

On one occasion, Perry Jones, Ben Roden's right-hand man and the person who would later become Vernon Howell's father-in-law, arranged for a newspaper reporter to interview the prophet of Mount Carmel. It was a hot summer's day when the reporter came to meet the messenger of God. When he arrived, he found Ben in the kitchen, swatting flies. According to Perry, the reporter was amazed that a prophet of God would show himself to the press, swatting flies in his kitchen.

Ben appeared unpretentious on the surface, but his claims about himself were not. He held absolute sway. Nothing was done without his consent or knowledge.

Ben Roden was also a baseball fan. Watching baseball was forbidden under the Branch, because of strict interpretations of Ellen White's writings. On some occasions, however, Perry would find Ben watching the occasional baseball game. "I know it's a sin," Ben would say, "but I can't help but watch it sometimes."

It was Roden who introduced the concept that the people of God needed also to keep the feast days: namely Passover, Pentecost, Day of Atonement, and Tabernacles. He began teaching this doctrine in 1964, nine years after he began his ministry. He did not believe sacrifices were necessary but that the feasts should be kept in a Christian context. Roden's message dealt mainly with these feast days, and the harvest motifs of Scripture.

It must be pointed out that there was one statement made by Victor Houteff that characterizes Branch theology. That statement simply reads as follows.

> He makes wise the simple and confounds the prudent by showing that where there is **no type** there is **no truth**.

Because of this statement Branch theology was based entirely on types. This has been carried to ridiculous excesses.

Isaiah 8 provides a good example. This chapter actually speaks of an alliance between Syria and the northern kingdom of Israel, against the Jews in the south. This alliance took place in the 8th century BC. Isaiah the prophet tries to convince King Ahaz not to hire the Assyrian empire to break up this alliance. But Roden applied this chapter to the future, and defined antitypes for all the nations, people, and objects found in the biblical passage.

The antitypical Assyrian	= USA
Antitypical Syria	= USA government
Antitypical ten tribes	= SDA [Seventh-day Adventists]
Antitypical two tribes	= Branch
Antitypical butter and honey	= truth
Antitypical cow	= Spirit of Prophecy writings [inspired writings not belonging to the Bible]
Antitypical two sheep	= Old and New testaments
Antitypical Immanuel	= Antitypical David

All this from Isaiah 8. The land was, however, seen as literal Jerusalem.

Roden also believed that God's people should migrate to Israel. To Roden, Waco, Texas was only a way-station, a transition between the United States and Israel. He managed to acquire land in Israel and there were even a few who moved there. Finally, Roden concentrated mainly on reaching Davidians and Seventh-day Adventists. Although the Branch, as it was known, was the largest splinter group of Davidians, it did not boast a large membership.

In 1977, his wife, Lois I. Roden, claimed to have had divine inspiration. She claimed that while praying one day she saw an angel move by her window with silver wings. From this she deduced that the Holy Spirit was the feminine part of the Godhead. She had actually tried to teach this as early as 1974 but that doctrine had been rejected among Branch members.

Ironically, the main opponent to her 1977 "vision" was her husband, Ben Roden. By this time he was sick and it was generally expected that he would die. Despite the fact that the vision had come to his wife, Ben Roden opposed the doctrine of the femininity of the Holy spirit. Perry Jones said that just before his death Ben Roden accepted the prophetic gift of his wife, along with her message. Perry said that Ben accepted this privately and that not many Branch members knew about it.

Lois Roden assumed power in 1978, and led the sect until 1983.

– Marc Breault and Elizabeth Baranyai, May 1993

Appendix 2

The Rise and Fall of the Branch Davidians: A Chronology

1831 William Miller, an atheist turned Baptist preacher, begins studying the end-time prophecies of the Bible.

1833 William Miller concludes that the end of the world will occur in 1843, and begins preaching his doomsday message.

1843 Miller discovers that he has made a mistake in his calculations, and revises his end-of-the-world date to 1844.

October 22, 1844 Christ fails to appear in the clouds of glory and the Millerite movement begins to disintegrate.

December 1844 Ellen Gould Harmon (later Ellen G. White) receives her first vision.

1863 Seventh-day Adventist Church becomes a recognized denomination.

1929–1930 Victor Houteff, in Los Angeles, California first begins to preach a message that would later cause his disfellowship from the Seventh-day Adventist Church.

1930–1931 Victor Houteff writes *The Shepherd's Rod*. After being disfellowshipped from the Seventh-day Adventist Church, Houteff forms his own organization, the Davidian Seventh-day Adventists, more popularly known as "The Shepherd's Rod."

1938 With headquarters already established at what is now known as Old Mount Carmel in Waco, Houteff begins to teach that God will establish a literal kingdom in Israel ruled over by Jesus Christ and his lieutenant, who Houteff terms as the "Antitypical David." This is perhaps the most important theological development of the sect. It appears that Houteff and his followers believed he was the Antitypical David.

1939–1955 The group confines its recruitment activities to the Seventh-day Adventist Church membership. The Shepherd's Rod becomes one of the most notable thorns in the Seventh-day Adventists' sides.

1955 Death of Victor Houteff. His widow, Florence Houteff, assumes the office of Vice President and initiates a three-and-a-half year prophecy that culminates in a literal divine slaughter of wicked Seventh-day Adventists, the resurrection of her late husband and the establishment of God's earthly kingdom. This begins a massive and somewhat successful recruitment drive. Benjamin Roden first proclaims that God has inspired him to take the mantle of leadership vacated by Victor Houteff. Ben Roden condemns Florence Houteff saying that the actual slaughter etc. will take place in 1960, not 1959 as she predicted.

1955–1959 Ben Roden founds a movement called the Branch Davidian Seventh-day Adventists (BDSDA). He tries to recruit

Davidian Seventh-day Adventists to his cause. Other splinter groups emerge as well, but Roden's is the most successful of these.

1959 At the appointed time predicted by Florence Houteff, many Davidians gather at the New Mount Carmel Centre (then run by Branch Davidians) ready for translation. When her prediction fails, the movement founded by Victor Houteff begins to disintegrate.

August 17, 1959 Birth of Vernon Wayne Howell.

1962 After a long legal battle, Ben Roden and his followers buy out the Davidians and take possession of the New Mount Carmel Center. The Davidians scatter and never arise again as a cohesive entity.

1962–1977 Ben Roden teaches that he is the Antitypical David, the king of Israel. He teaches that Christians must observe the various Hebrew feast days, including Passover, Pentecost, Day of Atonement, and Feast of Tabernacles. The last "feast" to be introduced was called the daily, now abandoned, which consisted of a twice-a-day, one-hour-long worship service.

1977 Ben Roden's wife, Lois, claims to have a vision from God in which she sees that the Holy Spirit is the feminine aspect of the trinity.

1978 Death of Ben Roden. Lois Roden assumes the presidency of the organization. A few dissatisfied Australians leave the movement.

1978–1983 Lois Roden's message attracts many believers. She travels widely and is interviewed by a number of talk shows and news agencies. The BDSDA organization launches a magazine called *Shekinah*.

1979 Vernon Howell is baptized into the Tyler Seventh-day Adventist Church in Texas.

1981 Vernon is disfellowshipped from the Seventh-day Adventist Church. He arrives at the Mount Carmel Center, which is under Lois Roden's leadership. He becomes the handyman at Mount Carmel.

1983 Vernon Howell first claims divine inspiration. He convinces Lois Roden, through Isaiah Chapter 8, that he must have sexual relations with her and the two begin to cohabit. This generates open friction between Vernon and Lois's son, George B. Roden. George begins to claim inspiration.

1984 A conference of Branch Davidians takes place in which a number of would-be prophets say their piece. The invitation is sent originally by Lois Roden and Vernon Howell to come and here the "truth." Nothing is accomplished and the group begins to fragment. George Roden eventually forces Vernon and his followers off the Mount Carmel property at gunpoint. Vernon and his band wander through various towns in Texas. God tells Vernon to marry Rachel Jones, daughter of longtime Branch minister, Perry Jones. Only 14 years old at the time, Rachel becomes Vernon's legal wife.

1984–1985 Vernon acquires a property in Palestine, Texas where he and his followers settle.

1985 Vernon Howell receives a major revelation from God in Israel. He is shown that he is the Antitypical Cyrus and the Antitypical David. Vernon attends the 1985 General Conference session of Seventh-day Adventists in New Orleans. Through a weird combination of his rejection there, and the popular song by The Animals, "House of the Rising Sun," Vernon sees this as the official beginning of his ministry and the beginning of the "time of the end." Vernon begins to formulate a ten-year prophecy after which Christ will appear again.

January 1986 Marc Breault joins the group.

February 1986 Vernon Howell's first trip to Australia. He recruits a number of Melbourne, Australia residents who belonged to the old Branch Davidians under Ben and Lois Roden. Elizabeth Baranyai, Lisa Gent and Jean Smith decide to travel to the United States to visit Howell's headquarters.

March 1986 Vernon first sleeps with Karen Doyle, aged 14. He claims her as his "second wife." Vernon begins teaching polygamy.

June 1986 A number of people from Honolulu, Hawaii join Vernon's group.

Vernon first teaches that he is a second intercessor for mankind and that Christ only died for those before the cross.

July–August 1986 Vernon secretly begins sleeping with Michele Jones, his wife's youngest sister. Michele is only 12.

August 1986 Recruitment drive in Wisconsin meets with initial success but eventually fails.

September 1986 Marc Breault argues with Vernon over his doctrine that Christ did not die for our sins. Vernon appears to change his mind but Breault is tricked. Vernon begins to teach that he is entitled to 140 wives, sixty women as queens, and eighty as concubines. He uses the biblical book of the Song of Solomon to teach this.

December 1986 People from Hawaii begin settling in Palestine, Texas.

December 1986 Sherri Jewell, Kiri's mother, introduced into the group.

Early 1987 Robyn Bunds joins Vernon's harem.

September 1987 Sherri Jewell joins Vernon's harem.

November 3, 1987 Shoot-out with George Roden at the Mount Carmel property. This results in the arrest of eight of the Vernonites, including Vernon himself.

April 25, 1988 After a trial, seven of the eight are acquitted. The jury vote is hung 9–3 in favor of Vernon's acquittal. The state drops charges against Vernon.

March–May 1988 George Roden goes to prison on unrelated contempt-of-court charges. An elderly couple pays back taxes owing on the Mount Carmel property, thus allowing Vernon and his group to move in.

July 1988 Nicole Gent recruited and soon after joins Howell's harem.

September 10, 1988 Birth of Howell's first child born by a woman other than his legal wife.

November 1988 Robyn Bunds' child Shaun (originally named Wisdom by Vernon) is born.

Early 1989 Friction between Vernon and Breault develops. Nicole Gent leaves for Australia to have her baby.

April 1989 Vernon makes the now infamous dream tape. This audio tape contains damaging evidence against Vernon Howell.

April 28, 1989 Elizabeth Baranyai and Marc Breault are married.

May 1989 Elizabeth returns to Australia and Marc awaits migrant's visa to join her. He tries to reconcile himself to Vernon one last time. For a while, it works.

August 5, 1989 Vernon teaches all women belong to him and only he has the right to procreate.

September 1989 Marc Breault leaves Vernon's group, never to return.

September 29, 1989 Marc Breault arrives in Australia.

September–June 1989 The battle for Australia begins in earnest. By June 1990 most Australians break from Vernon, leaving only a few who still follow him. Although the New Zealand membership of the cult is small, that battle is almost as fierce, and eventually, some New Zealanders break away from Vernon.

October 1989 Vernon makes his "Foundation" tape and sends it to Australia in an effort to scare Australian defectors into staying faithful to him. This tape contains the most damaging hardcore evidence against Vernon.

Spring 1990 Vernon Howell changes his name to David Koresh.

February 1990 Breault's first trip to New Zealand to free people from Howell's influence.

May 1990 Breault's second trip to New Zealand. Leslie and Poia Vaega are free from Vernon.

June 1990 Breault flies to Waco, Texas where he first alerts police to cult's activities. He is ignored by the Waco Police Department. Enough Australians break away from Vernon to begin a united effort to alert the authorities. Geoff Hossack, an Australian private investigator, becomes involved.

July–August 1990 Robyn Bunds, one of Vernon's women, breaks from the cult. This provides Australians with more ammunition. The approach to the authorities begins at this time. Raid by the La Verne Police Department, La Verne, California yields results. According to Hossack, La Verne issues three warrants against Vernon for statutory rape. These warrants have since disappeared.

October 1990 Steve Schneider visits Australia in a last effort to convince defectors to return to the Vernon fold. It fails.

October 1990–June 1991 Stalemate with American authorities.

June 1991 First confirmation of Kiri Jewell's danger. First rescue attempt fails. Ruth Mosher, Kiri's grandmother, approached to take action.

September 1991 Jeannine Bunds, Robyn's mother, leaves the sect.

October 1991 Australia's "A Current Affair" (Nine Network) shows interest in story and begins research.

November 1, 1991 With the help of the local Seventh-day Adventist Church, David Jewell of Niles, Michigan tracked down and warned of his daughter's situation.

November 1991–February 1992 Preparations for the Jewell custody case are carried out in secret. Evidence is gathered and affidavits are prepared.

December 28, 1992 Kiri Jewell travels to Michigan from Anaheim, California to visit her father. David Jewell granted temporary custody of his child until the full custody hearing, which is set for February 24, 1992.

December 30, 1991 "A Current Affair" Australia interviews the Australians involved. Reporter Martin King is assigned the story.

January 5, 1992 "A Current Affair" Australia visits and interviews Vernon Howell at Mount Carmel. An interview with Robyn Bunds is also conducted in California.

January 7, 1992 The Vernonites, including Sherri Jewell, receive official notification of the temporary custody order.

January–February 1992 Final preparations for Kiri Jewell's court case.

February 20, 1992 Marc Breault and Elizabeth Baranyai arrive in Niles, Michigan. Court date postponed to February 25.

February 25–27, 1992 Court case. After two days of testimony the Vernonites concede defeat and full custody is awarded to David Jewell.

February 20–March 6, 1992 Breault learns of Vernon teaching about suicide and martyrdom from five independent sources. A cult member flees in panic after death notices are issued by Vernon.

March 6–April 15, 1992 Further information confirms that cult members think they will die shortly. Fears of a mass suicide/martyrdom escalate.

April 15–18, 1992 Intensive media coverage by both Channel 9 and the *Herald-Sun* in Australia. This coverage, along with some American coverage, seems to cause Vernon to back down. Event seems to have been called off.

May 1992 *Waco Tribune Herald* begins an in-depth investigation into the Branch Davidian cult.

May–June 1992 ATF investigation begins.

February 28, 1993 ATF raid on the compound. Four ATF agents are killed and sixteen wounded. Six cult members, it is believed, have been killed too. Vernon claims his 2-year-old daughter is dead.

March 1–April 18, 1993 Several adults and twenty-one children are released from the compound. They are usually released two by two. Of the children released, none are those fathered by the cult leader. Adults who left the compound during the siege include: Brad Branch (charged with conspiracy to commit murder), Livingstone Fagan (England), Oliver Gyarfas (Australia), Victorine Hollingsworth (England), James Lawter (United States, Margaret Lawson (United States), Sheila Martin (United States), Katherine Matteson (United States), Gladys Ottman (Canada), Anita Richards (England), Rita Riddle (United States), Ophelia Santoya (United States), Kathryn Schroeder (United States), Kevin Whitecliff (United States). The children released include David Jones's three children, Kathryn Schroeder's three children from a previous marriage, Mike and Kathryn Schroeder's child, three of Douglas Wayne Martin's children, Natalie Nobress, Scott and Floracita Sonobe's two children, Stan and Lorraine Sylvia's two children, Neil and Margarida's child, Mark and Jaydeen Wendel's four children, and Livingstone Fagan's two children.

April 19, 1993 The compound explodes into flames after the FBI tries to end the fifty-one day siege with tear gas. Eighty-six people, including seventeen children fathered by Vernon Howell, are presumed dead. Only nine people survive the blaze. They are Renos Avreem (England), Jaime Castillo (United States), Graeme Craddock (Australia), Misty Ferguson

(United States), Derrick Lovelock (England), Ruth Ottman-Riddle (Canada), David Thibodeaux (United States), Marjorie Thomas (England), and Clive Doyle (United States).

April 29, 1993 Investigators have pulled a total of seventy-two bodies out of the rubble. Fourteen are still unaccounted for and speculation runs wild that David Koresh might have escaped. Only seven corpses are officially identified, and only five names have been released: David Jones, Shari Doyle, James Riddle, Stephen Henry and Livingston Malcom. Of these, four appear to have died from gunshot wounds to the head. Children presumed dead in the fire (all fathered by Vernon Howell) are Rachel Koresh's children (Cyrus Koresh, 8; Star Koresh, 6; Bobbie Lane Koresh, 16 months), Michele Jones-Thibodeaux's children (Serenity Sea, 4; twin girls, age unknown), Lorraine Sylvia's child (Hollywood, 2), Judy Schneider's child (Mayanah, 2), Nicole Gent-Little's children (Dayland, 3; Paige, 15 months), Kathy Andrade's child (unknown name and age), Aisha Gyarfas-Summers's child (Startle, 1), and Shari Doyle's child (unknown name and age). Vernon Howell has four surviving children, who were not in the compound at the time of the siege.

May 2, 1993 The body of Vernon Wayne Howell, leader of the Branch Davidians, is officially identified using dental records. It was found in the kitchen area of the compound near a number of other bodies. He died of a gunshot wound to the head.